Middle East Studies
History, Politics, and Law

Edited by
Shahrough Akhavi
University of South Carolina

A Routledge Series

Middle East Studies: History, Politics, and Law

Shahrough Akhavi, *General Editor*

New Pythian Voices
Women Building Political Capital in NGOs in the Middle East
Cathryn S. Magno

Turkey in Germany
The Transnational Sphere of Deutschkei
Betigül Ercan Argun

Islamic Law, Epistemology and Modernity
Legal Philosophy in Contemporary Iran
Ashk P. Dahlén

Gender, Literacy, and Empowerment in Morocco
Fatima Agnaou

Trapped Between the Map and Reality
Geography and Perceptions of Kurdistan
Maria T. O'Shea

Kurdish Nationalism and Political Islam in Turkey
Kemalist Identity in Transition
Ömer Taşpinar

Organizations, Gender, and the Culture of Palestinian Activism in Haifa, Israel
Elizabeth Faier

Palestinian Identity in Jordan and Israel
The Necessary 'Other' in the Making of a Nation
Riad M. Nasser

Strategies of Resistance in the Dramatic Texts of North African Women
A Body of Words
Laura Chakravarty Box

Islam, Democracy, and the Status of Women
The Case of Kuwait
Helen Mary Rizzo

Legislating Authority
Sin and Crime in the Ottoman Empire and Turkey
Ruth A. Miller

Legislating Authority

Sin and Crime in the Ottoman Empire and Turkey

Ruth A. Miller

Routledge
New York & London

Published in 2005 by
Routledge
Taylor & Francis Group
711 Third Avenue
New York, NY 10017

Published in Great Britain by
Routledge
Taylor & Francis Group
2 Park Square
Milton Park, Abingdon
Oxon, OX14 4RN

First issued in paperback 2013

International Standard Book Number-10: 0-415-97155-1 (Hardcover)
International Standard Book Number-13: 978-0-415-97155-3 (Hardcover)
International Standard Book Number-13: 978-0-415-65542-2 (Paperback)
Library of Congress Card Number 2005001384

Library of Congress Cataloging-in-Publication Data

Miller, Ruth Austin.
Legislating authority : sin and crime in the Ottoman Empire and Turkey / Ruth A. Miller.-- 1st ed.
p. cm. -- (Middle East studies: history, politics, and law)
Includes bibliographical references and index.
ISBN: 0-415-97510-7
1. Criminal law--Turkey--History. 2. Criminal justice, Administration of--Turkey--History. 3. Criminal law (Islamic law) I. Title. II. Series: Middle East studies (Routledge (Firm))

KKX3800.M55 2005
345.561--dc22 2005001384

T&F informa

Taylor & Francis Group
is the Academic Division of T&F Informa plc.

Visit the Taylor & Francis Web site at
http://www.taylorandfrancis.com

and the Routledge Web site at
http://www.routledge-ny.com

Contents

Acknowledgments

This book grew out of a dissertation written for the Near Eastern Studies Department at Princeton University, and I am indebted to the department for its material and intellectual support. I am particularly grateful to Şükrü Hanioğlu and Michael Cook for their guidance and encouragement as I conducted my research. I would also like to thank Abraham Udovitch, Negin Nabavi, and Heath Lowry for their insightful comments on the finished dissertation.

I am similarly grateful to my colleagues in the History Department at the University of Massachusetts, Boston, who have provided a congenial environment in which to continue my scholarship. Woodruff Smith especially has been unfailing in his support of my work, while David Hunt and Lester Bartson have made me feel more than welcome in the department as a whole.

Tom Green at the University of Michigan spent a great deal of time commenting on an early version of the book manuscript—his advice and his suggestions have been invaluable to me as I have revised and reformulated my argument. Shahab Ahmed, Jocelyn Sharlet, Kristin Jensen, and John Parry have all likewise given me excellent advice on all or part of the manuscript.

Finally, I would be remiss if I did not mention Miles and Betsy Miller, who have been patient, sympathetic, and understanding throughout the entirety of this process.

Introduction

There has been a great deal of debate among historians of the modern Middle East surrounding the region's nineteenth and twentieth century legal transformation. The role of secularism in post eighteenth century legal change has received much scrutiny, for example.[1] Likewise, the extent to which the legal codes that were developed in the Middle East over this period were "real"—that is, appropriately modern—has been a subject of discussion since the mid nineteenth century.[2] As to whether or not Middle Eastern legal systems have remained "authentic"—that is, appropriately "Islamic"—in the modern context, this has become both a scholarly and popular trope, invoked in monographs and newspapers, as well as in the political speeches of a vast array of leaders and intellectuals.[3] There has also been a great deal of attention paid to Islamic legal doctrine and its implications—especially legal doctrine in the so-called "classical" period. The debate, for example, on whether the gate of *ijtihad* (legal interpretation) is or has been closed, whether it was ever open, or whether *ijtihad* is in any case really what we think it is, has now entered its second or third generation.[4] This book will not be discussing any of these issues.

Instead, the following chapters will be looking at the discourse of law in and of itself—law as it was understood apart from its social context. Some would argue that separating law, in this case Islamic law, from the dynamic environment in which it grew up essentializes it, and that adopting this approach is both politically and intellectually irresponsible. Over the nineteenth and twentieth centuries, however, Ottoman and Turkish law was in fact detached from its social context. It did become essential. And—more to the point—it was deliberately made so.

This does not mean, of course, that Ottoman law was not changing and had not changed over the preceding five centuries. It changed in the eighteenth century, in the seventeenth century, and, for that matter, in the fourteenth century as well. But in the nineteenth century, the character of this change was different. Whereas before there were periods of centralization and decentralization, periods of secularization and call it de-secularization, periods in which *kadı*s (judges of

Islamic law) held sway and periods in which governors held sway, in the nineteenth century the primary characteristic of legal change was the law's increasing abstraction. The other trends that I mentioned came into play in the nineteenth century as well—indeed, they performed key roles in the creation of an abstract system of law—but the overall legal trend from 1839 onward was the system's movement away from the concrete.

What exactly do I mean by an abstract system? First of all, it is a system divorced from its social relevance. Second, it is a system in which purity of function or purity of idea is more important than utility of function or utility of idea. Finally, in the context of criminal law, it is a system in which crime is purely discursive.[5] Before, there were crimes against victims, which defined the limits of an individual's freedom of action. There were victimless crimes, which defined the boundaries of social morality. But in 1839, the year in which the Ottoman government set out to "reorganize" itself, these two categories began to collapse into discursive crime, which defined only the legal system against which they had been committed.

It goes without saying that the Ottoman legal system was not the only one undergoing this change in the nineteenth and twentieth centuries. In France, the "correctionalization" movement against the jury system was primarily about protecting the purity of the law from contamination by jurors who wanted to decide cases according to shifting moral standards.[6] In China, the judicial functions of provincial administrators were eroded in an attempt to create an un-corruptible—that is pure—legal system.[7] In Argentina, a criminal was no longer someone who contravened a specific law, but instead someone who was simply "known" in the abstract to be criminal.[8] The transformation of the Ottoman legal system can therefore be seen as something of a case study. The ways in which this transformation occurred, however, and its implications are unique.

To begin with, there was the Tanzimat. A great deal has been written about the Tanzimat, the "Reorganization" (literally "Regulations") which began with the 1839 Edict of Gülhane and ended with the 1876 Ottoman Constitution. Most agree that it was a period of centralization, in which the government in Istanbul began to influence more and varied aspects of provincial administration.[9] Many agree that it was a period of secularization,[10] although this argument has been questioned with increasing frequency of late.[11] A main theme in this book will in fact be the extent to which the Ottoman legal system rapidly de-secularized over the course of the nineteenth century. All agree that it was a period of reform. What exactly "reform" means, however, is the subject of some debate—as well as the subject of a second major theme in this book.

A final and related commonly held view about the Tanzimat is that more change or reform occurred over the years between the Edict of Gülhane and the Constitution than had occurred in any half century preceding them. This view is problematic. When people talk about the quantity, frequency, and rapidity of change over the course of the Tanzimat (and post-Tanzimat) periods, they are usually referring first of all to institutional change. During the Tanzimat period, a number of new ministries were created and then repeatedly renamed. The educational system was divided into sections, much of it was brought further under the control of the government, and these sections were, again, repeatedly renamed. The military was reorganized and renamed. Institutional change in the Tanzimat period was, in other words, very, very well documented.

A second characteristic of reform during the Tanzimat that tends to get highlighted is the response of civil society to these institutional changes. People get very excited about the multiplying printing presses and newspapers—both official and unofficial—over the course of the nineteenth century.[12] A great deal has been written about the growth of social organizations (and their publications) as well as the spread of secret philosophical societies (and their publications) during and after the Tanzimat period.[13] The changes that occurred in civil society between 1839 and 1876 were indeed almost as well documented as the institutional changes that occurred over the same period.

What this means is that when one walks into the Ottoman Prime Ministry Archive in Istanbul, the section of wall space taken up by catalogs referring to the Tanzimat and post-Tanzimat periods is about twice as great as the section of wall space taken up by the rest of Ottoman history combined. But it is a mistake to think that this excessive documentation is an indication of more change or more frequent change happening between 1839 and 1876 than had happened between 1739 and 1776 or, for that matter, between 1439 and 1476 when, for example, the role of the Sultan, the role of the *ulema* (religious legal scholars), the system of taxation, the system of commerce, and the Empire's capital city all underwent monumental, if lightly documented, alterations.

If the quantity of paper produced by Tanzimat reform does not necessarily indicate more or greater change happening in the nineteenth century, however, it does indicate a different quality of change. Again, centralization and de-centralization had occurred in previous periods. The influence of the religious establishment on governance and law had waxed and waned as time passed.[14] But until 1839 the amount of data produced by these changes remained relatively constant. And then, suddenly, it spiked. The real difference between nineteenth and twentieth century reform and earlier reform therefore seems to be the fact that in 1839, reform became self conscious. The documentation indicates not more change, but rather highly aware change. With the Tanzimat, you have for the first time reform for the sake of reform.

This self consciousness led in the end to the abstraction of function I mentioned above. At first, the papers produced by the Tanzimat reforms, the documentation of institutional change, the membership rosters compiled by the secret philosophical societies were produced for the sake of the reforms, the institutions, and the societies. The purpose of the paper was to record the changes that had taken place in the institutions. Very soon, however, this relationship shifted. Instead of documentation produced for the sake of the institution, the institution existed for the sake of the documentation. Functionaries performed and their functions existed because they were part of an abstract system, and that is all.[15]

Indeed, it is arguably as a result of this transformation that we see in the nineteenth century the obsession—not just in the Ottoman Empire, but everywhere—with the corruption of functionaries and the consequent disorganization of function. Corruption and disorganization are part and parcel of a system that exists for a practical purpose. If everyone on the ground knows that one pays x functionary y amount of money to perform his task—even if z functionary wants a different amount to do the same thing—and if everyone is content with this situation, then the behavior of x functionary is hardly questionable. In fact, the behavior of such functionaries was not (often) questioned prior to the nineteenth century. If x functionary tries to behave in such a way in a system that exists not for the people on the ground, but for its own ideal self, however, x functionary is in trouble. A self conscious, abstract system can tolerate neither corruption nor disorganization.

Once again, though, Ottoman institutions during the Tanzimat period were certainly not unique in this transformation. Max Weber has argued convincingly that the defining characteristic of the modern period everywhere was the creation of self-sufficient bureaucracies in which functionaries performed for the sake of the system.[16] Michel Foucault has similarly argued with reference to criminality and power that discipline—which resides in these self-sufficient systems—replaced law in the modern period as the true mechanism of control.[17] Neither, however, has explored the implications of these institutional transformations toward law as a whole in the modern period. If, as Foucault implies, law becomes obsolete with the rise of a disciplinary system, what then is the purpose of law? It still exists. It is still legislated. Presumably there is some reason behind it. If, as Weber argues, modern functionaries exist for the sake of their bureaucracies, what does this mean for legal systems? What does it mean especially for criminal law systems, whose purpose is either to define the limits of individual freedom, or to define the boundaries of social morality? Is there no longer any connection between legal function and these social issues?

More to the point, in the case of the Ottoman Empire, did this bureaucratic transformation actually affect the working of criminal law at all? In order to answer that question, we need to look at the growth of Ottoman law from its inception. To start with another truism, therefore: Ottoman law was Islamic law interpreted for the purposes of Ottoman governance. Even those who favor an essentialist definition of Islamic law, who see it as a single, unchanging entity, increasingly misunderstood and debased over time, will sometimes agree with Joseph Schacht that in the midst of all of those troubling, "secular" early modern Ottoman codifications, Ottoman *kadı*s were successful—and according to Schacht, more successful than others—in their application of Islamic legal precepts.[18]

Whether these legal precepts addressed the primary concerns of criminal law is, however, another question. As for the first concern—that criminal law define the limits of individual freedom—it is difficult to have a legal system that does not include some legislation in that direction, and the Ottoman legal system was no exception. Any society or government that condemns, for example, murder is to some extent limiting individual freedom. The Marquis de Sade may not have been the only philosopher to make this point, but he was certainly one of the most adamant. A true product of the Enlightenment and the ideals of the French Revolution, he noted quite logically that a completely free society would have not a single law constraining it. Indeed, he seemed more distraught by the existence of laws which limited individual freedom—not just laws against murder, but laws against wounding, rape, and theft—than by the existence of laws that defined social morality.[19]

The second concern of criminal law is to set society's moral boundaries. Defining any activity as a victimless crime is essentially drawing a moral line in the sand. Legislation against suicide is a prime example of such a line. For Roman aristocrats under Nero, and for European Romantics who liked to read about Roman aristocrats under Nero, suicide was an acceptable, indeed a laudable, thing to do. For Medieval Europeans, and in Anglo-American systems, however, suicide was both a sin and until recently a crime. Possessing heroin—if not perhaps selling it—is a victimless crime. In general, wherever there are laws against adultery, pornography, or smoking, these laws define society's moral boundaries.

But the line between crimes against victims and victimless crimes is, of course, a fuzzy one. Usually those who want to legislate against an activity argue that this activity falls into the former category, and those who want to block the legislation argue that it falls, if anywhere, into the latter. American anti-abortion activists, for example, argue that abortion is a crime against an unborn victim. Pro-abortion activists argue that calling abortion a "crime" at all is imposing an outmoded moral code on society. Are pornography and prostitution really victimless crimes, or are their subjects being violated? Similarly, victimless crimes tend to be the ones that pinpoint rifts in society. Suicide may not have been a crime among bourgeois Victorian poets, but among the Victorian working classes, it remained so, and the "perpetrator's" property was consequently seized by the state.[20] It is a commonplace that fashion models who possess heroin are rarely prosecuted in the same way that the urban poor who possess heroin are. Why is there this relationship between purely moral crimes and social rifts, and when did this relationship begin?

These are questions that receive a great deal of attention in legal studies generally, and they deserve consideration in Middle Eastern studies as well. One of the more intriguing byproducts of Ottoman and Turkish legal reform, in fact, is the extent to which various crimes shifted categories as the criminal law system became more abstract. For the most part, we see a movement away from the "crimes against victims" category and toward the "victimless crime category." Simultaneously, we see the state replacing God as the implied victim of the latter category. Before this shift occurred, however, did the Ottoman legal system legislate morality? Again, it is difficult for a criminal law system to exist without doing so. In the Ottoman case, we need merely note that of the basic Islamic *hadd* crimes, two—apostasy and drinking alcohol—are victimless, and one—fornication/adultery—is arguably so.

Prior to the Tanzimat era reforms, therefore, Ottoman criminal law performed the two basic roles required of it. What about during and after the reforms? Recall, to begin with, that the defining characteristic of the Tanzimat period was the increasing self consciousness of functionaries and the increasing abstraction of their function. The changing criminal law did not escape these trends. As I noted earlier, starting in 1839 the Ottoman legal system began to separate from its social context. It began to function in the name of an abstract ideal of itself rather than in the name of the society that had created it.

As a result, first of all, "crimes against victims" became the crimes of least importance. This is not to say that murder, for example, ceased to be a crime in the Tanzimat period, it means simply that the focus of the legal system was on other issues. Again, one of the more intriguing trends over this period is the transference of most major crimes into the "victimless" category. Second, the morality that this victimless crime was defining was no longer a flexible, changing morality—morality as it was lived—but a pure, abstract, and crystallized morality that existed apart from its social context. The two architects of moral boundaries, therefore—law and society—began to go in completely different directions at this point. We consequently begin to see in this period the collapse of these two types of crime into a third category—discursive. As the Tanzimat period progressed, crime began to define not individual freedom or even moral boundaries, but simply the legal system itself.

What about the place of religion in this system? For a long time, when people talked about modern reform, they meant secular reform. The French revolutionaries had smashed both altar and crown in their transformation of society—even if a few years later they rehabilitated both under slightly changed circumstances. All subsequent change, therefore—it being a given that anything that occurred in Europe (and often elsewhere) after the French Revolution was somehow a product of this revolution[21]—necessarily had to be similarly secular. More recent discussions of change in the modern period have stepped away from this rather blunt model. But these more recent discussions have still not dealt explicitly with the role of religion in modern legal transformation. Instead, religion is either ignored, or it is dealt with summarily. Religion, much like law, becomes obsolete in a bureaucratic, disciplinary society.

In the Ottoman Empire, however, religion not only continued to play a role in society, but was a motivating force behind the reform movement. This is not because the Ottoman Empire was an Islamic, and therefore somehow more religious, state. In the same way that the Tanzimat reforms and the transformation of the Ottoman legal system can be seen as case studies for similar transformations occurring in a global context, the role of religion in these reforms was not unique to the Ottoman situation. France, the birthplace of secularism, to some extent reunited religion and state in the mid nineteenth century.[22] Italy, Austria, and England had never separated them.[23] Various nineteenth and twentieth century Chinese governments attempted to reinterpret Confucian tenets in support of their reform movements.[24] The list is quite long. The point, though, is that in the Ottoman Empire, as elsewhere, religion played a key role in the reform of the modern legal system.

At the same time, the role that religion played changed drastically over precisely the same period. Reform along less than secular lines was certainly nothing new to the Ottoman Empire. With very few exceptions, all legal change in the Ottoman context had occurred under the aegis of the religious establishment.[25] Indeed, religion had been one of the tools with which the legal system had defined shifting social norms. Legislation of criminal law had arisen in response to specific changes in individual freedom or moral boundaries, and the religious establishment had supported this legislation.[26] When *kadı*s tried criminals according to these laws, they were showing in a very practical way where exactly the new boundaries had been set. Throughout the early Ottoman period, in other words, state and religion had worked together, but always as separate entities. Religious leaders had lent legitimacy and even authenticity to state-sponsored legal reform that had arisen in response to changes in society.

When the legal system and its institutions became self conscious and abstract, however, so too did the position of religion with regard to this system. In the nineteenth century and afterward, religion still acted as a support for the legislation of criminal law and the trying of criminals. But the nature of this new legislation meant that the religious establishment was tied to the bureaucracy and state in a way that it had never been before. When criminal law became about defining the legal system, its institutions, and the bureaucracy, rather than about defining shifting social norms, the religious establishment was forced to reinterpret its role. Again, religion was still a primary source of legitimacy and authenticity in the legislation of criminal law. But now, neither religion nor law was responding to social change—they were responding to institutional change. The purpose of the religious establishment therefore became first and foremost to define and to legitimize the legal system's institutions and bureaucracy. Instead of working alongside the state to facilitate social change, it became a pillar of the state, divorced from social reality. The religious establishment was an important element, that is to say, in the growing totalitarian nature of the modern Ottoman legal system.

Use of the word totalitarian sometimes makes people nervous. To be explicit, therefore: when I use it here, I am using it in its most basic form. That is, I am defining totalitarian as a system of law or government in which the individual, and every other aspect of life, is subordinated to the state. I am not, of course, arguing that the late Ottoman Empire was a totalitarian state. Abdülhamid II and the Committee of Union and Progress may have had fantasies in that direction, but they were certainly not realizable. The Turkish Republic's nature is more debatable, but we shall leave that alone for now. What I am arguing is that the development of the modern Ottoman criminal law system exhibited totalitarian tendencies. And it is these tendencies that lead us to the conclusion of this story, the moment at which Mustafa Kemal Atatürk, president of the new Turkey, adopted Mussolini's fascist code of criminal law for Turkish Republican use.

One of the more striking indicators of the increasing totalitarian nature of the Ottoman legal system was the Ottoman government's attitude toward political crime. The number and types of crimes that could be committed against the Ottoman state rose dramatically over the course of the nineteenth and twentieth centuries. Once again, this is not an occurrence that was unique to the Ottoman Empire. Political crime had become a pressing issue for governments from Japan to England to Argentina. Where there was no obvious conspiracy against the state, the state tended to make one up. In general, therefore, totalitarian law was the fashion all over the world.

In the Ottoman case, however, this growing emphasis on political crime can be easily traced back to the trends I have been describing thus far. When law becomes discursive and relates only to the legal system that created it, when morality becomes crystallized and no longer relates to social norms, and when religion becomes a pillar of the bureaucracy, the only sort of crime that can be relevant is political crime. Law, morality, and religion are all pillars of the state in such an order. The state is consequently the only "victim" truly worthy of the legal system's notice.

There are all sorts of implications to this transformation, of course. Most of them will be covered in the following chapters. I do, though, want to make note of David Streckfuss' analysis of discursive crime in Thailand, in which he writes:

> certain modern political crimes, such as lèse majesté, sedition, or insulting national symbols are purely discursive crimes. Such crimes do not physically threaten the state, but erode the state's construction of what it contends is a sacred national identity. Moreover, the prosecution of these cases produces its own peculiar convoluted logic . . . In a regular slander case, the central issue is substantiating the truth—that is, a statement of truth that sullies one's reputation is not slander . . . in lèse majesté cases, however, it is not necessary to substantiate the truth, for the truth of what was said is not at issue. Ascertaining guilt remains at the level of its hypothetical impact, determined by the projected effect the words would have on the listeners.[27]

In other words, in a discursive legal system, not only are individuals not obviously protected by the law anymore, but they can be prosecuted for committing imaginary crimes. Individuals are either completely free—in the sense that the Marquis de Sade desired freedom—or they are not free at all. It does not matter, because the focus of the law is no longer on individuals.

After the fall of the Ottoman State and the coalescence of the Turkish Republic, Atatürk set out to reform—once again—Turkey's legal system. He was not as constrained by traditional checks and balances as earlier reformers had been. Consequently, when he decided to adopt various European codes of law in their entirety, or to a great extent in their entirety, very few people protested. Those who did protest were not heard. And so the German commercial code and code of criminal procedure were adopted. The Swiss civil code—with some rather major alterations—was adopted. And the fascist Italian criminal code was also adopted.[28]

Why did Atatürk adopt Mussolini's criminal law? He did so because such a law was the logical conclusion to the trends I have been describing. He did so because he could. And he did so not least because in the 1930s totalitarianism was in fashion. When the new codes of law were approved by the Turkish parliament, a number of members got up and made a number of speeches. In these speeches, the members of parliament noted that the Italian code was the newest, the most modern, and the most civilized code around. Many historians like to find underlying meaning behind the words of such politicians. That is, the politicians may have said "new, modern, and civilized," but what they *meant* was "conservative, traditional, and barbaric." Such an interpretation is not necessary, however. In the same way that politicians and scholars in a variety of countries saw fascism as the way forward, so too did their counterparts in Turkey.

Fascist law was, after all, simply positivist[29] law tweaked to some extent. And positivism by the 1920s and 1930s had a long and distinguished tradition in a variety of different countries. In general, positivist law defined crime as the behavior of a biologically determined criminal type. The activity, any activity, of someone classed as a "criminal" according to pre-determined scientific indicators was necessarily a crime. The purpose of criminal law, therefore, was not to define "crime," certainly not to rehabilitate criminals who were, after all, biologically predestined to act in a criminal manner, but to protect the social body from these evolutionarily disadvantaged parasites.[30] Replace "social body" with "state" or "party" and you have, essentially, fascist criminal law. Indeed, when Jacob Landau notes the ease with which former pan-Turkist poets were incorporated into the early Republican intellectual framework, merely by their replacement of the word "Turan" (the Turks as a people regardless of political borders) with "Vatan" (the Nation),[31] the issue is not just one of scansion. There had indeed been a shift in the understanding of what was to be worshiped and protected. Before, it was the positivist conception of the Turks as a social body. Now, it was the fascist conception of the Turkish nation-state.

Perhaps a more appropriate question to ask, therefore, is why did Atatürk adopt Mussolini's criminal law, whereas, say, Raymond Poincaré did not? It will sound like something of an evasion, but Atatürk adopted a fascist law, whereas Poincaré did not, because under the historical circumstances, Atatürk could. Again, totalitarianism appealed to people everywhere during the 1920s and 1930s. But the clean slate from which totalitarian structures could be imposed required certain prerequisites. First, the country had to be independent. A government that sought to create such radical new institutions had to have a completely free hand in doing so. That leaves out the colonized world. Second, the country had to be in a situation in which traditional checks on a leader's power were temporarily curtailed. That leaves out France, England, the United States, and other states. The countries that lost the First World War, or were seriously destabilized by it, however, are another story.

The final two chapters of this study will go into more detail about this eventual adoption of the fascist code. For now, it is simply worth repeating that the Turkish adoption of a fascist criminal code should be in no way surprising given the trajectory of criminal law reform for the century leading up to it. Nor should it be considered anomalous. Atatürk adopted the code because he was able to. Any other leader in his position would likely have done the same.

It will not have escaped the notice of the more observant that I have built up an edifice here with little or no evidence to support it. The following chapters will set out to rectify this problem. In general, these chapters will follow a chronological framework, with each section bounded by a new legislation of criminal law. After two brief chapters discussing historical and legal background, that is, Chapter Three will cover the period (1840–1850) overseen by the first "reformed" code; Chapter Four will cover the period (1851–1858) overseen by the second, even more reformed code; Chapter Five will cover the period (1859–1876) overseen by the third, extraordinarily reformed code, and so on. Each chapter will also tackle one major element of the argument I have sketched out above.

In the first decade we shall see the creation of an abstract criminal law system and the positioning of the religious establishment within this system. The chapter covering this decade will ask how early Tanzimat legal reformers viewed criminal law, and where they felt they ought to place religion in developing this law. The next chapter will look at the shifting focus from crime against victims to victimless crime between the years 1851 and 1858. It will discuss, that is, the creation of a discursive criminal law system in the Ottoman context. How, it will ask, did mid Tanzimat legal reformers use the system they had created to define what crime now was?

In Chapter Five, I shall trace the growing importance of political crime between 1859 and 1876. In general, this chapter will cover the bureaucratization of criminal law in the years leading up to the promulgation of the Constitution. Chapter Six will return to the question of religion and law. It will look at the role of the religious establishment in turning political crime into sin between 1877 and 1908. How did *ulema* help to define the post-Tanzimat trajectory of Ottoman criminal law, and how were they trained to behave in this system? In Chapter Seven I shall examine the positivist and totalitarian tendencies of Ottoman criminal law between 1909 and the end of the First World War. Finally, Chapters Eight and Nine will cover the early Republican period. They will look at the Turkish adoption of Mussolini's fascist code of criminal law, and whether or not this adoption really was the logical conclusion of earlier legal reform.

All of these chapters will explicitly or implicitly challenge a number of theses about late Ottoman and early Turkish Republican development. First, there is the idea that Ottoman legal reform was an essentially secularist undertaking,[32] that as time passed, secular and religious law—especially criminal law—separated, with the former eventually pushing out the latter. This book sees exactly the opposite phenomenon occurring. Far from a separation and a battle over jurisdiction, the reorganized system simply incorporated the institutions, personnel, and ideology of the religious establishment as it developed. Second, many still hold to the belief that there was a definitive break between the Ottoman period and the Turkish Republican period,[33] that Atatürk's reforms created an Anatolian Turkey completely divorced from its Ottoman past. This book instead sees more continuity than change. The legal system that arose in Republican Turkey was a direct result of the legal system that had been created in the late Ottoman Empire. And then finally, there is the idea that legal reform in the Middle East somehow went in a hugely different direction than simultaneous legal reform in Europe or elsewhere.[34] Again, it will for the most part be implicit and contextual, but the questions that the following chapters raise should apply as much to France, Italy, or Argentina as they do to the Ottoman Empire and Turkey.

Which bring us to the issue with which we started. This book also seeks to look at law and the modern development of law in a new way. The creation of abstract institutions divorced from social reality in the nineteenth and twentieth centuries is something that has been discussed in some detail before.[35] Analyzing the legislation of criminal law (if not criminality and punishment) in the Ottoman Empire in this context is therefore a nice case study, but to some extent derivative. Placing the religious establishment in the foreground of this process, however, and drawing from it the development of a fascist legal system is, I think, a new twist. If the bureaucratization and abstraction of the criminal law system leads to a fascist understanding of crime and criminality, if it turns political crime into sin, then the purpose of law in a supposedly disciplinary society becomes clear: to rationalize the apparently irrational desire of individuals to be dominated by a party or state.

Chapter One
Historical Context

The period with which this book concerns itself—the nineteenth and twentieth centuries—marked the culmination of 600 years of uninterrupted political rule by a single dynasty. In the late thirteenth century, Osman I, the eponymous founder of the Ottoman ruling house, began to consolidate military power in central Anatolia. He was one of many competing Turkic princes in the area, but a combination of strategy, geography, and ideological creativity helped him to transform his principality into the nucleus of an empire. Osman I and his descendants quickly expanded Ottoman rule into the Balkans and eventually into eastern Anatolia. By 1453, the Ottomans had replaced the Byzantines as the rulers of Constantinople and its environs. By 1529, they were besieging Vienna for the first time.

By the early sixteenth century, the Ottomans had also conquered much of the Arabic speaking Middle East, and in traditional accounts of Ottoman history, this century is seen as the "classical" Ottoman century. By the beginning of seventeenth century, these accounts continue, Ottoman military power was waning and the Empire as a whole was in decline. Starting in 1683, with the second siege of Vienna, Ottoman borders began to collapse, and throughout the eighteenth century, the Austrian Empire and the Russian Empire began to expand at Ottoman expense. By the beginning of the nineteenth century, threats to Ottoman sovereignty came not just from the Austrians, Russians, British, and French, but also from internal nationalist movements.

The reform movements of the nineteenth century, undertaken first by autocratic Sultans and then later by various factions within the bureaucracy are often seen in this literature as responses to the post seventeenth century territorial contraction.[1] Ottoman leaders and intellectuals looked around, it is argued, saw that their Empire was in decline, acknowledged the superiority of European or Western technology, governance, law, and eventually world view, and attempted in their reforms to "copy" Europe. In the same way, however, that more recent scholarship has convincingly challenged the decline thesis, noting in particular the dynamic nature of social, intellectual, and political life in the later centuries of Ottoman rule,[2] this "reform as reaction" thesis has been increasingly questioned over the past few years. But before addressing the problematic elements of this argument, I want to describe the nature of the late Ottoman political and bureaucratic transformation.

In 1839, Reşid Paşa, the Ottoman Foreign Minister and later Grand Vezir under Sultan Abdülmecid I (1839–1861), initiated the Tanzimat (1839–1876) by reading an imperial decree in Gülhane, the "Rose Chamber." The decree promised all Ottoman "citizens"—a newly defined category—the right to "life, honor, and property," an equitable system of taxation and military conscription, and an organized system of law and legal procedure.[3] All of these reforms were couched in a rhetoric of Islamic political philosophy and Islamic law, and all of them were set up against a modernist and quasi-liberal backdrop.[4] The Tanzimat was thus an attempt at reinterpreting and repositioning earlier Ottoman ideals of justice and legality within a mid nineteenth century context.

Following the reading of the Gülhane decree, the Ottoman government began to reorganize its bureaucracy. A number of ministries were created and bureaucratic hierarchies and salary structures formed. The most relevant of these for our purposes is the legislative council (the *Meclis-i Vâlâ-yı Ahkam-ı Adliye*),[5] which became the Ministry of Justice in 1868.[6] This council promulgated new land laws, commercial laws, a civil code (not inclusive of family law, which remained un-codified until 1917), and a number of criminal codes. It—and eventually the Justice Ministry that replaced it—also oversaw the implementation and staffing of the "regular" (*nizamî*) [7] courts that were supposed to implement the new laws. Finally, in 1876, the Grand Vezir, Midhat Paşa, read the new Ottoman Constitution, based roughly on a Belgian model, and with that the Tanzimat ended.

The Constitution remained in effect for less than a year. A combination of rapid territorial contraction, European diplomatic maneuvering, and ideological repositioning led the new Sultan, Abdülhamid II (1876–1909), to dismiss the parliament and to engage in his own version of reform. Traditional historiography often paints Abdülhamid II as a reactionary. It sees the Sultan's anti-liberal bent, his less than tolerant minority policy, his politicization of Islamic identity, and his dismissal of European diplomatic intervention as evidence that what had started off "modern" during the Tanzimat had gone wildly off course.

Again, more recent scholarship has effectively challenged this take on Abdülhamid II. Indeed, it was only under his rule that Tanzimat era plans and legislation took effective form.[8] The Ottoman law school opened in 1878 and started actual operation in the 1880s, the regular court system was efficiently staffed and instituted in the provinces, and the overall bureaucratization of the law—the promised "organization"—became an Empire wide phenomenon. It might also be pointed out that Abdülhamid II's reinterpretation of political identity, the structures that he destroyed, and those that he created were certainly not out of place in the late nineteenth and early twentieth centuries. In fact, he would arguably have been far more "reactionary" if he had clung to a late eighteenth century liberal understanding of the state/citizen relationship, rather than taking part in the authoritarian nationalism that was the trend in so many other states.

Whatever the case, Abdülhamid II's take on political authority did nonetheless create an environment in which challenges to that authority were equally strident. And in 1908, the Committee of Union and Progress, the Young Turks, brought about a successful political coup. The CUP had started as a student organization in the Ottoman medical school—a group of sociological positivists with an obsessive belief in the morality of science, who wanted to test their political theories in an empirical context.[9] After 1908, they got their chance. Chapter Seven goes into greater detail about the interplay between Young Turk positivism and the trajectory of Ottoman law. For now, it suffices to say that for the most part, the CUP maintained most of Abdülhamid II's legal and bureaucratic structures, merely infusing them with a more self consciously "scientific" tone.

In 1914, the Ottoman Empire ended up on the wrong side of the First World War, and in 1919 a representative of the Sultan's government (the CUP leaders had fled) signed the Treaty of Sèvres. Sèvres effectively destroyed the Ottoman state, leaving the Sultan as ruler of slightly less land than that with which Osman I had started out in 1299. 1919 was not 1299, however, and by the twentieth century a number of Turkish speaking intellectuals and military leaders had constructed and developed a sense of Turkish ethnic identity. One of these, Mustafa Kemal (eventually Atatürk) (president 1923–1938), refused to accept the terms of Sèvres, and set about creating a Turkish nation state within the "traditional homeland" of the Turks.[10] In less than four years, Mustafa Kemal and his associates had managed to re-take almost all of the land that they had designated in their National Pact as "Turkish," and in 1923, a representative of the Turkish government signed the Treaty of Lausanne, which abolished Sèvres and established the Republic of Turkey.

Before going into detail about the direction of early Turkish Republican law, I want to return to the question of the nature of late Ottoman reform. I mentioned before that traditional historiography has depicted Tanzimat era and post Tanzimat era reform as a frantic reaction to the supposed military, political, and intellectual superiority of Europe or the West. This is a problematic take for a variety of reasons. On a basic level, the chronology does not work. If we assume that the Ottoman government was playing a constant game of catch up with various European governments, we would expect modern ideas or institutions to appear in these European countries before they did in the Ottoman Empire. This was not the case. To pick a few key issues closest to the heart of this study, the Ottoman reinterpretation of the citizen/state relationship occurred simultaneously with, or before, similar reinterpretations in European countries, as did the codification and organization of Ottoman legal systems.[11]

Perhaps more to the point, we see a self consciousness about what is modern and what is not in the Ottoman Empire before or alongside similar self consciousness in most European states. The Tanzimat was an official, explicit "regulatory reorganization."[12] The regular courts, were, again, explicitly "regulatory" or "organized." Even the *nizam-i cedid,* the troops that were supposed to supplant the "corrupt" Janissaries in the reign of Selim III (1789–1807) were not literally "new troops," as they are often called but "the new *order.*" This fixation on organization, rationality, and order—arguably one of the most important defining characteristic of the modern mindset—would not become evident in many European states until the end of the nineteenth century.

Finally, if we follow the "reform as reaction" thesis to its logical conclusion, we have to assume that similar trends were not occurring in the "stronger" European states. If, that is, these processes were the result of a consciousness of imperial decline, then those states not "in decline" would presumably not be interested in them. Obviously this was not the case. The governments of the British and French Empires, militarily the strongest of the day, were constantly attempting to reform themselves and their subjects, constantly bemoaning the "corrupt" and "weakened" state of their current systems, and constantly looking both backward and forward to a pure tradition upon which a progressive future might be built. Modernity, that is, was in no way geographically situated.

I am emphasizing this point not for reasons of sensitivity or politics, but because it is at the heart of my argument. Tanzimat and post-Tanzimat reform in the Ottoman Empire was part of a larger process occurring for the most part on a global scale. Yes, by the beginning of the twentieth century the Ottoman Empire was in a quasi-colonial relationship with various European powers. Yes, there was a definite sense of military imbalance. But the internal workings of the Ottoman state were still very much in Ottoman hands.[13] "Reform" was a self conscious and self reflective process. And in the same way that the British state and the French state used bureaucratic transformation to define for themselves British and French political identity, the Ottoman state did the same.

With the coming of the Turkish Republic, this intrusive style of social engineering became even more pronounced. More so than Ottoman reformers, Turkish reformers were certain about what Turkey was, and intent upon creating a state and citizenry that conformed to this definition. "Reform" in fact became "revolution" under Turkish auspices—although it remained very much a top down transformation—and every aspect of social, political, or personal life that could be monitored was. Among other Republican era changes, the alphabet went from the Arabic to the Latin; the language was purged of "foreign" words; Ankara became the capital city and was rebuilt using a fascist/neo-classical architectural model; a great deal of sartorial legislation was enacted, most of which is still hotly contested today; and, of course, the legal system underwent massive changes.

Between 1926 and 1938 Ottoman law almost completely disappeared and was replaced by Turkish versions of the Swiss civil code, the Italian criminal code, and the German code of criminal procedure. The law school in Ankara—teaching modern, nationalist legal methods—quickly overshadowed the law school in Istanbul that had been set up under Abdülhamid II. Both political law and criminal law were reinterpreted such that they could support a Republican presidential/dictatorial system. But most important, law in general—much like every other early Republican structure—had to conform to a radical, state-based notion of Turkish nationality that could tolerate the existence of no competing ideologies of identities. And arguably, this is where Republican legal change was the most "revolutionary."

Even under the CUP, Ottoman political philosophy had acknowledged, if not necessarily tolerated, the existence of alternative ideologies and political identities. Under the Turkish Republic, this was not the case. Turkey was a modern, radical nation state, and its government had no interest in, and no need to conform to neo-liberal standards of state behavior or even to recognize that these standards existed. It was only in such a context that the trends in legal philosophy that had begun in the early nineteenth century could come to fruition. Mussolini's criminal code could not have functioned in a state hampered by the 600 year old imperial legacy of the Ottoman ruling house. In a compact nation state with a legacy of less than a decade, however, the fascist understanding of criminality operated, for a time at least, quite smoothly.

Chapter Two

Legal Context

Nineteenth century Ottoman criminal law was very much a product of earlier trends in legal thinking. It was without question a break, a disruption of "the traditional," but at the same time a self consciousness about "tradition" influenced its growth. Modern Ottoman criminal law was thus largely a reinterpretation of what had come to be seen as authentic and classical—a reinterpretation, however, effected for thoroughly modern aims. This chapter will attempt to define this "traditional" or "authentic" conception of law for the purposes of late Ottoman legal reform. In particular it will ask two questions: first, who was "the victim"—the individual, society, God, or the state—that the early Ottoman penal system attempted to protect? And second, how did the relationship between religion and state play out over this period?

Since the second question is more structural than the first, I am going to start with the issue of religion/state interaction. The Ottoman legal system was, again, Islamic law interpreted for Ottoman purposes. As such, we cannot really talk about "state" law and "religious" law, or a division between the two, at any period in Ottoman history. The state—along with its criminal law system—operated according to Islamic political theory, and necessarily there was a great deal of interaction between religious and temporal authority.

This interaction, however, looked quite different prior to the nineteenth century than it would after the Tanzimat era incorporation—unification—of the two spheres.[1] Whereas in the nineteenth and twentieth centuries, political crime took on distinct and deliberate religious overtones, in the earlier period political crime and religious crime remained largely separate—to the extent that the religious and the temporal did interact, it was the state that put into effect rulings produced by the religious establishment.

This pre-Tanzimat relationship between religion and state was very much a legacy of "classical" Islamic jurisprudence. The Abbasid caliphs in the ninth century were the first to create a hierarchy of *kadı*s, concerned solely with divine law.

The Abbasids also developed the *mazalim* system, an alternative judicial system based upon the authority of the political leader, to bolster the *kadı* hierarchy. They thereby involved temporal state power in the administration of religious law, attempting in the process to apply a "purely" religious understanding of criminality to the daily practice of imperial rule.

There were also, however, a number of logistical difficulties that the Abbasids had to overcome in their application of this system. First of all, religious criminal law addressed only a few key issues, most of which were not crimes of the day to day sort, and none of which concerned issues of administrative irregularity or abuse.[2] Second, the rulings of *kadı*s could not be appealed to other *kadı*s. Once a decision had been made in a *kadı*'s court, it was set.[3] Finally, the evidentiary requirements needed to try criminals accused of the major crimes against God were nearly impossible to meet, and *kadı*s were not allowed to risk a miscarriage of divine justice by relaxing them. The *mazalim* system therefore existed primarily to deal with minor crimes, with abuses of temporal power, with complaints against, or "appeals" of, *kadı*s' rulings, and with cases that called for relaxed procedural rules.[4] The *mazalim* system also legitimized the state's role in effecting the punishments decided in the *kadı*s' courts—courts that in and of themselves had no power of enforcement.

The Ottoman version of this system was not as different from the Abbasid version as has sometimes been argued. Under Sultan Murad I (1359–1389) the *kadı*s were organized into an administrative hierarchy,[5] and linked to the temporal bureaucracy by the fact that their effective power was in the hands of the Grand Vezir. The Sultan oversaw his *divan,* or council—the Ottoman equivalent of the *mazalim* court—as did each of the provincial governors appointed by him.[6] And even though *kadı*s did often have the power to enforce as well as to judge in the Ottoman context, any punishment of a serious sort had to be confirmed and administered by the Sultan's temporal arm.[7] In general, *kadı*s were always answerable to state authorities (governors and vezirs),[8] even if the rhetoric of a separation of the two spheres remained. But this rhetoric was not meaningless. The *kadı*s had "judicial" power. It was the *kadı*s who were responsible for "justice." The governors and vezirs had "disciplinary" power,[9] and to the extent that they punished wrongdoers, this wrong-doing was crime rather than sin.

At the same time, it is worth highlighting the fact that of the duties of the original *mazalim* court, the ones that interested the Ottoman government almost to the exclusion of all others were, first, eliminating the abuse of administrative power, and second, seeing to it that *kadı*s and their rulings were not "mistaken." Rather than concerning itself with minor crimes committed by or against individuals, or with major cases that called for relaxed procedural rules, that is, the Ottoman version of the *mazalim* court existed to a large extent to police the Ottoman bureaucracy. Indeed, as Uriel Heyd points out, the early criminal law's "main emphasis [was] placed on the protection of society and not . . . on safeguarding the rights of the individual,"[10] and "the chief object of the [sixteenth and seventeenth century] Ottoman penal codes . . . was not the protection of society against criminals but the protection of the common people against oppressive officials and fief-holders."[11]

Although the increasingly interactive relationship between religion and state that we shall see in the modern period by no means existed at this time, in other words, its antecedents did. The *mazalim* system had been reinterpreted even by the early Ottomans as a means of increasing state control over the legal system as a whole. To the extent that it could be, the religious establishment was incorporated into the bureaucratic structure—or at least the bureaucracy was used to control religious judges.[12] Over the course of Sultan Selim III's reign (1789–1807), in fact, *kadıs* were tried with greater and greater frequency by the administrative council for activities "contrary to law"—including not just mistaken rulings, but bribe taking, partiality, and similarly "corrupt" practices.[13]

By the late eighteenth and early nineteenth centuries, the stage was thus set for the Tanzimat era re-interpretation of the religion/state relationship. The religious establishment was not playing the ideological role that it eventually would—turning bureaucratic crime into sin—but the structural change that would lead to this shift was underway. What eventually made the complete shift possible is the focus of the second section of this chapter—the modern reinterpretation of "the victim." Whereas prior to the Tanzimat era, criminal law sought to protect, variously, society, the individual, God, or an abstract morality, by the late nineteenth century, it sought to protect the state.

The structural separation implied in the pre-modern *kadı/mazalim* dichotomy is reflected in the sorts of crimes that each adjudicated. The *kadıs*' courts oversaw *hadd* crime or crimes against God—divine law as it was articulated in the Quran. The *mazalim* courts oversaw crimes against "the public"—crimes that had not been enumerated in any fundamental text, but that were nonetheless dangerous to public welfare. The two "victims" protected by pre-Tanzimat criminal law were, therefore, on the one hand God, and on the other hand the public. Crimes that could be committed against the first—the *hadd* crimes—included rebellion, apostasy, drunkenness, theft, banditry (highway robbery), adultery/fornication, and false accusation of adultery/fornication.[14] All of these crimes were defined explicitly, as were their punishments and the evidence required to produce a conviction. The punishments were harsh, usually death, lashings, or amputation, but the evidentiary requirements necessary to inflict these punishments were next to impossible to meet—four "morally upright" witnesses who would swear to having seen a couple committing adultery, for example. In general, prior to the modern period and the violent spectacle of authenticity that so frequently accompanies modern identity formation, states tried to restrict the meting out of *hadd* punishments as much as possible.[15]

In addition to punishment and evidence, intent played a key role in distinguishing sin, or an attack against God or morality, as opposed to crime or an attack against public welfare. Children and the insane, for example, were not subject to *hadd* procedure.[16] Since they were not capable of differentiating between good and evil, they were exempt from the attribution of sin associated with the *hadd* punishments. Similarly, if a criminal repented before being arrested, he was sentenced not in a *kadi*'s court, but in a *mazalim* court. Repentance implied the existence of "good" intent alongside "evil" activity, and it was the purpose of the *kadi*'s court to punish only the "evil." In general, that is, the defining characteristic of crimes tried by *kadi*s in the pre-Tanzimat Ottoman courts was the intent to commit an act against God. As such, they were relatively small in number and, to reiterate, had very little to do with administration or the functioning of bureaucratic structures.

The second category of crime—that tried in the *mazalim* courts—occupied almost exactly the opposite position in legal thought, existing solely to protect society and by extension the individual. This type of crime (*tazir* crime) included the misbehavior of functionaries and administrators, *hadd* crimes whose evidentiary or definitional requirements could not be met, homicide when the heirs forgave the murderer, and various petty crimes not enumerated in the Quran. In adjudicating these crimes, intent was less important than damage done, and the punishments were less severe than the *hadd* punishments. In general, the victim of these crimes was understood to be the public, and the purpose of punishing them was to serve the public welfare.

This concept of "public welfare"—*maslaha*—deserves some elaboration, however.[17] First of all, it was a collective concept. Although *tazir* crimes were usually brought to trial by the injured party, they also implied the existence of a more abstract victim in the form of a social whole, represented by the Muslim community. Even though *tazir* crimes were usually torts, therefore, to the extent that they were about damage done specifically to an individual, this damage had to represent an attack on public welfare as well.[18]

In the pre-Ottoman and early Ottoman period, this understanding of public welfare and benefit remained a relatively conservative one. Defined as anything that helped to avert damage, *maslaha* was determined by scholars such as Ghazali to be the maintenance of "religion, life, offspring, reason, and property."[19] It was, in other words, a concept that preserved social norms rather than one that challenged them. In the nineteenth and especially the twentieth centuries, this understanding of *maslaha* began to change—its original meaning giving way to a more "modern"[20] one that undermined both individual interests and the maintenance of the status quo. In the twentieth century, in fact, *maslaha* came to be defined not as "public welfare," but as "national interest,"[21] with all of the political, moral, and legal notions that the concept implies. Prior to the Tanzimat, that is, the "public" victimized by *tazir* crime was an amalgam of individual and group consciousness—set up in distinction against the God and the morality that were the victims of *hadd* crimes. By the nineteenth century, the two had begun to overlap, with the modern state—the national interest—coming to represent both.

A final category of crime—homicide—was also tried by Ottoman *kadıs* and occupied a tenuous position between *hadd* and *tazir.* Homicide, although also usually a tort in Islamic law, was simultaneously invested with a definite moral weight. In general, the heirs to a homicide victim would bring the case to trial, and the role of the judge was to determine solely whether the accused had committed the act. If the defendant was guilty, the heirs/plaintiffs had the right to choose among *lex talionis* (*kısas*), blood money (*diyet*), or forgiveness. Although if the heirs chose to forgive a convicted murderer, the state could step in and try him in a *mazalim* court.

The Hanafi school of law—the school followed by the Ottomans—was particularly concerned with the role of intent and morality in addition to social harm in homicide cases. First of all, the Hanafis argued that in a straightforward murder conviction, the heirs had to ask for *lex talionis* rather than blood money, since *lex talionis* benefited society as well as the next of kin.[22] Second, unintentional killing as opposed to murder could never be punished by *lex talionis,* nor could a homicide that had been committed under coercion. Both of these situations implied an absence of the obvious intent necessary to a completely guilty frame of mind. Finally, the Hanafi school emphasized the importance of deliberation—a homicide committed with, for example, a blunt instrument, rather than with a more obvious weapon could not be punished with *lex talionis,* they argued, because such a homicide was implicitly "a mistake," or at least not fully deliberate.[23] In general, that is, homicide was understood to be both a social and a moral crime. The role of the *kadı* was largely to determine the "frame of mind" of the accused, and the "victim" of the crime was a combination of the individual, the heirs, society and abstract moral values.

Prior to the nineteenth century, that is, Ottoman and Islamic law sought to protect the individual, God, and society. The institutions threatened by criminals were not the state or the bureaucracy, but the public and an abstract morality. It is true that the relationship between the religious structure and the temporal structure was constantly shifting, and that the role of the Ottoman *kadı* was likewise in a perpetual state of flux. But the two concepts that required legal protection—

morality and society—retained their distinctive position for the most part until the Tanzimat era transformations. Sin was a well defined and severely circumscribed concept—even if codified, it was limited to activities explicitly forbidden by the Quran. Crime, likewise, was largely circumscribed. If an activity was not contrary to "public benefit," the temporal authority had no right to legislate against it. It was only in the modern period that both victimhood and sinfulness began to expand as concepts. As we shall see, this, along with one final re-articulation of the religion/state relationship, set the groundwork for the emergence of bureaucratic sin, and for the creation of a criminal law system intent largely on the policing of itself.

Chapter Three

1840 to 1850: Crime and the Bureaucracy

England is one of the only European nation states without a codified legal system—a situation that has baffled people both inside and outside of the country since the mid nineteenth century, when legal codification became the mark of a civilized society.[1] Some of the most vocal proponents of legal codification—Jeremy Bentham in particular—came out of the British legal tradition, and yet their ideas were heeded only in other countries, or "at best" in British colonies. Why then did the British government not codify its legal system? And what produced the collection of confused observers? A variety of responses have been proposed in answer to at least the first of these questions. Scholars have argued variously that codification is not part of the English tradition, that the English legal establishment is inherently conservative, or that English common law is more flexible than codified law and therefore simply a better system.[2] The second question tends to attract less scholarly attention. Max Weber is usually held up as the exemplar of confused outside observers in the same way that Bentham is held up as the exemplar of irritated internal supporters of a "rational" system of law. The question is thus distilled into one about law as performance—into a discussion of the relationship between legal transformation and modern identity formation, between codification and political re-birth.

Lindsay Farmer, for example, in her discussion of "The English Codification Debate" argues the following with regard to legal reform in the British context:

> Logically, the [codified] criminal law is seen as the key to the completeness of the law, but in practice (at the level of signs) it is recognized always to be incomplete. Due to both the limitation of language and the changing nature of the social, the positive law will never succeed in establishing a closed, universally valid, system of values. Thus the need for reform is introduced as a constitutive feature of the law, constituting a new rationality of reform through the foundational recognition of the imperfection of the law.[3]

Although her point has more to do with the relationship between law and society in England specifically, the connection that she makes between systematization and reform can apply anywhere. It is generally accepted that a codified law is *easier* to reform. But Farmer goes a step further and argues that a codified law demands reform. It is not just that codification is progressive and purifying, that is, it is also that codification presupposes future progress and future purification.

Making the law "rational" is meaningful, in other words, only if we assume first, that the social context in which it was formerly operating is productive of imperfection, and second, that the law ought to be pure. If we do accept these notions, however, then a perfect legal code would be one that represented an equally perfect social/national structure—one that was both derived from and the norm for a static social ideal. The goal, in other words, would be a codified law that was valid despite the "limitation of language" and despite "the changing nature of the social"—a law that could represent an essential national or social character. Rational, codified law is therefore necessarily a law that is undergoing a continual process of re-definition and refinement—codification upon codification of social and political norms.

In England, this process was half hearted at best. The Ottoman Empire was a different story. Throughout the Tanzimat period, Ottoman criminal law was codified and reformed a number of times. And each time it was codified, the ways in which reformers defined and rectified previous imperfections shifted according to new—usually authoritarian—notions of the state/citizen relationship. Even as their understanding of criminality became increasingly radical and rigid, however, these reformers never strayed far from the liberal rhetoric of progress. Between 1840 and 1850, that is, as the modern Ottoman legal system was established, as the concept of criminality was idealized, as criminal law came to protect the purity of bureaucratic function rather than the rights of the individual, it was the rational, humane, and modern nature of the state that was invoked. It did not matter that criminal law was being detached from the messy reality that was Ottoman society—in a progressive state, bureaucratic institutions would completely replace social or moral ones.

DEFINING "THE STATE" IN THE 1840 CRIMINAL CODE

Although Tanzimat era legal reform was decidedly different from that which had preceded it, it did not develop out of a vacuum. As early as the sixteenth and seventeenth centuries, the legislation of Ottoman criminal law had aimed not at protecting the individual *per se,* but at limiting or defining the powers of administrative officials.[4] The Ottoman penal codes developed during this period operated within overlapping religious and temporal spheres, where the power of both *kadı*s and governors were repeatedly redefined. But the law in general remained within the realm of Islamic jurisprudence (*fikh*). A number of fifteenth and sixteenth century *ulema* and *Şeyhülislams*, for example, wrote treatises explicitly placing the new criminal codes within the overall sphere of Islamic political theory. Likewise, the mutual support of the *Şeyhülislam* and the Sultan—the former issuing legal decisions (*fetvas*) in defense of temporal sentencing practices, and the latter requesting this support—kept early Ottoman criminal law rooted within the realm of "classical" Islamic legal theory.[5] In the end, both the legislative and sentencing bodies that supported the pre-nineteenth century Ottoman codes were branches of a legal system self consciously "inherited" from the Abbasids.[6]

The intellectual starting point of the Tanzimat era codes was similarly "classical"—their aim being to redefine but not replace earlier administrative and legal authority. [7] Where things went upon leaving this starting point is another matter. Local elites and erratic *kadıs* remained one target of Ottoman criminal law. But they were joined by deviant bureaucrats and treasonous ideologues. Likewise, the goal of criminal law quickly became the creation of a pure, rational, centralized, and uniform state structure—a state structure that would be proof against any conceivable political, social, or intellectual attack.

The precursor to the 1840 code, for example, a short and pointed text from 1838, concerned itself almost exclusively with bribery and how to bring lawsuits against civil servants.[8] The individual, classical ideas about sin and social mores were not of any interest—instead, from the beginning of the Tanzimat period, the legislation of criminal law was about defining and policing the bureaucracy and its servants. Not much had changed by 1840. First of all, of the thirteen articles that make up the 1840 code, six have to do with state or bureaucratic crime.[9] Second, and more to the point, the 1839 Gülhane Edict and the bureaucratic reorganization that it embodied show up with increasing frequency throughout the code.

After their appearance in the introduction, for instance, in which "justice is joined" to "the imperial decree read at Gülhane," the edict or the ideas contained within it occur in almost all of the following articles.[10] The bureaucracy, that is, was beginning to play an increasingly central role in defining what Ottoman criminality was. To emphasize, "justice" is not joined here to ethics or to protection from murderers, thieves, and brigands. "Justice" has nothing to do with the rights and duties of Ottoman citizens. Instead, "justice" is joined to an administrative document, a hyperbolic version of a bureaucratic "regulation," the primary purpose of which was to redefine state institutions. Indeed, after this reference to the edict, we almost immediately come to a striking example of the codification/reform relationship described by Farmer. The code, it is noted in the introduction, is incomplete because of its rushed promulgation, and thus additions to it will continue to be made.[11] Now that the law has been codified, that is, it demands reform. Reform in turn demands the continuing existence and growth of the bureaucratic institutions devoted to this process—in this case, the Council of Judicial Ordinances (the *Meclis-i Vâlâ-yı Ahkam-ı Adliye*).

The articles that make up the body of the 1840 text continue in this vein. Chapter One, article one reads:

> His Imperial Majesty has solemnly promised and sworn that without exception the life of no subject of the Sublime State may be deliberately targeted, either secretly or publicly, by execution or poisoning. But those who openly venture to commit such acts as treachery against the Sultan, the Islamic legal (*şer'î*) sovereign of their allegiance, inciting rebellion against the Sublime State, or murdering humans [may be subject to execution] only after the necessary investigation and required inquiries are made, their cases have been heard many times, and a verdict has been pronounced upon the establishment of their guilt without prejudice; [aside from these situations] without exception, no functionary of the Sublime State or any other person may attempt to kill another person; for instance, should a vezir murder a shepherd, let *lex talionis* (*kısas*) be inflicted upon that vezir.[12]

This article is first and foremost a personal promise on the part of the Sultan to protect his subjects from murderers: the introductory sentence seems to be a straightforward attempt to define and protect society from the most basic personal crime around—murder. The sentence is immediately followed, however, by a conflation of murder and state crime. Murder in this subsequent section is not so much a question of individual rights or the protection of the individual—it is a question of the rights and protection of the state and the Sultan. The article indeed concludes—as nearly all of the articles in the code do—with a discussion of bureaucratic functionaries and what their role in the process ought to be. Even the specific example—the vezir murdering the shepherd—is seemingly addressed to misbehaving civil servants rather than to "ordinary" citizens. Starting with the introductory article, that is, the code's purpose is clear—first to define, and then to police, the new Ottoman bureaucracy. The rights of the individual do appear, but they appear in a tangential way, and are overwhelmed by an interest in the rights of the state and its institutions.

An article of the code in a section ostensibly having to do with slander continues in the same vein:

> Chastity and honor are as sacred and dear to a person as his life, and the safety and protection of these are among the necessities of patriotism and humanity. For instance, to dishonor a person with words, to beat a man, or to curse a person, mean violating that person's honor. Therefore, from now on, military and other law enforcement personnel such as soldiers, guards, and others shall

> not beat and swear at anyone as they wish. Thus, in the event of a fight or a quarrel in the streets, the duty [of law enforcement personnel] will be to apprehend the accused people and bring them directly to the appropriate police station without doing anything to them. From now on, regardless of his rank, whoever, whether he is a soldier or guard working in the service of law enforcement, swears at any other person or dishonors a person with words [will be punished]. If, for instance, such an event takes place in Istanbul and the person who dares to commit such an act happens to be a functionary of the Sublime State or a member of the ulema, let his case be heard at the Council of Judicial Ordinances, and let him be imprisoned for five to twenty five days, according to the importance and degree of his offence, and if it is established that his offense is very light, let the Council reprimand and scold him.[13]

Once again, what starts out as an article seemingly about crimes against personal honor turns into an article about the role of state functionaries. We have an oblique reference to the Gülhane Edict in the coming together of life, honor, and patriotism, a mention of personal dishonor, and then a definition first of the role of the police, second of the role of state functionaries, and then finally of the role of the *ulema.* This article goes a step further than the earlier one, however, noting that state functionaries will be tried by a simultaneously administrative/legislative and judicial institution—the Council of Judicial Ordinances—rather than by a court, thereby placing the bureaucracy once more at the apex of the system. The purity of bureaucratic function is in this manner tied to the apparent, if not actual, external manifestations of a rational judicial power.

And this focus on the system and on the purity of function continues throughout the 1840 code. There are a number of articles on murder, for example. But never do we see a definition of murder, a specific discussion of what its punishment might be, and certainly never an analysis of a murderer's relationship to society. Instead, the articles on murder emphasize the importance of sending appropriate reports on the cases, the proper procedure for investigation, and the role of the provincial and central councils.[14] Questions of intent, of hierarchies of violence, of the quality of moral transgression are never raised in these articles, moving the code gradually away from its "classical" Islamic foundation. There is rather an emphasis on uniform procedure, on the importance of institutional reform, and on provincial and central councils—underlining the necessity for increasing bureaucratic centralization. The only power or violence of interest to the criminal code is the power and violence wielded by the new bureaucracy. Violence committed by individual actors is neither targeted, nor for that matter admitted.

The articles on personal or individual crime are thus characterized by vague and sometimes non-existent definitions wed to specific, self conscious procedural instruction. Procedure, in fact, almost completely overwhelms definition in these sections of the criminal code. This situation, however, changes when we get to the chapters devoted to political crime. In these chapters, the primary focus of the text is still the institutional process, but defining criminal behavior also becomes important: what exactly constitutes a crime is suddenly spelled out in detail. First of all, such crimes are divided into two sections—crimes by word and crimes by deed. On the one hand, a person might encourage others "with rebellious words to actions against the Sublime State or its laws and regulations." On the other, a person might supply others with weapons or gunpowder or himself engage in a conspiracy. Whatever the case, the jurisdiction over such issues falls once again to the Council of Judicial Ordinances, and not to a purely judicial court.[15]

Both definition and procedure are explicit here. Procedurally, jurisdiction over political crime falls to the simultaneously judicial and legislative/administrative Council of Judicial Ordinances. The bureaucracy, rather than a court, is once again called upon to protect the rights of the state. Of perhaps more interest is the fact that political crime includes rebellion not just against "the Sublime State," but also against "its laws and regulations." This is a bit strange. If any "rebellion" against any law is a political crime, then theft, murder, wounding, and every other personal crime is simultaneously treasonous. In later years—as we shall see—this is precisely the direction in which law begins to develop. In this first decade of the Tanzimat, however, the coming together of personal and political crime is in its earliest stages. The article simply shows the extent to which the 1840 code is geared toward the state and the bureaucracy rather than society or the individual. The "laws and regulations" of importance are those relating to the state. Law indeed exists solely to define and to protect the state. It makes sense, therefore, that the adjudication of "important" cases remains in the hands of an administrative rather than a judicial council.

This situation and the way in which criminality as a concept developed within it were not, however, unique to the Ottoman Empire. The British government in North India, for example, had a similar attitude toward personal and state crime. Sandria Freitag notes in her discussion of collective crime in India, for instance, that the "elaboration of legal codes and police establishments to deal with individual crime conveyed the impression that 'the rule of law' had been introduced into British India; yet the annual compilation of crime and police statistics makes clear the minimal state resources committed to policing individual crime."[16] In British India too, that is, modern criminal law focused on crimes against the state and its institutions. Crime perpetrated by and against individuals, contrarily, dwindled into pointlessness. Indeed, to the extent that individual crime put in an appearance, it was the impression of dealing with it, rather than its actual policing, that was important—establishing the "rule of law" and that is all. Instead, the bureaucratic apparatus was taking center stage—if the law itself existed, it did so solely to justify the expansion of this apparatus.[17]

DEFINING "RELIGION" IN THE 1840 CRIMINAL CODE

To return to the Ottoman Empire, however: this expansion of political crime after 1840 did not owe its success exclusively to the appeal of "rationality." As Ottoman reformers used criminal law to re-invent and re-define the state's personality, they also invoked the moral authority of the ostensibly irrational religious establishment. This is hardly surprising, however, given the way in which law in general is almost always indebted to a religious tradition or a religious establishment. Especially to the extent that law defines morality—and in the modern period "common" or even national morality—religion plays a key role in providing the intellectual foundation for this relationship. What is interesting in the creation of modern criminal law systems—systems that are not, as we have seen, necessarily about classical moral issues—therefore, is the degree to which religion continues to be a part of the equation.[18] In the Ottoman case, even in the first decade of the Tanzimat, the religious establishment was acting as a pillar of the new legal system. "Islam," in an essential—and eventually normative—way, began to be used in the legitimization of not just the bureaucratic transformation, but the criminalization of those who acted against this transformation. As a result, *ulema* and the ideology they represented became both more powerful—in the sense that they guided the state's self definition more directly than they ever had before—and less powerful—in the sense that they no longer had an even remotely independent existence.

I am deliberately qualifying these statements with the word "began." It is true that the incorporation of the religious establishment started with the 1840 code and the institutions that supported it. This relationship between the religious hierarchy and the new legal system, however, only became fixed in the decade following the 1851 codification. What, however, did the foundation set by the 1840 law look like? Most important, it is in the introduction to the 1840 code that the Gülhane edict, its invocation of the legal rights of the Ottoman people, and its subordination of these rights to the personality of the state are linked explicitly to "Islam." It is in this section of the 1840 text, that is, that Islamic law (*şeriat*) and the ideals of the Gülhane edict come together in support of the new bureaucratic processes, thereby endowing these processes with a moral and religious, as well as rational and administrative, logic.[19] The code in fact seamlessly integrates the necessity of bureaucratic transformation and the concept of a legitimate state based upon Islamic political theory. It invokes Islamic law, temporal law (*kanun*), and administrative regulations together as the three foundations upon which judges, scholars, and functionaries ought to understand crime as well as sin.[20]

The result is a situation in which religious morality and political loyalty are inextricably linked in the same way that murder and treason had been. Recall, for example, that the first article of the 1840 code, on "murder," effectively conflated violent crime against the individual and treasonous activities against the state.[21] This section continues by insisting that the investigation and trial of either case follow the rules of *both* temporal law and Islamic law (*kanun* and *şeriat*). What exactly this means in practice remains unclear, but the symbolic intent of the requirement is obvious. Rhetorically, bureaucratically, and in the ideal, any murder/treason investigation or trial will occur simultaneously in a religious and a political framework.

The three legal concepts discussed in the article—equality before the law, the inviolability of the state, and the protection of the individual against violent attack—are the concern of both religious and temporal functionaries. Anti-state activity thereby becomes as much of a sin as murder, and murder is likewise reimagined as an attack upon the health of the state—the civic and the moral occupying the same intellectual sphere.

In almost all of the articles of the 1840 code, Islamic law concepts and the office of the *Şeyhülislam* appear similarly prominently. And in almost all of these articles, there is little or no detail about the role that the religious establishment will play. The *Şeyhülislam* and "Islamic law" have jurisdiction along with the bureaucracy, but the nature of this jurisdiction is never spelled out.[22] Again, however, the day to day practice of criminal law was not the focus of Tanzimat era legislation. Instead, it was the institutional, abstract role of the religious establishment that was essential—the procedure, as an ideal. As the bureaucracy became gradually inviolate, that is, religion and religious functionaries lent authenticity to this transformation.

TRYING CRIMINALS AND QUELLING REVOLUTIONS

This creation of a sacred bureaucracy brings us inexorably back to Max Weber. The chapter began, recall, with Weber looking in a confused manner at the legal situation in England. England was a manifestly modern, industrial nation, and yet it did not fit into Weber's theoretical schematic at all. Simultaneously "modern" and "disorganized," the administration of English law simply made no sense. The Muslim world was a bit easier. Weber saw industrialization as the key to modernity, and he therefore felt himself to be on firmer ground when discussing Islamic law—law that was being systematized (or not) in less industrialized areas. To begin with, Weber argues in his discussion of "*imperium*" and law first, that *imperium* must include the ability to discipline subordinate officials and to deter disobedience in general; and second, that it is the intrusion of *imperium* into the legal system that leads to a systematization of the law.[23] In other words, the systematization of law is an inherently bureaucratic process which, he continues, is not possible in an Islamic context.[24] Islamic law is fundamentally irrational in his view, and in any case, a strong bourgeoisie is an integral part of what he describes as the legal systematization process.[25]

Despite the fact that he does not consider Islamic *imperium* relevant to his theory, Weber's description of the interaction between political authority and the systematization of law is of some interest in describing the late Ottoman development of an abstract legal hierarchy. He argues, for example, that the systematization and the unification of the law benefit two actors in particular. The leader himself benefits from a "clarity" and "orderliness" in the law and bureaucratic officials are also freed from regional constraints. In a modern legal framework, that is, neither leader nor functionary is required to take into consideration the aberrant needs of a local population. With the systematization of the law, an official can suddenly be employed in every province of the empire, and at every level.[26] In other words, Weber sees a direct relationship between the creation of a codified law and the creation of abstract legal institutions.

In his article on Weber's discussion of "Sultanism" in the Ottoman context, the historian Halil İnalcık brings the religious establishment into the picture. İnalcık notes that one element of the classical Ottoman sultan's "patrimonial power,"[27] was his hold on judicial authority.[28] Throughout the Ottoman period, he continues, judicial power remained a prerogative of the sultan rather than a prerogative of his provincial administrators,[29] although, again, the sultan did delegate judicial authority to both governors and *kadı*s via the *Şeyhülislam*. As time passed, however, the personal powers of the sultan began to diminish. Over the last decades of Ottoman rule İnalcık suggests that "by emphasizing their spiritual domination as caliphs and integrating the *ulema* into their bureaucratic apparatus, [Ottoman sultans] were attempting to compensate for their loss of power."[30] And compensate they did.

Indeed, from the earliest days of the Tanzimat, Ottoman reformers were completely up front about the fact that the primary goal of their reform was to develop an abstract, centralized state power. They wanted to use law as a symbol of this power, to create legal institutions, the sole purpose of which would be to emphasize the role and personality of the state and its bureaucracy.[31] In the same way that the codification of the law demanded its constant reform, that is, this reform demanded the growth of bureaucratic institutions. In the same way that legal reform was a performance, so too was bureaucratic power. But these new institutions in turn reflected the self consciousness and state-centered nature of the original code. In other words, the state policing itself became one of the most important symbols of central power.

İnalcık notes in another article, for instance, that one of the more effective means of "reducing the great authority of the governors of the provinces,"[32] was

> to demote, or to fine, or even to imprison governors, muhassıls, and other officials as prescribed by the newly established penal code if they were found to be unlawfully collecting fees, demanding services and taking bribes as before. According to the registers in the archives, especially those dated 1256/1840 and 1257/1841, punishments for this kind of offense were abundant.[33]

It is worth emphasizing as well the fact that those who were convicted of "crimes against the Tanzimat" were not sentenced according to the new "regular" stipulations, but instead according to "Islamic law."[34] The religious establishment thus also played a key and influential role in the proceedings. By the 1840s, that is, as the *legislation* of criminal law became a question of defining the bureaucracy and incorporating the religious establishment into this bureaucracy, its *implementation* became a question of demonstrating to peripheral areas the bureaucratic power of the imperial center.

Out of approximately 900 trials—ostensibly for personal or social crimes such as murder, wounding, and brigandage—conducted between the years 1840 and 1875 (1256–1293), for example, the greatest proportion[35] occurred in areas that were posing a political or administrative threat to the central government's self definition.[36] Although such cases did occur in every part of the Empire, that is, they were clustered most prominently in three locations: the southwestern Balkans between Greece and Austria; western Anatolia and the Aegean islands in particular; and south eastern Anatolia plus Mosul.[37] More to the point, the periods during which trials of "personal" crimes occurred with the most frequency coincided almost without fail with periods of political instability in these regions.

The primary years of "criminal law" activity in western coastal Anatolia and the Aegean Islands, for example, were the 1840s and 1850s[38]—precisely the years that these areas were posing a political threat to Ottoman central power. The Aegean Islands and Cyprus especially had been areas of discord throughout the century, but things had come to a head only in the late 1830s. Cyprus, for example, had first been occupied in the 1830s by the rebelling governor of Egypt, Mehmet Ali, and was later the subject of an increasingly worrisome British colonial interest.[39] The Ottoman government therefore spent the 1840s and 1850s putting into play any and all possible symbols of its authority, including its newly articulated criminal law. The highest proportion of criminal trials in Aydın, İzmir, Menteşe, and Saruhan coincide exactly with the Ottoman government's new and stringent measures for economic centralization in these areas.

In İzmir, for example, there was a particularly high proportion of criminal law activity between the years 1842 and 1866, whereas in Aydın this activity occurred between the years 1848 and 1860. This is the same period during which the Ottoman government was attempting to undermine local economic and political authorities, both for its own reasons and in reaction to international pressure. By the late 1830s competition between European merchants supported by the center and local authorities had become particularly heated. This competition continued between the mid 1840s and the late 1850s, until finally the local authority had been successfully undermined by the central.[40]

Other centralizing measures over the same period included the restructuring of the Aydın and İzmir provinces in 1847 and 1850, as well as the drawing up of plans to build a railroad during the late 1850s and early 1860s.[41] By the early 1860s, all of this economic and political restructuring, as well as the tightening of administrative control had been completed to the extent that it was going to be completed. That is, its *discussion* if not its actual implementation had been completed. And so, along with the easing up of the economic policies and the cessation of territorial re-structuring, there is a simultaneous decrease in the number of criminal cases being tried and sent to Istanbul for confirmation. After 1860, only four recorded cases appear at all.

In the more interior areas of Western Anatolia—the Teke, Hamit, Karahisar, Kütahya, Bursa, and Karesi regions—an equally high number of criminal court cases were sent to Istanbul. Once again, the earliest clustering of cases in the region occurs simultaneously with a redefinition of the borders and political relationships among these provinces.[42] In the 1850s, these administrative changes had come to a halt, but by the 1860s, a new series of territorial restructuring was underway—especially in Karesi, the region with the highest proportion of legal cases to population of the entire empire. In the 1840s and 1860s, the status of Karesi changed repeatedly from independent entity to part of Hüdavendigar to part of Aydın.[43] As each of these changes took place, a new spattering of criminal court cases was tried. The only explanation for this pattern is that the trials were undertaken at least in part to emphasize the new political status of the region, and to demonstrate the presence of a central, bureaucratic authority.

No area, however, saw criminal law activity like southeastern Anatolia and northern Iraq. The provinces of this area had always been notorious for their independent and "ungovernable" nature, and the Kurdish and Arab tribes in the Mosul and Urfa regions especially were constantly fighting government policies, usually with a great deal of success. Even in the more settled areas, the absence of an urban infrastructure in much of the region and the local population's lack of interest in bringing cases to government courts had previously led to a relatively low number of trials conducted in these provinces. By the mid nineteenth century, however, this situation could no longer be tolerated. Institutionally, at least, these provinces had to be brought into the larger imperial structure.

As a result, criminal cases were tried with frequency after 1840, especially in Mamuretülaziz, Muş, Diyar-i Bekir, Urfa, and Mosul. In Mosul, for example, the activity of criminal courts spiked in 1853, 1855, 1856, 1859–60, and 1872. Given Mosul's "special" history, this pattern makes a great deal of sense. In 1851, the region had ceased to be an independent entity and had become a province of the Bağdad *vilayet*—apparently in an attempt to deal with the Yezidi tribal rebellions.[44] The frequent trials of 1853 and 1855 seem to have been a follow up to this territorial restructuring. The territorial restructuring was less than successful, however, and a second series of tribal revolts took place throughout 1859.[45] These too were followed immediately, in 1859–60, with another flurry of criminal court trials. Finally, the mission of the Grand Vezir, Midhat Paşa to the Mosul area between 1869 and 1871—and his more personal attempt to assert bureaucratic hegemony over the area—likewise coincided with a final series of cases tried and sent to the center. These trials, however, had little or nothing to do with the personal crimes—murder, theft, kidnapping—they were ostensibly targeting. Criminal law in Mosul was a spectacle, a symbol—its purpose was to demonstrate the existence of a uniform and rational central power, to play up the hegemony of bureaucratic institutions. Linking these institutions to any sort of social reality in the region was of no importance at all.

The southwestern Balkans—in particular the provinces of Tırhala, Yanya, Manastır, Üsküp, Prizren, Berat, and Drama—were likewise the site of frequent criminal court trials, the areas of highest activity being Berat and Tırhala. Both of these provinces were strategic, the former with its fortress and coastal access and the latter situated on the border with Greece. Tırhala became especially problematic after 1830, with the creation of the modern Greek state, and the growing appeal of a Greek national ideology and identity in neighboring Ottoman provinces.[46] By the late 1840s and early 1850s, in fact, the growing communication between the Greek state and the Ottoman Macedonian and Albanian territories[47] was well on its way to undermining the ideological power of the Ottoman center. Criminal court activity in the Macedonian and Albanian provinces was thus spread evenly over the years 1840 to 1870, as regular as the Macedonian uprisings against the imposition of a uniform Ottoman identity: 1840, 1856, 1868, and 1878.[48]

As for the more northern Albanian provinces of Manastır, Prizren, and Berat, a similar situation had developed. In the 1830s, the Ottoman government had already attempted to limit the power of local Albanian leaders.[49] By the early 1840s, a competition between Greek language and Turkish language schools had arisen in the Albanian territories. By the mid to late 1840s, a native Albanian movement in favor of its own language instruction had emerged.[50] At the same time, uprisings against Tanzimat policies had taken place in 1844, 1845, and 1847. The fact that the highest levels of criminal law activity in the Albanian provinces were first in the mid 1840s to the mid 1850s should not therefore be surprising. Nor should it be surprising that a second spate of criminal cases were tried between 1859 and 1864, in the years leading up to the provincial restructuring of 1865.[51]

At the same time, upon first glance, the geographical distribution of cases in the Balkans does not seem completely logical. One would expect the provinces on the northern frontier, such as Niş, Sofya, Vidin, Tırnova, Rusçuk, or İzvornik, to show high criminal law activity as well. It is important, though, to remember the purpose of this activity. The point, again, was not necessarily to try and to condemn revolutionaries—except perhaps tangentially. It was instead to demonstrate the existence of uniform bureaucratic control by means of policing and defining this very bureaucracy. And this the government did—but only in the south, where it could. In Albania as elsewhere, criminals were tried not necessarily or solely in response to crimes actually committed, but in response to the symbolic needs of the new bureaucracy and administration.

Once again, the Ottoman state was not unique in this respect. Rebellious and revolutionary behavior in China under the Qing, for example, prompted similar reactions from the Chinese government. In response to popular reaction against political centralization (in this case tax collection), the nineteenth century Qing state also put the symbolic power of its own new criminal law system to work: "the local political issue was simply reduced to pure legal terms . . . singling out one or two corrupt officials of the state, the law to some extent fulfilled its ideological and symbolic functions in preventing potential political harm."[52] Yes, there had been an actual rebellion. And yes, some revolutionaries had been condemned. But the thrust of the Qing state's response was to demonstrate its bureaucratic and legal power by policing its own functionaries. Both the Ottoman legal establishment and the Qing legal establishment, that is, tried criminals for far more abstract reasons than the mere elimination of the "criminal element." Law and its implementation in the criminal courts had come to symbolize an abstract ideal of uniformity, rationality, and progress.

A NEW BREED OF CASES

But what exactly did these "abstract" trials look like? The overview above goes beyond the decade covered by this chapter in order to show in a more general way the link between criminal law activity and bureaucratic self definition. The cases actually tried between 1840 and 1850 bring us more to the point. Starting in 1840, court procedure also began to promote first, an abstract understanding of criminality, and second the importance of religion in redefining the law. These trends are not nearly as pronounced in the 1840s as they are later on in the Tanzimat period, but without doubt, we can trace their origins to this decade.

At the same time, cases actually came to trial between 1840 and 1850 in much the same way that they had prior to the Tanzimat. First, the principals of a case or the police would bring the issue to the attention of either the local council or the governor. The council or the governor would then make a tentative decision and, if necessary, have Islamic legal writs legitimizing the decision composed. A report would then go to the central council (*Meclis-i Vâlâ*) for confirmation, and the writs, if necessary, would be confirmed by the office of the *Şeyhülislam*. Finally, everything would be sent back to the local council or governor for implementation.

So we can see here a situation in which criminal law has begun to relate more to bureaucracy than to society, but in which the transformation is by no means complete. The central council and the local councils—institutional arms of the Tanzimat—have begun at this point to encroach on the power of the local authority. The central council must see to it, for example, that the activities of the governor adhere to uniform and rational rules of procedure and practice. But it is also clear that the provincial councils at least are still defining themselves according to local conditions, rather than against an abstract definition of what "Provincial Councils" are supposed to be.[53]

We can simultaneously see the beginnings of an incorporation of the religious establishment into the larger bureaucratic system. Again, though, the incorporation is by no means complete. At the local level, the two systems overlap—the governor and the local council try both traditional or religious and new or regular cases. But at the center, things remain separate. The office of the *Şeyhülislam* sees the Islamic legal writs and confirms them, the central council looks at the reports and confirms them, neither consults the other, and the confirmation is sent back to the local authorities. This would change in later years.

Between 1840 and 1850,[54] however, the cases themselves also point to the growing importance of the religious establishment in the redefinition of law. In a murder/treason (*katl/fesad*) case from 1839–40, for example, a defendant on trial for both crimes is sentenced "by the requirements of Islamic law" [55] to a harsh regular penalty. What this means is, first of all, that the defendant cannot be pardoned, as he could have been if sentenced only according to the regular principles. Second, if any heirs appear and demand *lex talionis* (*kısas*), he can be immediately executed. The state, in other words, has used Islamic law ideology as a means of ensuring an execution of the sentence, and the regular ideology as a means of retaining some jurisdiction over a treason case. The primary issue of concern in this case is the defendant's treasonous threat to the state and its bureaucracy. But the religious establishment is key in supporting the claims of the bureaucracy and in seeing to it that the threat is dealt with. This use of both philosophies does not, however, mean that in this period Islamic law ideology was somehow "abused." In a similar case just a few months later, in which an individual's sentence is under dispute, a point is made to keep the *Şeyhülislam* informed and effective within the case. The religious establishment, that is, is always on hand to administer those parts of a case "related to murder and to general law in the context of Islamic law (*şeriat*)."[56]

Two apostasy cases from 1841 and 1843 are similarly interesting. The first is listed innocuously among a number of murder, theft, brigandage and treason cases tried in the Filibe area.[57] In it, the defendant, upon being arrested for banditry, converts to Islam, later apostatizes, and therefore, according to the requirements of Islamic law, must be examined and interrogated by the office of the *Şeyhülislam*. The document continues that if he persists in his apostasy, he will be executed. In any case, it concludes, both the Grand Vezir's Office and the *Şeyhülislam* must see the response before it is forwarded to the Istanbul *Kadı*, so that both might have a say. Apostasy in this case clearly trumps banditry in terms of jurisdiction. At the same time, however, the functionaries of both the regular and the religious hierarchies remain involved in the case—both the Grand Vezir's Office and the *Şeyhülislam* are to be kept informed.

A similar case from 1843[58] concerns a defendant accused of blaspheming and acting against Islamic law, who, after having done so, is summoned to the Manastır council and asked to retract his statements. He does not, and is therefore put into prison to await a response from Istanbul. The office of the *Şeyhülislam* issues a declaration stating that death *siyaseten* (by the political authority) is legitimate—drawing upon the power of the Sultan and his bureaucracy to support its case. The general council decides not to request an authorization for the execution, but at the same time makes no comment about the requirements of Islamic law. The eventual fate of the defendant is never made clear.

In both of these cases the jurisdictions of the two systems overlap, and they overlap in a telling and meaningful way. In the second, the *Şeyhülislam* calls for an execution *siyaseten* for a blasphemer, whereas in the first, a bandit who has apostatized is executed according to the requirements of Islamic law. Apostasy and blasphemy are no longer crimes simply against divine law, but against the new bureaucracy. Religious and regular law work together to create a larger, totalizing system, in which self definition and the preservation of this definition is the goal.

In fact none of these cases concerns itself directly with what we would normally consider the interest of criminal law—murder, theft, wounding, etc. Instead we have two murder cases. The first becomes a treason case, concerned with defining the rights of the state and threats posed to those rights. The second becomes even more abstract—a question of procedure, concerned with defining the proper institutional behavior of the court. We also have a banditry case and a blasphemy case. The first becomes an apostasy case, concerned with defining the rights of the religious establishment, threats posed to these rights, and where the state stands in eliminating these threats. The second, which should by all rights be a straightforward issue of the honor of the religious hierarchy also raises questions about the relationship between this hierarchy and the new bureaucracy. To what extent is the bureaucracy interested in protecting the newly defined religious establishment?

Bentham and Weber were particularly disturbed at England's lack of a codified system because this omission placed England outside the bounds of the civilized, rational world. There are, however, a variety of different ways in which to be irrational. Legal systematization does not necessarily ensure a utilitarian situation—at least not a socially utilitarian one. In the Ottoman Empire, as elsewhere, the early codification movement instead sought first and foremost to define the new legal system in an abstract form that would likely have shocked Bentham's practicality. Worse, this redefinition happened above and apart from society. As, however, the reform demanded by the new system continued, its definition and purpose gradually came into sharper focus. The abstraction of criminality as a concept created criminals whose sole relationship was with an equally abstract political authority and bureaucratic apparatus. This still left society without a role to play—but, again, as long as state institutions could replace social ones, as long as bureaucratic purity could replace idiosyncratic as opposed to normative religious morality, the logic of the system, as a foundation for future social engineering, remained intact.

Chapter Four

1851 to 1858: The Disappearance of the Victim

In late nineteenth century Buenos Aires, the trying of criminals took a distinctly positivist turn. Crime became a question of an individual's threat to the larger social body, and not the contravening of a set hierarchy of rules and regulations. Around the same time, the Devil began to make increasingly frequent appearances in Argentinean courts.[1] Female deviants in particular—that is, women flouting society's moral dictums—were especially prone to demonic corruption, their anti-social behavior apparently the result of supernatural prompting.[2] Indeed, as Kristin Ruggiero argues, "the very shift of focus to the criminal from the crime was the context in which the devil secured a place in the late nineteenth century courtroom."[3] In other words, it was sociological positivism—that scientific, atheistic ideology—that let the Devil into the late nineteenth century Argentinean legal system.

Sociological positivism also became the framework in which Argentinean criminology began to focus on victimless crime. It was, again, deviants—those who offended social norms, rather than those who attacked other individuals—who were the primary target of positivist legislation. Positivist criminal law was, again, not about defining a crime and measuring its severity according to damage inflicted on people or property. It was instead about defining a criminal and measuring that criminal's actual or potential threat to the abstract notion of a social body. At the same time, however, when phrenology and other such scientific methods of determining an individual's potential or actual threat to society were not sufficient, it seems that in Buenos Aires at least, a leaf *was* taken from earlier legal strategy. Abstract evil, immorality, threats to society's self definition—victimless crimes—began to be determined not only according to scientific data, but also according to "traditional" notions of sin and wickedness.

Ottoman legal scholars in the 1850s were not influenced by positivist philosophy in the way that they and their counterparts in Argentina would be in the 1890s. But they would be later on. And it is in the 1850s that the shift in focus from crimes against victims to victimless crime begins to occur. It is also in the 1850s that the role of the Ottoman religious establishment, like its Argentinean counterpart, is fleshed out. The Devil was not much of a player in the nineteenth century Ottoman courtroom. Religious understandings of right and wrong, however, were essential components of new Ottoman interpretations of crime and criminality.

SHIFTING "BLAME" IN THE 1851 CRIMINAL CODE

At the same time, the 1851 criminal code was not developed and written from scratch. It was instead a supplement to the original 1840 law—a compilation of ten years of rulings by the High Council of Judicial Ordinances (*Meclis-i Vâlâ-yı Ahkam-ı Adliye*),[4] an institution with a relatively fluid role in late Ottoman legal culture. Although the Council did oversee some murder and theft cases,[5] for example, its basic purpose was to adjudicate "all cases involving sedition and subversive action against the government, physical or verbal abuse committed by government officials and ulema, and corruption within the bureaucracy."[6] It concerned itself, that is, with state crime. The 1851 code was thus the 1840 code, inclusive of ten years of rulings on crimes committed against the state and bureaucratic purity.

As such, the 1851 code was a giant step forward in the creation of an authoritarian Ottoman criminal law. In it, personal crime—against victims or property—became of even less importance than it had been before, although this does not necessarily mean that the tension between popular and political ideas of criminality decreased. The 1851 code in fact began to rely heavily upon the Ottoman religious establishment for the distinct moral value it could bring to the realm of administrative crime. And in general, as Ottoman criminal law became increasingly abstract, the influence of religious morality in the legal sphere grew proportionally.

The 1851 code, for example, like its predecessor, begins with the 1839 Gülhane edict. There is, however, an immediate difference between the two. Whereas in the 1840 text, the ideas presented at Gülhane are "joined to justice," in the 1851 version they are the "companion of Imperial Majesty." Obviously this does not mean that justice is no longer an issue in the 1851 law. What it does point to, though, is the repositioning of law, and criminal law in particular, as the protectors of bureaucratic or state power. By 1851, the personification of political power had become equal to if not synonymous with the concept of "justice." Life, honor, and property—the tenets of the Gülhane decree—no were longer functioning on their own, but were instead re-imagined as the "companions" of the state. This slight shift in emphasis sets the tone for the rest of the new code.

Recall, for example that the first article of the 1840 code emphasized explicitly the equality of all Ottoman subjects under the will of the Sultan. Anyone who made any attempt on the life of another, even a "vezir who tried to murder a shepherd," was subject to *lex talionis* (*kısas*).[7] The 1851 version of the article blurs the distinctive setting of this concept. The vezir/shepherd example, for instance, disappears completely, and the general reference to equality—repeated even in a separate article in 1840[8]—is reduced to a single sentence.[9] At the same time, whereas in the 1840 text it was the Sultan who was the "sovereign of [the people's] allegiance according to Islamic law," in the 1851 text, the Sultan is replaced by the "Sublime State, the sovereign of [the people's] allegiance according to Islamic law."

We see first of all, therefore, a waning interest in the equality of individuals under the law. More important, however, is the simultaneous movement away from traditional absolutism as represented by the monarch and toward modern authoritarianism as represented by the state. Not only will crime no longer be committed against victims, it cannot even be committed against the person of the Sultan. Gradually, the state was becoming the single relevant point of reference in the legal system.

But this trend toward victimless and discursive crime becomes far more obvious when considering the changing nature of articles on sedition and homicide. In the 1840 text, the articles on sedition and those on homicide were, with a few notable exceptions, divided into two separate chapters. One chapter concerned itself with crimes against victims, the other with crimes against the state's self definition. By 1851, however, all of these articles had been subsumed under a single heading, "life." Over the course of a decade, that is, the need to protect the "life" of the state and the bureaucracy had intruded into and undercut what had been before a section concerned purely with the "life" of the individual. The articles that fall under this heading in the 1851 code consistently place homicide and political crime into the same organizational category, and indeed they are often addressed simultaneously or in the same sentence.[10]

The second chapter of the 1851 code, on "honor," goes in the same direction. In this case, however, the focus of the law is on the purity and organization of the bureaucratic hierarchy—crimes against "honor," that is, are repositioned as crimes primarily against the ongoing legal and political systematization.[11] The foundation for this transformation had been set in 1840, with five articles from the earlier text discussing slander and showing a healthy if not overriding concern for the position and purity of high ranking officials.[12] By 1851, the transformation was complete.

The section on "honor" in the 1851 text, for example, consists of seven articles, each of which discusses in one way or another various distinct administrative groups and what happens when each is involved in a slander case or a case of non-violent "dishonor." The first article, although set up to some extent in the same way as its 1840 predecessor, abandons the more meticulous mention of the various social groups which were prominent in the earlier version. It declares instead that all people are subject to "Islamic law" punishments.[13] Although a quick analysis of this change would seem to point to a more egalitarian situation, when reading the article in the context of those which surround it, it becomes clear that "all people" means actually "The People." Members of the other ranks of Ottoman society appear to be almost completely exempt from these "Islamic law" stipulations.[14]

If the crime occurs in Istanbul, for example,

> social status will be taken into consideration, since the correction should be in accordance with this. If the [guilty] person happens to be a member of the illustrious ulema or a noble seyyid or a rank-possessing personality, let him be summoned to the Central Council and reprimanded there, and let average people be dispatched [to courts] and imprisoned or banished.

Those members of society not attached to the state, in other words, are subject to "Islamic law" in slander cases. For "average people," that is, slander remains a personal crime—a crime against a victim. Functionaries, however, are operating within a different framework. In their case, slander is a discursive crime. They have committed an act against the hierarchy itself—the self definition of the new system—and they are consequently under the sole jurisdiction of the state.[15] It is true that in the 1840 text a division does exist between ordinary and ranked people. But the explicitness with which social status is noted in the 1851 articles, and the deliberate division of "average people" from the others demonstrates the extent to which criminal law had been further detached from its social relevance in the intervening decade.

Again, however, Ottoman legal reform was not unique in this respect. In the Netherlands as well, the pure and rational administration of law had overwhelmed in importance its social relevance. Contemporary Dutch observers of the system noted, for instance, that "people know a neighbor has been charged, but perhaps they will never learn the outcome . . ." One study of Dutch criminal justice likewise cites an example of "a working class woman [who] inquired with the parquet how her case stood, only to discover that her case had already been followed up and that the offender had been convicted."[16] Both Ottoman and Dutch legal reformers, that is, were well on their way to perfecting a system in which the population and the individual were of secondary or no actual importance. In the Ottoman case, the "average" people were explicitly placed into a different, "traditional" framework.

In the Dutch case, they were left out of the process altogether. Both legal systems were focused on the rationality and purity of legal procedure, and both denied or attempted to eliminate any possible contamination of the process posed by idiosyncratic individual behavior.

Indeed, the final chapter of the 1851 Ottoman code, on "property," seems to assume the complete absence of the discrete, active citizen. The introductory article to this chapter[17] discusses, as might be expected, what constitutes crimes against property: in general, the state does not have the right to confiscate property without reason, and no one may take someone else's property by force with the intent of selling it. Both forms of misbehavior are understood, however, within distinct, if interrelated, "official" and "ordinary" spheres. There is repeated differentiation, for instance, between state functionaries who contravene the law and regular people who do so. As for punishment, if the convicted person has an official position, he will be expelled from it; if he is not an official functionary, he will be banished and exiled for one year.[18] Although the article does discuss "both" types of criminal behavior, that is, by distinguishing between the two within a single article it is creating an overt dichotomy—and in the process, it is attributing to the political and to the bureaucratic the authority of the personal. In the same way that attacks on "honor" came to mean attacks on smooth bureaucratic function, in other words, attacks on "property" were likewise understood as attacks by corrupt bureaucrats on the state's legitimate confiscation of property. Theft was problematic. It was far more problematic, however, if it involved a dishonest official undermining the state's legal right to take and to own property.

In general, in fact, state authority occupies a very different position in the 1851 law than it had in the 1840 text. In the1840 code, for example, it was "His Imperial Majesty" who "promised" that the goods and property of no one would be seized.[19] By 1851, the sultan's personal promise had disappeared, and the article read "let the goods of no one be confiscated by the state . . ."[20] With this change in vocabulary, there was a distinct shift in ideas about political power. By 1851, the state was no longer simply the entity which put into effect the "will of the sultan"—it had become instead the overreaching personality for which the system was operating. As a result, "crime against property" came more and more to mean "the corruption of official functionaries." Articles 2 through 5 of this chapter,[21] for instance, discuss bribery, corruption, faulty official bookkeeping, and the general responsibilities of all Ottoman officials. They go into no detail whatsoever, contrarily, talking about what happens when, say, one's neighbor steals one's horse. The law and its institutions indeed become almost completely self reflective in this new context—their concern more and more their own increasingly harsh policing.

And the symbolic value of this self-policing was clearly not lost on the drafters of the new code. At the end of the first article of the 1851 chapter on "property," for instance, the punishment for corruption is changed from three years of hard labor[22] to banishment, hard labor for an undetermined period, or a chastisement "according to the degree of the offense and the social status [of the criminal] ..."[23] The stipulated punishment for bribery in article 8[24] likewise goes from three years of hard labor to an undetermined sentence according to, among other things, the social status of the individual who committed the crime.[25] Members of the bureaucratic hierarchy were thus definitely able to protect themselves by emphasizing their social status. At the same time, however—subject to open ended sentences and notions of "rank"—they were also rendered completely beholden to the state structure. In a basic way, the new article was thereby creating a situation in which individual crime was replaced by the crime of being individual—in which deviant bureaucratic behavior became almost the sole focus of the law.

Article 9 continues in this vein, turning corruption into a far more serious state crime than it had ever been before. In this article, for example, a person who gives a bribe is placed into the same criminal category as a person who accepts it for the first time—whether or not the person offering the bribe compelled or threatened the person he was bribing. In the 1840 version of the law, only if an individual threatened the official while offering his bribe was he committing a serious crime. The 1851 code thus transformed bribery from a personal crime into an abstract threat to the system as a whole. It had to be stopped and punished regardless of levels of individual culpability. Rank, in other words, was important—a high ranking corrupt official was more of a threat to the state's self definition than a low ranking one or an ordinary citizen. But intent and circumstance—so important to determining the severity of personal as opposed to discursive crime—ceased to play a role at all.[26]

RELIGION AS THE "VICTIM" IN THE 1851 CRIMINAL CODE?

Religion, like rank, similarly remained a key concept, with sinfulness and evil becoming crucial components in the new articulation of criminality. Compared to its predecessor, for example, the 1851 code is far more concerned not only with bureaucratic purity, but also with attaching to bureaucratic structures a religious moral value. Indeed, attacks on bureaucratic authority gradually became morally and religiously reprehensible acts over the 1850s. And by the end of the decade, the religious establishment and an increasingly essential understanding of "Islam" were playing vastly different roles in the discourse of criminality than they had been playing just fifteen years earlier.

Recall, for example, that the introduction to the 1840 text brought up the 1839 Gülhane edict, the legal rights of the Ottoman people, and the necessity of a just state, all against a separate but nonetheless rhetorically important discussion of Islamic law.[27] While Islamic law was prominent, that is, it was as a system of legal thought more parallel to, than part of, the philosophy of the Gülhane edict. It is emphatically placed upon equal footing with regular law,[28] but it is not considered a basis for the development, reform, or moral authority of this law.

This is not the case in the 1851 text. The introduction to the 1851 code mentions the 1839 Gülhane edict with far more rhetorical flourish and goes into more detail interpreting Tanzimat era philosophy.[29] It then situates Islamic law within the regular system, drawing upon its moral influence to support the reform of the system. In addition to using the word "*mansus*" ("supported by divine authority" or "authoritative")—a word which is ordinarily used in exegeses of the Quran—to describe the ideas contained in the Gülhane decree, for instance, it also states the "obvious" fact that these principles are "tied to Islamic law" and an element of Islamic legal philosophy.[30]

There is in fact a concerted effort in every aspect of the code to understand Islamic legal philosophy as an integral part of the regular system[31]—a change in emphasis that is also a distinct movement away from the ideology of *pre*-Tanzimat era criminal codes. It is true that in these earlier codes the religious and temporal systems had overlapped administratively. But ideologically, it was clear to which sphere any activity belonged. Evil and sin were evil and sin—religious concepts and nothing else. Crime—even if it was not "evil" in this way—was certainly punished, but it was a disciplinary punishment, having little to do with an individual's moral stature or lack thereof.[32] By 1851, however, sin and crime were coming together, and Islamic legal thought was becoming a motivating force behind the legislation and reform of all aspects of criminal law.

The first article of both versions of the code, for example, discusses crimes against the state. We have seen the 1840 rendition of this article a number of times already—vezirs can not murder shepherds, and murder is conflated with treason. But the 1851 version of the article deserves further investigation. Conceptually, it remains to a large extent the same.[33] There is, however, some blurring of the lines between what is regular and what is religious. Islamic law plays a larger role in the latter part of the 1851 article, for example. Instead of merely noting that murder is subject to *lex talionis* (*kısas*), as in 1840, the 1851 text goes into detail about the process of both *lex talionis* (*kısas*) and "blood money" (*diyet*), as well as who is allowed to claim them.

But state-centered concepts also sneak into the text in that area. The article stipulates, for instance, that if the heirs choose to forgive the murderer, the state has the right to step in and execute a sentence both "*siyaseten*" (by the political authority) and "*nizamen*" (by the regular system). Finally, the will of the Sultan disappears completely in the 1851 version of the article,[34] and Islamic law occupies a much more prominent place in protecting the health of the state. It is not just an investigation according to the rules of Islamic law which must be undertaken, but also a verdict according to these rules which must be pronounced.[35] The point, again, is not which system necessarily has more power in this situation—it is the extent to which the two systems are overlapping and working together to eliminate the line between what is immoral and what is deviant.

This overlap continues throughout the rest of the 1851 code. In the 1840 code, the articles on homicide and those on sedition were divided into two chapters. The first of these obliquely referred to state crime, but was primarily concerned with capital punishment and homicide. In it, Islamic law concepts and the office of the *Şeyhülislam* did appear, but only to the extent that they had a vague and undefined jurisdiction over murder cases.[36] In the second chapter, dealing solely with sedition and state crimes, Islamic law and the office of the *Şeyhülislam* did not come up at all. All legitimacy rested with the state's right to protect itself through punishments executed by the political authority (*siyaseten*):

> Once verdicts of execution have been pronounced for such men, these [verdicts] will be submitted to His Imperial Majesty and the sentencing of a guilty person to a life sentence of hard labor [rather than execution] is up to His Imperial Majesty's merciful discretion.[37]

By 1851, the situation had changed. The first completely new article in the 1851 text, for example, requires that the legal functionaries[38] responsible for capital murder trials ground their sentencing in the precepts of Islamic law, even if the accused is an officer of the state. If the functionary ignores these precepts, he himself is subject to a regular punishment.[39] In other words, the jurisdiction of Islamic law over murder trials is not only highlighted, it is protected by the threatened application of a regular punishment. At the same time, this is a new twist on the "classical" concept of the temporal authority putting into effect Islamic law decisions. Rather than acting as a) an administrative support for the *kadı* or as b) a de facto "appeals" court for a mistaken ruling, the regular system is protecting the ideological overlap that the original system was supposed to prevent. Judges here are not *allowed* to choose the relaxed sentencing and procedure associated with the pre-Tanzimat era *mazalim* courts. Instead, the religious trial must remain a religious trial, whatever the judge himself might think—its moral weight is too important to undermine.

Articles 9[40] through 17 of the chapter cover sacking railroads, rebellion, homicide, attempted murder, discharging a weapon at another, and defying the police.[41] Each makes frequent use of aspects of both the religious and the regular systems to support new notions of criminality. Article 10, for example, details the exact limits of Islamic law jurisdiction. *Lex talionis* (*kısas*), it states, cannot be applied to law enforcement personnel who kill brigands during a violent clash. It can, however, be applied if a brigand is killed without a trial, but after capture.[42] In other words, if the police fail to follow the proper bureaucratic procedure after capturing a criminal, they too become "average people" and are subject to Islamic law. As long as they are acting in their capacity as officers, however, they are exempt.

Articles 11 and 12 reaffirm the state's right to step in and sentence a murderer by its own authority, should the heirs of a homicide victim demand "blood money" (*diyet*) or forgive the murderer. The state also confirms its right in this article to apply *lex talionis* (*kısas*) as the representative victim, in cases where the heirs are absent or missing.[43] As long as Islamic law conforms to the needs of the state, that is, "Islamic law" has jurisdiction. When Islamic law does not uphold the bureaucratic ideal, however, it can be reinterpreted. Finally, article 14, on hiring intermediaries to commit murder, notes the primacy of Islamic law requirements, but then supplements them with state punishments as well, emphasizing that the requirements of both the Islamic legal system and the regular system must be carried out.

> If a man makes an attempt on the life of another man, and has the latter murdered through the assistance of an intermediary, either by paying [the intermediary] money or by deceiving him, let the necessary requirements of the Islamic law (*şeriat*) and regular law be applied to the actual murderer. Therefore, let the person who ordered the murder receive, according to the degree of his [crime] one to five years of hard labor, and similarly let the individual who assisted the murderer receive one to three years of hard labor and be put into fetters.[44]

Compare this to the 1840 text, in which there is not a single such qualification. The second chapter of the 1851 text, on "honor," is no different. In the 1840 version of this chapter, five articles[45] cover the punishment of slander and dishonoring another, and there is almost no mention of Islamic law[46] concepts at all.[47] In the 1851 text, the chapter on "honor" consists of seven articles, each of which discusses in one way or another various distinct social groups and what happens according to the rules of Islamic law when each is involved in a slander case.

But the third and final chapter of the code—on "property" rather largely defined—changed the most between 1840 and 1851.[48] Theft, for example—what we would ordinarily consider the primary interest of a chapter on "crime against property"—gets almost no play in the 1851 text. In fact, only one article refers to it specifically.[49] The rest of the chapter discusses taxes, state seizure of property and, most importantly, bribery and corruption—all of this couched in a newly articulated religious morality. Article 8,[50] for instance, elaborates on the theme of bribery, adding a note to the beginning of the original 1840 text stating that bribery is, according to both Islamic and regular law not allowed (“*münker*”). Indeed, anyone who commits the crime is committing a religiously reprehensible (“*mekruh*”) act.[51] That bribery is a very bad and immoral thing had already been emphasized in the Gülhane edict and the 1840 code. That it was a religiously reprehensible thing is something new. But other articles—11 through 19, for example—go in the same direction. These articles, completely new additions, cover the paying of taxes—especially the religious *zakat* tax and the *öşr* tax (art. 14 and 19)[52]—and the forging of imperial, regular, and Islamic law documents (art. 12).[53]

In other words, the fixation on a regular, rational bureaucracy had also been adopted by the religious establishment. It is not just state taxes, but religious taxes that must be paid in an official and uniform manner. It is not just the forging of imperial and regular documents, but the forging of Islamic law documents that is unsanctioned. Islamic law and regular law were thus working together to support the new system. They were also, however, given the logic of that system, subject to the same insults—with bureaucratic regulations taking on the moral weight formerly held only by the dicta of Islamic law.

CASES WITHOUT PLAINTIFFS

Indeed, the moral authority of the religious establishment became increasingly necessary to the continuity of legal reform throughout the 1850s. As the focus of the law switched from crime to the criminal and to the latter’s threat to an overall system, defining a criminal as religiously evil or immoral in addition to administratively deviant or criminal was a necessary support to the reform movement. Criminal law procedure reflected these changes. Although the procedure for bringing cases to trial in the 1850s remained similar to the procedure followed in the 1840s,[54] for example, the internal structure of criminal cases changed dramatically. There was an increasing reliance, first of all, on religious legitimacy in both the trying and the sentencing of cases over this decade,[55] with far more Islamic law writs being issued in support of regular decisions than had ever been before. The jurisdiction of the regular and the religious systems likewise began to overlap, and defendants were repeatedly shuttled between Islamic law judges and their regular counterparts.

In three corruption cases from 1852, 1853, and 1857, involving both *naib*s (judges in the religious court) and local *müdürs* (functionaries),[56] for example, the legal procedure followed a new and newly circuitous route: the functionaries were first brought to the local council on corruption charges as outlined in the 1851 criminal code. Reports were then sent to Istanbul, and reviewed by the central council. Following this initial review, the situation of the *naib*s was also examined by the office of the *Şeyhülislam*. The central council then decided upon the punishment (banishment) for the *müdürs*, in keeping with the criminal code, whereas the office of the *Şeyhülislam* decided upon the punishment (less severe banishment or dismissal) for the *naibs*, in keeping with the spirit of the criminal code.

What is occurring here is a blending of religious and regular jurisdiction. The servants of Islamic law were, especially upon first instance, subordinate to regular administrative structures. But they were also associated explicitly with the religious framework. The servants of the regular system were likewise designated by the code as religiously reprehensible. But they were then banished upon the authority of the central council. Islamic law and regular law were in this way linked together, but they also worked together, each in its own way protecting the bureaucracy from impurity and from the idiosyncratic behavior of deviant functionaries.

A case from 1856 raised the question of religious and regular jurisdiction once again, and in response to it, the government issued a decree clarifying the matter, at least for the province of Işkodra. This decree stipulated that for all "blood" cases—murder and wounding—the heirs or the police would first appear in a court of arbitration (*sulh* court), so that it could be established without question that Islamic law jurisdiction did not override regular jurisdiction. If it did, then the question of "blood money" (*diyet*—for wounding there was no other option) or *lex talionis* (*kısas)* would be decided in the arbitration court.[57] If it did not, only then would the case proceed to a regular court. The important point to emphasize here is the decree's primary focus. It is not the actual murder trial, or how it might turn out—it is instead the specific boundaries of religious and regular jurisdiction, what sort of violence each is allowed to inflict on behalf of state power, and whether these boundaries in turn conform to the legal system's new self definition.

Finally, a case from 1851[58] describes a situation in which a governor is investigated for issuing lashes to people convicted of various crimes committed under his authority. The document goes on to say that this sort of punishment is "contrary to the Tanzimat," and that "from now on, accused individuals—aside from those to be punished by the application of Islamic law punishment—should not be beaten, but sentenced to hard labor and imprisonment according to the legal code."[59] The issue at stake here once more is not the crimes committed. It is not even the violence of arbitrary punishment—hard labor, although legal, is not exactly "humane." It is instead the local authority's irregular threat to the rational organizational structure demanded by the Tanzimat. The crime is not against a victim or against social mores—it is against the system's self definition. Regular punishments are fine, Islamic law punishments are fine, combinations thereof are encouraged. But arbitrary punishment on the part of the local governor is absolutely not fine, and must be curtailed.

Once again, positivist ideology did not begin to influence Ottoman reformers until a good 30 or 40 years after the period we have been discussing. Similarly, the wide open doorway through which the Devil could enter a courtroom was equally far off. But in the 1850s, we can see the scene being set for this eventual conclusion. Between 1840 and 1858, the Ottoman legal establishment's understanding of crime changed drastically. The concept of the victim lost any importance it may once have had, and instead the "life" of the state overrode the "life" of the inherently deviant individual. As a result, by 1859, political crime and state crime began gradually to take center stage, while attacks on the self definition of both were endowed with religiously evil overtones.

Chapter Five

1859 to 1876: Crimes Against the State

Discussions of modernity seem to return inexorably and inevitably to France. It was in France that the "liberal revolution" happened, in France that these "liberal ideals" were either betrayed or reached their logical conclusion in Napoleon Bonaparte, and in France that modern popular authoritarianism arose with Louis Napoleon. The Napoleonic legal codes that accompanied the rapid political changes were equally modern in their outlook, and were adopted in whole or in part by a variety of governments around the world—many of which were unfortunately "not ready" for such revolutionary legal change.

The "not ready" epithet deserves a bit of attention. These countries were not "not ready" because they lacked liberal, democratic institutions. Although many did indeed lack liberal, democratic institutions. Again, France's "liberalism" had lasted only a decade, to be replaced first by a military regime, then by a classical monarchy, and then finally by a modern dictatorship. The Napoleonic legal codes had been written in support of the first and the last. They were revolutionary, therefore, to the extent that they envisioned a modern authoritarian state which communicated with a modern entity called "the masses" by means of a charismatic dictator. But liberal individualism had very little place in their texts. The countries that adopted the Napoleonic codes, however, could easily manufacture a relatively modern authoritarian state, and in many instances, the charismatic dictator was equally viable. "The masses," though, were more of a difficulty, and it is here that these governments "naturalized" French law. In the absence of "the masses," the already state focused Napoleonic Codes became even more so.

This is not of course to say that France under Louis Napoleon was in any way a functional example of citizen rather than state-based "democracy." As one scholar has noted in reference to the dictator's legal ideology, for example, he

> distrusted juries, especially when it came to trying politically motivated crimes and crimes against agents of the state. In 1852, he returned jurisdiction over political or press crimes to the judges of the *tribunaux correctionnels,* who were much more reliable when it came to convicting enemies of the regime.[1]

It simply means that to the extent that the French judiciary had become obsessed with political crime, these other countries would become equally or in some cases more so.

This is also not to say that the governments that adopted the Napoleonic codes were the only ones going in this direction. The British legal system also began to interest itself primarily with crimes against the state in this period—especially when it came to the administration of colonized populations. And whereas the oddity of an imperial government sentimentally attached to its case-precedent system imposing codes on its colonial periphery has been noted by numerous scholars,[2] the codes that *were* enacted were quite "normal" given contemporary trends in legal thinking. The criminal code enforced in India, for example,

> *looked* much like that enacted for English society (although leaning decisively toward the authoritarian rather than libertarian side of utilitarianism)—hence the reassuring appearance of "rule of law." But alongside this overt, explicit legal structure (ostensibly geared toward individuals) grew up an almost covert legal structure elaborated expressly to deal with collective crime.[3]

We shall return to "collective crime" later on in this chapter. The point here is simply that the uncertain relationship between the abstract and the concrete, between appearance and implementation, between overt symbol and covert meaning that we see in the Ottoman case was clearly alive and well in a variety of other regions too.

"NAPOLEON'S LAW": THE OTTOMAN EMPIRE AND FRANCE AS LIBERAL STATES

In 1859, the Ottoman government chose to adopt the 1810 Napoleonic criminal code for its own use. The masses did not play much of a role in the Ottoman version of the code, but the increasingly abstract nature of the Ottoman legal system, as well as the trend in the 1850s toward discursive crime, made the adoption of precisely this sort of authoritarian law perfectly reasonable. Indeed, between 1859 and 1876, political crime and crime committed against bureaucratic purity became of paramount importance, and the text of Napoleon's law facilitated this transformation in a way that the earlier codes would likely have not.

Although, for example, there are proportionally more articles concerned with crimes against people and property in the 1859 law than there are in its predecessors, the first article of the text makes quite clear what its primary function will be: to punish infractions committed against the state or public order[4]—or at least to punish such infractions in the abstract. It is of some interest that whereas the law contains many provisions against those operating against state interests, an authority responsible for carrying out these provisions was not created until the promulgation of the Law of *Vilayet*s in 1864.[5] This situation suggests, if nothing else, that the actual target of the legislation was once more the concept of political crime, and not any one corrupt official—that the symbolic act of legislation was more meaningful to Ottoman reformers than the concrete act of implementation.

In comparison with the French model, similar themes emerge. To reiterate, the Napoleonic code of criminal law is not a text dominated by liberal or democratic thought. It is in fact a bit disingenuous on the part of some scholars, when comparing the Ottoman and French codes, to point out the Ottoman decision not to include the French section "Attacks on Liberty,"—about 1.9% of the total number of articles—as an indication of the former's anti-liberal bent.[6] Of the entire 68 article French "Resistance to and Disobedience against Authority" section—about 14% of the entire French text—the Ottoman government chose to adopt only 23 articles, making this section about 8.4% of the total Ottoman code. In general, though, it is true—the Ottoman code is even more concerned with the state and its protection than the French code had been.

Both the French and the Ottoman codes follow roughly the same outline, although the latter is about half the size of the former (484 and 264 articles respectively). First, there is a section in both on "general principles," followed by sections describing criminal and non-criminal penalties, criminal responsibility (in the French) and "exceptions to the general" (in the Ottoman). The specific crimes come next, including external and internal crimes against the state, fraud, crimes committed by functionaries and corruption, resistance and disobedience to authority, murder/homicide/wounding, crimes against morality, kidnapping of adults and children or trying to change the latter's civil status, false witness and calumny, theft, swindling and bank fraud, destruction and damage, and finally, crimes against public health (in the main body of the Ottoman code and in an added section on police contraventions in the French).[7]

Of the French sections not included in the Ottoman are those on recidivism, crimes related to the exercise of public rights, attacks on liberty, crimes committed by religious sects against the state (not to be confused with the articles protecting religious sects, which are present in both), murder (as opposed to homicide), crimes relating to associations and vagabondage, and crimes relating to the civil status of children. Of the sections in the Ottoman code not present in the French are violence and mistreatment committed by public functionaries, the obstruction of telegraphs, printing, publishing and opening schools without authorization, gambling (which exists in the French code, but is subsumed under "fraud," whereas it is its own section in the Ottoman), and most of the articles on the sale of drugs and alcohol.

These differences between the French code and the Ottoman code point first of all to a growing authoritarianism in the Ottoman version of the law. The articles on recidivism did not make it into the Ottoman code, for example, most likely because of the gulf that was opening up between Ottoman law and society by the late 1850s. Recidivism as an idea is centered around the individual and how to measure individual culpability.[8] That it did not become a part of Ottoman ideas about criminality at this time[9] is an indication of the extent to which Ottoman criminal law had begun to focus on an abstract state authority at the expense of the individual. It is also likely that the "responsibility" section of the French text was changed into the much shorter "exceptions to the general" section in the Ottoman for the same reason. Rather than defining the individual and his specific criminal responsibility, the reference point of this section of the Ottoman text is instead the law as an abstract in and of itself, and in what areas this abstract might be qualified.

The differences point secondly to a certain proto-totalitarianism in the Ottoman text, in which the needs of the religious establishment are subsumed under the needs of the state. There is, for example, no differentiation between murder and homicide in the Ottoman code, as there is in the French. This is most likely because of the various levels of culpability already articulated in Islamic legal theory. Again, it is intent and not will that determines the guilt of a defendant, and so whereas there is a distinction in Islamic law between intentional and unintentional homicide, there usually is none between "voluntary" and "involuntary" homicide.[10] Although "premeditation" is defined in the new law along much the same lines as it is defined in the "murder" section of the French code, therefore, it is immediately rendered meaningless by the two articles that follow it, and that secure the jurisdiction of Islamic law in such cases.[11]

At the same time, however, the fact, again, that homicide and treason were linked so intimately in Ottoman law meant that the moral authority of the religious law had to be maintained. Indeed, it is worth noting that of the entire twenty-four article section on homicide in the Ottoman code, only five actually derive from the French original. The rest are transplants from the 1851 text or concerned solely with defining the role of Islamic law in the newly articulated framework.[12] Islamic law was thus "maintained" but only so that it could support the bureaucratic transformation.

The final section of the French code which the Ottoman drafters discarded—primarily concerning crimes committed by religious sects against the state—would seem at first glance to point to a more authoritarian or totalitarian tendency on the part of the French. The French use criminal law to circumscribe the behavior of the religious establishment. The Ottomans do not. Upon closer examination, however, the situation becomes more complex. In fact, whereas some articles in this chapter discuss such issues as the failure by religious authorities to respect civil procedures in marriage,[13] most are about religious figures who criticize the state or attempt to influence state affairs.[14] The French laws are thus an attempt to maintain the rhetorically secular foundation of the new French government.

Including such articles in the Ottoman code would—whatever the case—have been impossible. One of the primary functions of the Ottoman religious establishment, as it had been defined not just in criminal law, but in political theory, was to support the state apparatus. By the Tanzimat period, *ulema* had in fact become fully integrated state functionaries, and articles limiting their role would have been at best meaningless and at worst damaging to the new political theory.

There are also sections of the Ottoman code which were not inspired by the French law but drafted independently. These sections in general underline the authoritarian and proto-totalitarian nature of Ottoman ideas about criminality. It goes without saying, for example, that the newly drafted section on violence committed by public functionaries derived directly from early Tanzimat ideas about the purpose of criminal law. The point here once more is for the bureaucracy to police itself, and thus preserve its functionaries as an entity apart from the "average." The inclusion of laws against publishing and printing without authorization are similarly an attempt to maintain the established hierarchy. Only those who held high positions recognized by the government had the right to create and distribute media. Likewise, the sections on gambling and the sale of drugs and alcohol, which would traditionally have fallen under the sway of religious law, indicate an interest in preserving public morality as well as state integrity.

Finally, a number of articles did make the jump from the French to the Ottoman code, but in an altered form. Ottoman legal reformers never claimed that their new criminal code was a direct translation of the French text (in the way that Turkish legal reformers would 60 years later). But the ways in which the articles changed can still tell us quite a bit about what the reformers wanted from their law.[15] Before going in that direction, however, it would be worthwhile to look at both the Ottoman and the French framework. The sections in either or both texts relating to individual crimes or crimes against victims or property include:

- murder
- wounding and homicide
- kidnapping

- swindling and fraud
- recidivism
- damage and destruction
- theft
- arson

The sections in either or both texts relating to state and public crime include:

- crimes against the state
- corruption and crimes by functionaries
- violence and mistreatment by public functionaries
- printing and publishing without authorization
- counterfeiting
- crimes by religious sects
- resistance to and disobedience of authority

Of the Ottoman code as a whole, 42%[16] of the articles concern themselves with political crime and 24%[17] with crimes against people[18] or property.[19] Of the French text, 36% of the articles deal with political crimes and 33% with private crimes. In other words, there is something of a balance even in the authoritarian French code between the individual and the state as subjects of legal interest. Less than a quarter of the Ottoman code, however, discusses crimes against victims or against their property. Moreover, of the articles that do address the individual, most are vague—the primacy of Islamic law ideology being noted, and then no detailed explication being offered—whereas the articles on crimes against the state are detailed and elaborate. Louis Napoleon, no doubt, would have been quite impressed.

ERASING THE LINE BETWEEN POLITICAL AND CRIMINAL LAW

He would have been even more impressed at the success with which Ottoman criminal law and Ottoman political law became gradually synonymous in the mid to late nineteenth century. The overlap between the two had started at the beginning of the Tanzimat, or even before, but the systematization of this overlap, and the effective incorporation of the religious establishment into the system were new, modern, and authoritarian. It is true that as far as political law goes, the 1876 Ottoman Constitution derived from a Belgian original. Like the 1859 "French" criminal code, however, the state-based nature of the Belgian Constitution merely intensified in the Ottoman context.

This Constitution, however, did not develop out of nothing. It was the result and the legacy of a number of Tanzimat era edicts, and we should look at them before jumping to 1876. Most important, it is not in any way an accident that directly following the edicts of 1839 and 1856, as well as the reinstitution of the Constitution in 1909, criminal codes were also proclaimed or renewed. The 1839 edict of Gülhane not only pops up in the 1840 and 1851 criminal codes, but also itself foreshadows the eventual promulgation of these laws.[20] Criminal law and the new criminal code appear in five of the eleven articles of the edict, and in article 8 the merging of criminal and political law in support of a just rule is advocated in detail.[21] Not surprisingly, the crimes of state functionaries were also of particular interest to the drafters of the edict. The question of bribery, for example, is the sole subject of one of the final articles of the edict. This may not be shocking in its own right, but within a short, general explication of the overall rights of the people and the government, the inclusion of such detailed issues of criminal law are at least worth noting.

The underlying purpose of the 1856 edict is slightly different from that of its predecessor, although it too gave rise to a new criminal code two years later. The 1856 edict was primarily an attempt to address European diplomatic pressure concerning the status of non-Muslim groups under Ottoman rule. And it does address this pressure—through a re-interpretation of legal theory, and especially the theory of criminal law.[22] The longest section of the text, for example, is composed of six parts, each relating to various aspects of courts and legal rights. Four of these parts cite criminal law. A second section also addresses the question of corruption and crimes committed by functionaries and how solving this "problem" might help in securing the equality promised by the edict.[23] Finally, although commercial law makes an appearance in the 1856 text, whereas it had not in earlier ones, all of the sections which begin with a brief mention of the commercial code, end with an in depth treatment of the criminal code and its relationship to the state.[24]

But it is only with the 1876 Constitution proper that criminal law and political law truly begin to overlap. The Constitution's drafting committee, composed of sixteen civil functionaries, ten members of the *ulema* corps, two military officials, three Christian notables, and presided over by the Grand Vezir, Midhat Paşa,[25] used the Constitution to define in detail what exactly the Ottoman state was, and where its subjects fit into this definition. The document consists of twelve parts, 116 articles, and details the rights of the Sultan, the rights of his subjects, and the duties of ministers, functionaries, the parliament, parliamentary councils, courts, the high court, and other related issues.[26] It is, again, roughly based on the contemporary 1831 Belgian Constitution, although—and this is key—articles from the French criminal code also show up in the text.

Midhat Paşa's edict introducing the new Constitution follows the pattern one might expect. In the first five lines, he links political reform to Islamic law and to the vaguely liberal ideals[27]—life, property and honor—that had been addressed in the first two edicts concerning more or less the same subject.[28] He goes on to discuss the specifics of why a Constitution is necessary—preservation of the rule of law, and prevention of tyranny—discusses why and how the council of parliament will be set up, and ends with thoughts about how the regular system and the religious system (equally weighted rhetorically) are calling out for such a document to be published.

In the actual text of the Constitution, the criminal code is mentioned prominently in twelve separate articles, commercial law shows up in four, and courts of arbitration in one.[29] Similarly, the section of the Constitution on "courts," discusses criminal law at length in the introduction and conclusion, as well as in one internal article. Other branches of law—commercial, civil, maritime, governance, land—are not mentioned at all. Ottoman citizens were thus defined largely according to what sort of crimes they might commit. Fundamental to and inherent in the articulation of the Ottoman citizen/state relationship was the idea that the citizen—indeed an individual of any sort, even a civil servant—was a threat to the functioning of the state. The modern state thereby developed as an organism constantly under attack—and in constant need of protection in all forms. But this focus on criminality in the Ottoman Constitution is not particularly unique. In the mid-nineteenth century, the French, German, Japanese, and Swiss constitutions all paid a great deal of attention to crime and criminality as well, and in general modern state formation had much more to do with the criminalization of the citizen than with his "freedom."

What is somewhat unique in the Ottoman case is the role of religion in bringing the two structures together. The religious establishment is still being incorporated into the political and penal legal structure—lending the Ottoman Constitution not just an authoritarian edge, but also a proto-totalitarian one. In the third article of the text, for example, on the "Inheritance of the sultanate and caliphate"[30] the Sultan swears to respect both Islamic law and the Constitution, each one again holding equal rhetorical weight.[31] Article 10 states that no one can be punished without a specific reference to either Islamic law or the regular system. Less obviously, article 118, on the existence of laws and regulations, states first of all that as long as regulations are not abrogated or amended they will be in force. It then continues,

> care shall be taken to base [regulations (*nizamat*)] upon the provisions of the judgments of *fikh* (Islamic jurisprudence) and *kanun* (temporal law), and upon public morals and customs, which should be in accordance with the interest and needs of the people at the time.[32]

Regular concepts are thus placed squarely upon an Islamic law foundation, and *fikh* is not so much proclaimed as assumed to be the framework in which they are operating.[33] These three examples do not of course show an overwhelming interest in Islamic law precepts. They do however make clear the extent to which religion was also a pillar of the emergent system of political/criminal law.

Once again, though, this attitude toward crime and the state was not unique to the Ottoman context. In early twentieth century China, for example, the proper relationship between the political establishment and the judicial establishment prompted similar questions. Under the late Qing, judicial independence—that is, a judiciary untainted by the needs of the state—became a fundamental element of constitutional reform.[34] Qing legal reformers, however, spent a number of years attempting to create a system in which political crime was *not* the only crime of relevance. As much as possible, they wanted to remove judicial powers from the hands of political administrators.[35] But by the 1930s, with the quasi-totalitarian Kuomingtang in power, the situation had come full circle and, for our purposes, began to look more familiar:

> In 1930, Hu Hanmin, a veteran KMT leader, emphasized that the legislation, based on the Three People's Principles was fundamentally different from modern legislation in Europe and America. The latter was based on individualism and took individuals as the object of law, which was even more backward than traditional Chinese law based on family. In contrast, the Three People's Principles legislation considered society as a whole to ensure social stability, economic development and a balance of various social interests. Since the KMT claimed to rule the country on behalf of society and the people, logically the party should make the law.[36]

Obviously China in the 1930s was different from the Ottoman Empire in the 1870s. This is not least because a twentieth century totalitarian state could be far more effective and self conscious in redefining the political law/criminal law relationship than a mid nineteenth century authoritarian one could be. In each of these cases, though, we can see a similar question being asked: is it the individual or is it the state that the law ought to protect?

"SILLY LOCAL PRACTICE": CASES AS EVIDENCE OF CENTRAL POWER

A number of governments asked this question in the mid nineteenth century, and most came up with the same answer. This answer was then articulated in the spread of "collective crime"—especially in the colonized world—over the later decades of the century. Collective crime is, as its name implies, crime committed by groups rather than individuals, almost always against state ideology or state institutions. Often, collective crime was subsumed under the concept of "banditry or "gang related" behavior, although it was a far cry from the banditry of the pre-modern period. Indeed, it was only after the 1840s that banditry—in its new, apparently virulent form—became a force to be reckoned with in Ottoman courtrooms.

It became a similar force to be reckoned with in Egypt. There was in fact according to one scholar an "epidemic" of banditry cases in mid to late nineteenth century Egypt, especially after the British occupation in 1882.[37] This was not because bandits suddenly became more active in the 1880s. In his study of criminal law in Egypt, Nathan Brown argues instead that the government simply began to focus more intently on the issue at this time.[38] The "discovery" of banditry on the part of the Egyptian government even before the occupation, he writes, was in fact fundamental to the state building process in Egypt.[39] Banditry was linked to the concept of public security, the crime question was "nationalized," and in the end it became "a matter for the attention of the central authorities."[40]

Moreover, once banditry had taken on this coloration, entire social groups fell under suspicion and often became guilty by association. Bedouin and migrant workers, for example, were associated with both bandits and rebels.[41] Rebellious attacks on railroads or telegraphs in fact prompted the British government to attribute collective responsibility to entire villages, which were then punished or pillaged.[42] Simultaneously, "the use of exile was not restricted to those who had been convicted of any specific crimes; the only qualification to deserve this punishment was a bad reputation . . ."[43]

If we switch focus to another British colony, we see that the creation of collective criminality and its association with crimes like banditry were not unique to Egypt. In India too, the British government created a category of collective crime that dealt specifically with those who threatened the new British Indian state. Earlier we saw that although the new Indian criminal law *seemed* to police individual crime, in actuality it was concerned with political crime.[44] The focus of this covert attention to political crime was more specifically, however, *thags* or migratory peasant "bandits."[45] The Raj soon "began defining whole tribes as 'criminal' to bolster sedentary values,"[46] and

> those who could be recognized as a collectively criminal group were "proclaimed" through a series of legal steps leading ultimately to their being considered "criminals" whether or not they had, as individuals, committed a crime.[47]

By the early twentieth century, this language was being used in an urban setting as well—"gangs" who operated against the state's social engineering could be convicted in the same way that "tribes" had been a few decades earlier.[48]

I bring up these examples simply to show that the growing focus on political crime in the Ottoman Empire in the mid to late nineteenth century was by no means an anomaly. Everywhere, the individual, or at least individual culpability, was becoming of less interest to criminal law and its institutions.[49] Threats to the state could of course still be posed by individuals. But serious threats were posed by groups or by the concepts that groups embodied—rebellion, treason, disorganization, anti-social values, impurity. In France, there was to some extent the mitigating feature of "the masses"—not, again, that the French record in this arena, especially in its colonies, was particularly different.[50] In areas in which "the masses" had not been defined or brought into the equation, however, any group could be a subject of suspicion.

In the Ottoman Empire, we can see this transformation playing out in a number of ways. The style in which cases were tried and the sorts of cases that were tried, for example, starts to change after 1859. First of all, there are in the post-1859 cases many more self conscious references to specific articles of the new code, as well as to Tanzimat philosophies such as the preservation of "*ırz* and *namus*" (honor). At the same time, detailed explications of the procedure followed in each case start to decrease—indeed to a large extent detailed procedure gets no attention at all. In other words, there is an understanding in these cases first, that the political establishment as defined by the Tanzimat has a distinct role and place in the trying of criminals. Second, it is not the details of the individual case that matter so much as the fact that a general procedure was followed. And in the 1870s, in fact, generic forms to record the testimony of witnesses in both religious and regular cases come into use, while cross examinations start to follow a specific, authorized procedure. Often these forms will contain only a few sentences—it is not the information contained in the form that is important; it is just the fact that the form exists.

Anecdotally, we see similar trends. A document from the year 1873,[51] for instance, describes a situation in which the Albanian population of Prizren is persisting in its adherence to a local form of judgment and sentencing. The document notes that this sort of local jurisdiction is not only "silly" (*vahiye*) but contrary to both the religious and the regular systems, and that the local authorities must stop it. In the end, the governor of the province requests an imperial edict to help him undermine local jurisdiction. He further asks that the edict carry the force of law and that it reinforce the authority of both the religious and the regular legal systems, taking power out of the hands of the "silly" local administrators. The conflation of the political and the penal, the religious and the regular here is obvious. Local variations on law have become a threat to the state—have become criminal in and of themselves. And not only are they criminal according to Tanzimat ideology, but also according to the newly defined religious ideology. Moreover, since the criminal code in and of itself is not working, a political edict with the force of law must come into play instead.

It is also in the 1860s and 1870s that the religious and the regular systems come together in earnest.[52] Capital cases from this period almost always end with the formula "by a regular investigation and an Islamic law trial,"[53] and there is a marked increase in the combined use of the religious and regular systems to prove and legitimize cases.[54] At the same time, however, any practical connection between religious law and the population disappeared, and cases post 1859 are also almost always sentenced according to the rules of the regular system, with religion marginalized, if noted at all. As the moral authority of the religious establishment gradually helped to turn insults and threats to the modern state into sins, that is, it was the bureaucracy that reserved the right to decide and to execute[55] punishments for itself.

As the legal system grew, these trends became more entrenched. In 1869, for instance, the regular courts in Selanik and Sivas drew the attention of the central government "for reasons of reform." The courts were not fulfilling their role in an appropriate manner, and so the following changes were instituted: the High Court and the Council of Cassation (as of 1873 run by Islamic law judges[56]) were attached; the High Court received a president appointed by the state as well as local members who knew the regular legal system; and the High Court would

> hear murder cases that took place in the central *sancak* (administrative unit) of a province as a first instance court and, along with the justice councils and Islamic law courts, it would see, as an appeals court, upon request, [criminal cases] that took place in the capital of the province and in the districts attached to it.[57]

The system was thus self consciously composed of functionaries from both the religious system and the civil bureaucracy. At the same time, autonomous entities from both areas, such as the councils and the courts, were merged together and overseen by bureaucrats sent from the center. Although the High Court would work "alongside" the Islamic law courts, the line between the two is fuzzy verging on non-existent. In the end, although the religious establishment has clearly become part of the regular system, effective power rests with the relatively political High Court. Institutionally as well as textually, the political establishment has become a part of—and given the code, the most important part of—the growing system of criminal law.

Less than a year after the promulgation of the 1876 Ottoman Constitution, Sultan Abdülhamid II suspended the meetings of the constitutional assembly. He then set about reforming the Ottoman state in a manner that scholars have since described as internally "Islamic" and externally "pan-Islamic."[58] Neither Abdülhamid's authoritarian tendencies, nor his interest in creating a newly defined "Islamic" state, however, should be surprising given the contemporary domestic and international trends in law and society. Indeed, Louis Napoleon, would once again have found the situation familiar and, likely, impressive.

Chapter Six

1877 to 1908: The Role of Religion

China in the 1930s made a brief appearance in the last chapter. Although it is a bit chronologically and geographically removed, I want to return to it now. When the Kuomingtang came to power, one of their first moves was to halt the trend in China toward creating an "independent judiciary." First and foremost, the legal system had to be "partyized,"[1] and only then could it function with any relevance. What exactly "partyize" meant is a little bit difficult to discern. But Ju Zheng, a KMT Supreme Court judge noted that the goal of the new policy was "not to make a judiciary of party members, but to make a judiciary of party doctrines."[2] "Partyizing" the law therefore involved creating a system that adhered only to official ideology. By the late 1930s, the government had issued a manual, "What Court Magistrates Ought to Know"—and this manual was very specific about what *exactly* they were supposed to know.[3] The reform of the system and the manual that went along with it indeed self consciously defined not only the roles of judges but how precisely these judges ought to perform them.

Some years earlier, in the nineteenth century, the concept of academic jurisprudence—what court magistrates ought to know—had likewise become a fetish among German civil servants. Jurisprudence was not just a skill that one learned on the job, while serving the population. It was a science that was higher, more noble, more meaningful, and, yes, more ideological than that. In other words, the process that had so excited Weber—the creation of a nation of clerks—was alive and well in nineteenth century continental Europe. The German bureaucracy stood above civil society and, like the KMT in the 1930s, "embodied the general interest."[4] Jurisprudence, that is, existed for the abstract general will, and not for the population. Legal functionaries in nineteenth century Germany, too, had an ideology to protect. Society could do what it wanted.

This question of the role of legal functionaries and how they were trained to reflect the general will is the focus of the following chapter. How did the Ottoman legal system manufacture judges? And once created, where did these judges work? In answer to the first question, the creation of legal functionaries was a very rational affair. Both the educational system set up in the late 1870s to train Ottoman functionaries, and the court system in which they performed their roles adhered to the model of which Weber was such a great advocate. In both, the two modes of legal instruction envisaged by Weber interacted. Law was simultaneously a craft, learned from practitioners in the course of actual practice, and an idea, taught in a special school, where legal phenomena were "given rational and systematic treatment."[5]

The manner in which the two modes interacted was, however, perhaps not exactly what Weber had in mind. At the same time, it was in no way unique to the Ottoman Empire. As Ottoman legal reformers began to populate their system in the late 1870s, as they defined the roles legal functionaries would play, they, like their counterparts in China and Germany, France and Argentina, had an ideology to protect. This ideology in the Ottoman Empire, as elsewhere, centered around defending the state's honor and expanding its power. And in the Ottoman Empire, as elsewhere, the religious establishment had already become a core element of the ideology. Not surprisingly, religion continued to play a role. Indeed, it was primarily *ulema* who populated the post-Tanzimat Ottoman criminal law system. As they performed their roles, however, Ottoman *ulema* genuinely *performed* them: the self conscious, theatrical nature of Ottoman criminal law did not change in the post-Tanzimat period, it simply sharpened its focus.

TRAINING FUNCTIONARIES

In 1878,[6] the Ottoman Law School (*Mekteb-i Hukuk*) began producing judges to operate the regular legal system. The regular legal system, however, had been in the making for 40 years prior to the Law School's opening, and it is worthwhile asking how the system had been populated throughout the actual Tanzimat period. First of all, prior to the Tanzimat, a legal scholar would have received his basic education in a local religious school and then later on at the hands of an expert attached to a mosque or a foundation. Between 1839 and 1876, this route was by no means phased out. At the same time, however, the government began establishing civil schools at the elementary and more advanced levels to create a corps of uniform civil servants who would better represent the regulations that were being promulgated with such frequency. In 1848, teachers' schools[7] began to open simultaneously with the military academies.[8] In 1853–1854 a special judges' school attached to the office of the *Şeyhülislam*—the *Mekteb-i Nuvvab* and *Medreset-ül Kuzat*—appeared.[9] In 1878 there was the Law School, and in 1900 *Dar-ül Fünun* (later Istanbul University) became the apex of the state's educational hierarchy.[10] The purpose of these schools, again, was to create civil servants who not only agreed with, but who could embody Tanzimat and post-Tanzimat ideology. Legal scholars, both as students and as judges, thus learned first, to protect the honor of the state and second, to use religion in the process.[11]

The Law School's focus from the beginning was on its students rather than on its teachers. As long as the appropriate type was recruited and as long as this type was properly molded by the educational process, it did not really matter all that much who was doing the educating. In the charter for the school, for example, whereas seventeen articles cover which students may or may not be accepted into the program,[12] not a single one mentions the necessary qualifications for the teachers. An earlier document discussing the establishment of the school does mention what sort of people ought to lead the classes, but this section of the text consists of only two short articles out of a total of thirty-five. Moreover, these two articles do not give any detail whatsoever about the preferred educational or professional background of the future professors, beyond noting that they will be appointed by the Justice Ministry.[13] As long as the students, somehow or another, managed to internalize the necessary legal ideology—if not perhaps the necessary legal skills—the Law School was doing its job.

If we do look at who taught there, though, it is of some interest that it was *ulema* in particular who were the mouthpieces of the ideology. By the beginning of the twentieth century, *ulema* were teaching *Mecelle,* Islamic Jurisprudence, Procedure of Islamic Jurisprudence, Legal Formulas, and Hadith at both the Law School and *Dar-ül Fünun.*[14] The religious establishment had already been coopted as the moral foundation for the new legal ideology and its focus on political crime. Its functionaries were now creating the judges who would be implementing this ideology.

But teachers need syllabi. In fact, in the case of the Law School, the syllabi were perhaps more important than the teachers—especially when we take into consideration the curriculum that was taught. Both the *kadıs*' school (*Medreset-ül Kuzat*) and the Law School aimed through their syllabi at the incorporation of the religious into the regular for the greater good of the state. The *kadıs*' school, for example, came into being in 1853 through a regulation (*nizamname*) that sought to render more uniform and bureaucratically correct the training of Islamic law judges. A number of articles in the regulation similarly stress the necessity of including both religious and regular elements in all aspects of course instruction. Also, as would occur twenty years later with the Law School, students would be required to pass an entrance examination to prove a minimum level of prerequisite knowledge before their matriculation.[15]

To emphasize, the religious *kadis'* school was founded upon and legitimized by means of a regular edict. Its entrance requirements were nearly identical to those that would be required later on by its purely civil counterpart.[16] Its courses explicitly imparted both religious and regular philosophies to future Islamic law judges.[17] The curriculum of classes to be taught upon the school's opening includes not only classes relevant to Islamic law like inheritance, Islamic law formulae, marriage and divorce, foundations (*evkaf*), and Islamic law procedure, or more general classes such as secretaryship, accounting, and penmanship, but classes relevant to the Tanzimat ideology such as "*kanunî* knowledge" (*Malumat-ı kanuniye*) and, more interesting, "laws of stamps and duties," (*Harc ve Damga kanunları*).[18] Were those who misused and forged stamps or those who trespassed on the state's authority as religiously and morally guilty as those who, say, apostatized or committed adultery? It would seem, given the focus of the bureaucracy's school for *kadi*s, that to a large extent they were.

But what about later on, with the opening of the more civil Law School? In its 1878 charter, the list of classes to be taught includes Roman, Commercial, Maritime, Penal, Public, and Administrative law as well as courses on Procedure of Islamic Jurisprudence, Branches of Islamic Jurisprudence, and the *Mecelle*.[19] Also, a 1295/1878 decree announcing the opening of the school mentions the *Mecelle*—the triumph of the religious/regular relationship—particularly prominently.[20] Finally, the curriculum of the Law School four years after its founding included such courses as "*Mecelle* and non-codified *fikh* relative to marriage, inheritance, cinayet, kisas, diet (sic), and foundations."[21]

In the following years, it became apparent that this particular take on legal education by no means put people off. In 1297/1880, eighty-five students were accepted to the first Law School class following their examination.[22] And the number of students after that remained healthy[23] as years passed and as the curriculum became increasingly religious. As late as 1908, the government was in fact reaffirming the rights of applicants trained in the religious system to enter the Law School without an entrance examination.[24]

Indeed, *ulema* made up a significant segment of the student body, and in 1886, when an extra year of study was added to the curriculum to accommodate a heavier class load, the administration noted that these changes must not cause hardship to the students, "many of whom were *ulema*."[25] In 1888, when the students staged a disturbance, the administration's solution was to replace the current administrator with "a religious, competent, and upright/direct person."[26] That is, the new director would embody law as envisioned by the post-Tanzimat bureaucracy. He would be simultaneously religious and competent, upright morally and direct or straight administratively. He would thereby be able to rein in the disorganized disturbances of the not quite fully formed students at the school.

In 1891, the curriculum of the Law School changed dramatically. First of all, a number of courses to be taught by visiting cassation court judges were introduced. Second, and more to the point, the list of "classes to be canceled," "new classes to be taught," and "current classes"[27] turned distinctly toward religious law:

- The first year classes to be canceled were: psychology (*ilm-i ruh*), literature (*edebiyat*), general history (*tarih-i umumi*), and French (*Fransızca*).
- The new first year classes were: *Mecelle,* the criminal code (*ceza kanunnamesi*), introduction to law (*medhal-i ilm-i hukuk*), and land law (*arazi kanunnamesi*).
- The second year classes to be canceled were: property law (*ilm-i servet*), rhetoric (*belagat*), general history, and French.
- The new second year classes were: *Mecelle,* criminal court procedure (*usul-u muhakemat-ı cezaiye*), international law, (*ilm-i hukuk-u milel*), administrative law (*hukuk-i idare-i mülkiye*), and the commercial code (*ticaret kanunnamesi*).
- The third year classes to be canceled were: logic (*mantık*), and French
- The fourth year classes to be canceled were: French.
- The new third and fourth year classes were: *Mecelle,* inheritance (*feraiz*), foundations (*evkaf*), civil/religious court procedure (*usul-u mehakim-i hukukiye*), foreign affairs (*muamelat-ı ecnebiye*), Islamic jurisprudence (*usul-u fikh*), the commercial code (*ticaret kanunnamesi*), the book of *diyet* and murder (*kitab al-diyat ve cinayat*), testimony about testimony (*kitabat al-şehadet 'ala 'l-şehade*), the book of *kadı* law (*kitab el kadı*), procedure for the preparation of legal writs (*usul-u tanzim-i ilamat-ı hukukiye*), and procedure for the preparation of criminal writs (*usul-u tanzim-i ilamat-ı cezaiye*).

What does this tell us? First, and most obviously, with the expulsion of French from all years of teaching there is a tendency here toward a more nationalist legal culture. The focus of the graduates was not supposed to be on comparative law or the roots of the Ottoman legal system. It was supposed to be on how the law could support the Ottoman state specifically. Knowing French or history was not necessary in developing this focus. With the expulsion of psychology, general history, literature, and logic from the curriculum, there is also a tendency toward specialization post 1891. This specialization explicitly discouraged Law School graduates from thinking about the context in which the law was operating. Psychology, history, literature, and logic are important if a judge wants to understand the environment in which plaintiffs and defendants are operating—in other words, if he wants to apply the law in a socially relevant way. It is not necessary, and even dangerous, if a judge is supposed to be administering the law in a uniform manner in support of an abstract ideology.

Finally, the new curriculum is clearly highly interested in the role of the religious establishment in the regular system. By the third and fourth years of instruction there is in fact more of a focus on Islamic law (*Mecelle,* inheritance, foundations, civil/religious court procedure, and Islamic jurisprudence) than there is on regular law (properly speaking, only foreign affairs, commercial law, and the preparation of criminal writs). Students would thus leave the Law School fully aware of the importance of religion in the increasingly nationalist, state centered Ottoman legal culture.

HIRING AND FIRING FUNCTIONARIES

But how many judges in the regular court hierarchy were graduates of the Law School and how many entered the system by other means? At a more general level, what did post-Tanzimat Ottoman legal functionaries look like? To begin with, the regular court hierarchy, leaving aside its commercial aspect, consisted of three levels: courts of first instance (*bidayet*), of appeal (*istinaf*), and of cassation (*temyiz*). Each of these courts was further divided into civil and criminal sections.[28] The civil sections remained Islamic law courts, and *naib*s, trained in the traditional system, presided over them. The criminal sections adjudicated matters relating to the new criminal codes, and their presidents were more directly members of the regular hierarchy than the civil court presidents were.

And then there were hierarchies within the hierarchy. At the level of first instance there were four stages—from the Istanbul courts to the local *kaza* (administrative district originally overseen by a *kadı*) courts. Officially, the president of all courts at the bottom two levels of the hierarchy was also a *naib* trained in Islamic law. Unofficially, *naib*s judged virtually all of the provincial cases, civil and correctional, at all levels of the courts of first instance as well. Such positions were officially open to *naib*s following a law of 1878 regulating the creation of the new courts.[29]

This law did not, however, mean that the courts of appeal were any more closed off to the *ulema* corps than the courts of first instance were. The primary president of the provincial court of appeal, for example, was usually a *naib* and members of the *ulema* corps undertook other tasks in the appeals court system as well.[30] On a theoretical level at least, therefore, *ulema* had jurisdiction over all civil and criminal law cases at all levels of the regular system.

I emphasize this point because an argument is often made that religious legal scholars were excluded from the Tanzimat and post-Tanzimat regular court hierarchy.[31] Following the establishment of the regular court system, the argument goes, job opportunities for *ulema* began to dwindle and to be replaced by appointments which could be filled only by "secularly" trained lawyers and judges.

After the establishment of the Law School, it continues, the only possible way for *ulema* to operate in the new system was to cast off their previous loyalties, to enroll in the new school, and to become fully-fledged "secular" functionaries.[32] This argument begins to fall apart when looking not only at the ideology of the Law School, but also at the composition of the regular court hierarchy. In the same way that religion was essential to the understanding of crime and criminality among earlier, Tanzimat era legal reformers, it was essential to the administration of the criminal law system after the Tanzimat had ended.

Between 1861 and 1908, for example, on average, 62% of the appointments[33] to the regular criminal court hierarchy were members of the religious establishment.[34] A further 30% of the appointments went to civil functionaries, and 8% went to non-Muslim graduates of the Law School. These averages did not change all that drastically over time.[35] Aside from the six-year period between 1876 and 1882, in fact, when the Law School had been established, but its ideology had not yet coalesced, the pattern in appointments to the court hierarchy indeed remained relatively calm. *Ulema* were almost always preferred to other functionaries in staffing the new courts.[36]

As time passed, however, it was not just *ulema,* but *ulema* who had been trained in and defined by the regular system who were employed. Between 1859 and 1876, for example, over a third of the appointments (38%) came from outside of the legal system—that is, for example, from governorships,[37] from the Finance Ministry,[38] or from the office of telegraphs and post.[39] By 1877, this number had dropped to 4%, and between 1891 and 1909 only 2% of regular appointments came from outside of the system. Over the same period, the percentage of appointments from criminal law positions to other criminal law positions[40] went from 38% to 62% to 81% of the total. Likewise, the percentage of appointments from civil or commercial law positions to criminal law positions went from 24% to 33% to 17% of the total.

In the later years, that is, someone already versed in criminal law was far more likely to be appointed to a criminal law position than someone whose experience was grounded primarily in the civil or commercial branches of the system. But these trends should look somewhat familiar. They are, in fact, precisely the patterns that we saw in the reform of the Law School curriculum. In both cases, the regular system became increasingly dependent upon the religious establishment and increasingly insistent upon specialization at the expense of the general.

To the extent that legal functionaries were responding to institutional and bureaucratic change rather than to social change, the law was also becoming gradually more authoritarian. By the beginning of the twentieth century, indeed, legal functionaries were acting out, with a great deal of energy, the self-policing advocated by all three of the Tanzimat era criminal codes. We can see this playing out especially in the rationale behind transferring and appointing criminal court members. Between 1859 and 1908, for example, functionaries received appointments and transfers for a variety of different reasons. These included, among others: the resignation, death, dismissal, or transfer of the previous office holder. As the twentieth century approached, however, the reasons advanced for appointing new functionaries began to coalesce into an interesting pattern.[41]

Between 1859 and 1876, for example, 56% of the appointments resulted from transfers, whereas 5% resulted from the previous functionary's dismissal and prosecution. By 1877, 44% resulted from transfers and 26% from dismissals. Finally, between 1891 and 1908, 37% of new functionaries replaced transfers, and another 37% replaced dismissals who were then prosecuted.

This is a remarkable change. By the beginning of the twentieth century over one third of the vacancies in the regular system were caused by the dismissal and often prosecution of the previous office holder. Fifty years earlier, the number had been negligible. There are two possible explanations for this. The first is that as time passed, judges and their staff became more corrupt, took more bribes, and in general flouted the system with more abandon than they had during the Tanzimat period. This is unlikely. The judges of this generation had been brought up within an environment bounded by Tanzimat and post-Tanzimat ideology. If anything, it would not have even occurred to them that any alternative procedure could exist.

The second explanation is more complex. By 1891, the self conscious, state-centered, performative nature of the Ottoman legal system had been set into place. *Any* irregularity, actual or perceived, was a danger to the state's honor and to the bureaucracy's self definition. By purging itself of impurities with such frequency, the bureaucracy was reaffirming its self definition. The documents that discuss the dismissal of these functionaries, in fact, rarely state in detail what exactly it was that the functionaries had done wrong. They had merely been "corrupt" and were thus dismissed. This purging of the legal and bureaucratic hierarchy—an activity that is one common denominator among the modern, twentieth century totalitarian states—further showed the functionaries themselves exactly the behavior that was expected of them.

We still, though, have not discussed in detail who the post-Tanzimat legal functionaries were. Most of them were *ulema.* But what else? The Ottoman government's new policy on appointments as of 1880 can help us out in answering this question. Starting in 1880 and ending in 1895, the Ottoman bureaucracy required that those appointed to the regular legal system fill out detailed *terâcim-i ahval*—résumés or biographies—before being hired. These biographies describe the applicant's family and educational background, previous work experience, subjects of interest, dismissals, and possible criminal record. They thus flesh out the picture sketched so far.

First of all, between 1880 and 1895 the religious establishment still provided around two thirds of the regular legal hierarchy's functionaries.[42] At the same time, however, only a little over half of the appointments were the sons of *ulema*.[43] This means that a good 10% of the regular functionaries between 1880 and 1895 chose independently to become attached to the *Şeyhülislam*'s office in order to further their careers. That the religious establishment had become an integral part of the regular system must have been obvious to these scholars. Otherwise they would likely have chosen another route.

But just any *alim* would not do—the system required specially trained *ulema*, who could properly embody post-Tanzimat ideology. Schooling, therefore, had to be in whole or in part the prerogative of the state. As a result, 56%, of the appointments mentioned attending civil primary schools of some sort without any (explicit) previous mosque, religious school (*medrese*), or other religious training. Only 28% of the appointments had received religious training alone.[44]

But when we look at those who went to the Law School, things become more interesting. Between 1880 and 1895, on average, only 30% of appointments to the regular legal system actually had Law School degrees. And this seeming lack of success on the part of the Law School in its early years may explain the curricular changes that occurred in 1891. Indeed, of those who did go to the Law School at least 40% had been trained in religious rather than civil schools at the primary level.[45] The Law School was thus not only ideologically dependent on the religious establishment, but administratively dependent as well. *Ulema* attended the Law School, learned the ways in which Islamic Law could be a pillar of the Ottoman state and bureaucracy, and then put their education to use as functionaries in the new system.[46] It was in the Law School, that is, that they learned to enact the symbiotic relationship between religion and state, to provide bureaucratic structures with the moral authority inherent to the Islamic legal system.

Things did not change much over time. The percentage of functionaries affiliated with the religious establishment, the percentage of functionaries whose fathers were *ulema*, the schools that these functionaries attended, the subjects of interest that they highlighted in their biographies, and the previous appointments that they had held remained stable, for example.[47] The only change worth commenting on is the fact that after 1885, more functionaries in the regular system came from families of *ulema* than from other backgrounds. Prior to 1885, the majority of the functionaries did not come (or did not mention that they had come) from *ulema* families. But this switch in 1885 is in keeping with all of the other trends we have seen thus far.

Education and previous work experience are a bit more complex. In the early years, at least half of the functionaries had received their education solely in religious institutions, although in 1882 this number dropped to less than a third of the total and remained there. At the same time, however, the number of applicants who combined a religious and a civil primary education grew gradually over the 15 year period, and there was certainly no elimination of those educated in religious primary schools. Similarly, although the applicants included non-religious subjects of study more than religious subjects in their biographies, by the late 1880s, emphasizing *fikh* (Islamic jurisprudence) was on the rise. By 1892, in fact, they were mentioning *fikh* more often than they had in 1880. Once again, though, given the change in the Law School curriculum in 1891, these trends seem reasonable. The religious establishment, its functionaries, and elements of Islamic Law all had become integral to the overall Ottoman legal system. *Ulema* worked both to represent and to put into effect this system, and their situation as *religious* legal scholars only helped them in this regard.

The state, that is, wanted *ulema* working in the criminal courts because *ulema* could keep to the party line. And in general, it was not *ulema* as a whole, but *ulema* who could not or would not work in the new framework who were excluded from the regular court hierarchy. Similarly, it was functionaries with neither regular nor Islamic legal background who could not find jobs. The number of civil servant appointments to the regular hierarchy, for example, drops to zero after 1885 as, with one exception, does the number of appointments from non-legal religious positions. Criminal law courts by the twentieth century had to be staffed by functionaries who were perhaps not "partyized," but who were definitely cognizant of their roles as the embodiment of the new ideology. If they were simultaneously *ulema,* it was simply that much better.

But *ulema* served equally well at the bureaucratic level—on drafting committees, court selection committees, and within the new Justice Ministry.[48] The typical example of *alim* made good in the regular system is Ahmet Cevdet Paşa,[49] the *ulema* corps member who not only oversaw the drafting of the Ottoman *Mecelle,* but also helped to write the criminal and land codes, and eventually became the first Justice Minister in the post-Tanzimat legal system. But other less well known *ulema* functioned with equal success. Some drafted codes and reform centered legislation, others oversaw the operation of both the religious and the regular aspects of the Ottoman and Turkish legal systems. All were fully aware of their pivotal roles in the modernization of Ottoman law and society.

A number of *ulema* helped to reform the legal and administrative system in Yemen,[50] for example, and many more worked in various positions, both temporary and permanent, in the immediate post-Tanzimat Justice Ministry.[51] At least eight *ulema* also became first or second presidents or members of the Istanbul court of cassation—positions held only by the highest ranking members of the Justice Ministry.[52] More to the point, half[53] of those who mentioned work in

Justice Ministry in their biographies were *ulema*. Of these, most had taken jobs in such explicitly regular departments as the *Muhakemat Dairesi*[54] (Department of Disputes), *Mücazat Dairesi* (Department of Punishments),[55] and the Justice Commission.[56]

Ulema also took positions at the higher levels of the bureaucracy—and indeed there was a certain self consciousness about employing them in this way. In 1888, for example, a council was formed to help in the selection of legal functionaries for the regular system. The nature and composition of the council, however, soon became the subject of debate and concern—who would play what role in the selection of judges and what would their background be? At first, the administration decided that the council ought to include five members of the Justice Ministry, one functionary from the office of the *Şeyhülislam,* and the Director of the Law School. But after some thought, it revised its decision and concluded that, since a *few* individuals had to be familiar with the "concerns of justice," a single functionary from the office of the *Şeyhülislam* was not sufficient. Eventually it was decided to include at least one more.[57]

In constructing this council, the two main themes of nineteenth century Ottoman legal reform collided. On the one hand, there was a committee, the sole purpose of which was to appoint judges and court functionaries. But it was really only as an afterthought that the "concerns of justice" even came into play. Everything was decided and agreed upon, and only then did somebody bring up the question of law and justice. The committee was far more concerned with its bureaucratic position than with its legal one. On the other hand, there was the religious establishment—brought in deliberately to deal with the tricky issue. It is intriguing, for example, that the five members of the Justice Ministry were presumably not familiar with "the concerns of justice," or at least not assumed to be. It is rather functionaries from the religious establishment who had to embody "justice" related aspects of the law—a twist on earlier Ottoman legal philosophy, in which the religious establishment was this time supplying a moral underpinning to a proposed bureaucratic change.

The selection of members for the partially administrative Istanbul court of cassation went in a similar direction. The most important immediate job, "court member," went to Abdülsettar Efendi, who is described as a *Meclis-i Tedkikat-ı Şer'iye* (Council of Religious Legal Inquiries) member, a *Mecelle Cemiyeti* (*Mecelle* Committee) Member, and a teacher from the Law School.[58] Similarly, in 1888, Ömer Hilmi Efendi,[59] an investigator at the Ministry of Religious Foundations became a cassation court member.[60] In fact, in the later years, there appears to have been far more of an interest in filling these positions with high ranking *ulema* than with anyone else. Earlier on, for example, when the *Divan-ı Ahkam-ı Adliye* (High Court of Justice) first came into being, *ulema*[61] were appointed to the highest positions far less often. And as late as 1873, an appointment to the *Muhakemat Ceza Dairesi* (Department of Criminal Disputes) went to the future Grand Vezir, Arif Paşa, who came from completely outside of the legal system. But in general, especially in the later years, it is *ulema* who are performing both the abstract bureaucratic roles in the regular legal system and dispensing discipline in the form of "justice" as judges and court functionaries.

PAYING FUNCTIONARIES

They were well paid to do so. In fact, as *ulema* were incorporated into the regular legal system, they were compensated for their work in a way that would have been quite familiar to them. It is true, as Halil İnalcık points out, that provincial *ulema* occasionally reacted to their "salaried" status.[62] But a closer look at this status leads one to wonder why precisely they were reacting. The official payment scale in the regular court hierarchy reflected almost exactly the less official, but nonetheless well established, payment scale among judges and functionaries in the purely Islamic law courts. The *Şeyhülislam*'s payment system for these courts circa 1909,[63] for example, was a five level hierarchy that started at 2,000 kuruş per month and ended at 5,000 kuruş or more, depending upon court function and geographical placement.[64] The office of the *Şeyhülislam* had also instituted a special retirement fund for those who had served a certain period.

The regular payment system likewise consisted of a five level hierarchy which differed from the above only in that it specified and limited the salaries of those who were at the 5,000 kuruş mark.[65] The primary presidents of the central provincial courts of first instance, as well as those in the capital, received 3,500 kuruş, the secondary presidents received 2,000 (in the provinces) to 3,000 (in the capital), and the judge-assessors received 400 (in the provinces) to 2,000 (in the capital). A similar but more lucrative pattern held in the appeals courts and, as for the court of cassation in Istanbul, the primary presidents received 10,000 kuruş per month, the secondary presidents 7,500 and the judge-assessors 5,000.[66]

It is worth pointing out that no specific salary was listed for the primary presidents of the provincial (*kaza* and *sancak*) courts of first instance or the provincial appeals courts[67]—an omission that would arguably never have occurred in Istanbul or one of the more visible urban centers. But the provinces were different. The bureaucracy had established its presence in the outlying areas merely by setting up the courts there, and this perhaps was enough. Since the functionaries who staffed the provincial courts were not as much in the state's eye, in fact, they could continue to collect money in the "corrupt" pre-Tanzimat style. *Ulema* merely needed to perform their roles in the new legal system properly. If they could do so, corruption in and of itself was apparently not so much of an issue.

In fact, the practical behavior of civil servants was quite officially not much of an issue. In 1890, for example, the state elaborated a salary policy on leaves of absence for civil servants, although only for those who were in need of a "change of scene," those who were on trial, and those who went on pilgrimage.[68] The policy was not particularly detailed: the first two lost half of their pay whereas the last, "due to the respect of the pilgrim's position," kept theirs intact for as long as might be needed.[69] What is worth emphasizing here, though, is that out of all of the possible motivations for leaves of absence, the state council reviewed only vacations, trials, and pilgrimages. This is an unusual assortment of issues. It makes sense, however, in the above context. First of all, putting civil servants on trial had apparently become as common as giving them vacation time or leave for pilgrimage. Secondly, civil servants who were on trial continued to receive at least part of their wages—indicating the performative nature of the trial. The point was not so much to punish a corrupt official, as to demonstrate that such a punishment was possible. And provided he played the role assigned to him, a corrupt functionary could indeed continue even to draw a salary.

FUNCTIONARIES PERFORMING THEIR ROLES

"Ordinary people" on trial were of course not so lucky. Between 1877 and 1908, the procedure for bringing cases to trial underwent a dramatic transformation, and with it, so too did the role of the defendant. First of all, the principals of a case or the police would bring the issue either to a civil court of first instance or to a Islamic law court. If the case was sent to a first instance court and turned out to be within Islamic Law jurisdiction, it was sent to the local *kadı*. If not, it could be appealed to an appeals court or decided and sent to the central Council. From the Council, a case could either be confirmed and sent to the Justice Ministry, confirmed and sent to the office of the *Şeyhülislam,* and then sent to the Justice Ministry, or not confirmed and sent for appeal once again to the cassation court. If the case went originally to a local Islamic Law court, a report was sent straight to the office of the *Şeyhülislam,* confirmed by the Council, and then sent to the Justice Ministry.[70]

Earlier, over the Tanzimat period, there had been a great deal of interaction between the religious and the regular systems at the local level, with the councils and governors hearing both types of cases. At the center, however, things had remained to a large extent separate. After the Tanzimat ended in 1876, the local religious and regular systems began to move apart, and it was at the higher level now that the interaction occurred. The jurisdiction of the office of the *Şeyhülislam,* the Central Council, and the Justice Ministry all began to overlap in many cases. All three also worked together to see to it that the outcome of each case conformed to their respective theoretical underpinnings—be it religious or regular or both.

A case brought against the Syrian followers of the Agha Khan at the beginning of the twentieth century helped to reinforce this new relationship.[71] In 1903, the Ismailis were charged in the Damascus court of appeals "with murder, attempted murder, use of violence in collecting money to be sent to the Agha Khan, violation of a girl, theft, and other 'common crimes.'"[72] In other words, everything. As the case progressed, however, it became clear that the real threat that the Ismailis posed was religious and political rather than moral or personal. The Ismailis had assaulted the state's self definition. The prosecution in fact relied upon the government's fear that the Ismailis considered the Agha Khan, rather than Sultan Abdülhamid II, their Caliph,[73] and in doing so attributed to this charge all of the moral weight attached to rape, violence, murder and personal or "common crimes." Eventually, after having been sentenced in the appeals court to hard labor, and in one case death, their case was brought to the cassation court. Surprisingly, the verdict of the high court did in fact overturn that of the appeals court. But it did so only because a) the Ismailis had been sentenced according to the wrong article of the criminal code and b) "they were all equally guilty." In the end, they all received life sentences.[74]

This case conformed in every detail to post-Tanzimat procedure. It was also grounded in—indeed would not have been possible without—the disjuncture between individual and political crime, between the abstract and the practical, and between the individual and the collective in early twentieth century Ottoman criminal law. The Ismailis were accused of many and varied crimes against many and varied victims. Their real crime, however, was their supposed threat to the state and to the religious establishment. The "common crimes" of which they were accused were just that—common—important for their moral weight but not even worthy of full enumeration. Moreover, when it came to appealing the case, the court of cassation did not re-consider the evidence, circumstances, or even legal argument. Instead it focused on the procedural minutiae of the code. Using this bureaucratic rather than moral platform, the court ended up by imposing in all but one case a harsher penalty than the appeals court had.

The movement in Ottoman legal ideology from personal crime to political crime—as well as the key roles played by both the bureaucracy and the religious establishment could not be more obvious in this case. By the beginning of the twentieth century, religious legal scholars and the philosophy that they espoused had moved to the center of legal reform. *Ulema* were apparently quite aware of the rules by which they were expected to play. But they were still not "partyized" in the way that their later Chinese—and Turkish—counterparts would be. At the same time, however, their role as representatives of a "general will" overseen by an abstract state was without question beginning to coalesce. It would become fully formed with the Young Turk Revolution.

Chapter Seven

1909 to 1920: The Reinvention of "Evil"—Positivists and Totalitarians

By the beginning of the twentieth century legal reform had become a self conscious and self reflective process in the Ottoman Empire, while notions of legal purity or criminal threat had become essential components in the Ottoman government's optimistic discourse of nation building and citizen shaping. But the implications of this self consciousness—the roles accorded to both the new nation and the new citizen—would be obvious only after the establishment of Young Turk rule. In 1908, the Young Turks, under the banner of the Committee of Union and Progress, overthrew what they saw as a backward and stultified Ottoman government and set out to construct a properly modern imperial state. In the process they ratcheted up the pace of "Ottoman reform" writ large and in particular intensified the relationship between legal transformation and political rebirth. Using a vocabulary of law, legal purity, and criminal deviance, the Young Turks re-imagined the Ottoman state and the Ottoman-Turkish social body as progressive and healthy, modern and pure, respectively. They then mobilized a simultaneously scientific and spiritual rhetoric to turn the "social organism" into something both inviolable and under constant attack. The individual citizen likewise became both the basic building block and the most insidious threat to the newly formulated universal ideal. The CUP government, that is, created a rhetorical space in which turn of the century notions of biological determinism and national purity could interact, eventually producing a self consciously modern, progressive, and protective legal discourse.

COMMON DECENCY: THE CREATION OF THE SOCIAL ORGANISM

The year 1908 marked, first of all, for example, the earliest moment at which the individual was re-imagined as a scientific and pseudo-biological threat to an abstract Ottoman-Turkish whole—a relationship that was in turn expressed in a distinct shift in legal vocabulary. Simultaneously, "Islam" as a normative concept began to play even more of a role in the articulation of a uniform national identity predicated on a universal notion of legality. Finally, in a movement away from the positivist and toward the—arguably—proto-fascist, the state became both the personality most in need of legal protection and itself the militarized protector of the newly conceived social organism. All of these transformations were effected deliberately, all in the name of the health, purity, and, again, uniformity of the social whole.

The Young Turks were, in other words, self-styled and self conscious sociological positivists.[1] Even before they took power, they had defined themselves deliberately against the liberal humanism that they saw as backward at best and a failure at worst.[2] They and their positivist counterparts believed that the liberal school of criminal law had grown from an inappropriate insistence upon an individual's free will and moral responsibility.[3] They saw notions of deterrence and even rehabilitation as unscientific and they believed that the liberal project of creating a system of equitable punishments for various crimes within a hierarchy of responsibility was misguided.[4] For the positivist Young Turks, the individual was nothing more than an irrational element within the social organism. Free will, especially, had no place in legal philosophy,[5] and the individual, they argued, as a biological entity, could and ought to be placed scientifically within a hierarchy of empirically established biological criminal types.[6]

The purpose of criminal law was thus to determine scientifically and empirically to which type an accused individual belonged. If convicted of a crime, the criminal would be rehabilitated or eliminated accordingly.[7] The Young Turks rejected in their legislation notions of free will, moral responsibility, justice as an abstract, and the metaphysical or spiritual aspect of an individual's—as opposed to a group's—behavior. They relied instead upon empirically measurable data in defining crimes and punishments. An individual's physical placement within a scientific hierarchy said far more to them than environment, morality, or responsibility. And as soon as they came to power, they began to legislate amendments and reforms to move the Empire's criminal law in the right direction. They needed above all, they believed, to transform Ottoman legal vocabulary into a proper foundation for the articulation of their philosophical position. The Young Turks thus self consciously turned Ottoman law into an arena for various expressions of positivist theory, deliberately altering not just the citizen's relationship to the state, society, and the nation, but redefining all four of these terms for their own purposes.

The earlier Ottoman criminal codes promulgated in 1840, 1851, and 1859 had been built upon a straightforward liberal or authoritarian vocabulary. They had been influenced by mid nineteenth century liberal or quasi liberal interpretations of the subject/state relationship,[8] and the tension in all of them had been between the ideal of the rational bureaucracy and the ideal of the classical monarch. The ideological battle was fought between those who supported a centralized, abstract rule and those who supported a local, socially meaningful rule,[9] between protecting the individual and protecting the state. The vocabulary that set the tone of the first two was either derived, or simply lifted from the quasi liberal 1839 Gülhane Edict. The vocabulary that set the tone for the third was influenced by both Napoleon Bonaparte's and Louis Napoleon's popular authoritarianism.[10] Things changed in 1908.

Rather than attempting to protect the rights of the subject and the state, or using spare terminology to set out as succinctly as possible the most humane and politically expedient relationship between institution and individual, Young Turk legislation instead went into great detail in order to create a new entity to safeguard. Legal change after 1908 was thus fundamentally an attempt to define and protect a new ideal—the social organism. The decrees instituting new legislation called repeated attention to the importance of uniformity and group identity, they mobilized a vocabulary of biological determinism to play up the ways in which deviant individuals threatened the purity of this group, and they redefined religious and social morality as quasi-medical barriers against this threatening deviation. All of these changes were then presented alongside detailed explications of the political and social philosophy that had apparently motivated them.

Two decrees from May and September 1911, for example, each discuss the logistics of reforming the criminal code, and are excellent expressions of both this transformation in legal thinking and the self consciousness that underlay it. The purpose of both was simply to note that a change was about to take place. The point of neither was to describe any amendment in detail, and indeed, prior to 1908 they would have run a sentence or two long, indicating that there had been an addition to the article, that it would be taking effect on such and such a date, and stopping there. The May 1911 decision, however, goes on at length, stating not only that the change was occurring, but explaining why it is necessary for the people (*halk*) to obey the new version of the law: obedience to the new law was important not just in strengthening the state (*memleketin takviyesi*), but in protecting common decency (*adab*), and general moral principles (*ahlak-ı umumiyye*) from defect (*halel*).[11] Variations on the theme of universality and generality (*umumi* and *amme*) show up repeatedly in the text, and the power and strength of the collective is deliberately set up against the threatening yet despicable individual deviant. The September decree likewise goes into far more detail than one would expect given earlier Ottoman legislation, also noting the importance of protecting and maintaining discipline toward "common decency and general moral principles." It likewise invokes religious duties and morals (*feraiz ve ahkam-ı celile-yi islamiyye*), common decency or etiquette (*adab-ı umumiyye*), and then eventually public opinion (*efkar-i umumiyye*) to support its position.[12]

Both of these texts are departures from earlier Ottoman legislation—the product of a post 1908 ideology. The consolidation and conflation in each of them of the state, common decency (or even etiquette), general morality, religious morality, and public opinion underlines, first of all, the collective nature of Ottoman society. It is not just that the state was becoming both the protector of and protected by "private" respectability in the form of decency, morality, religion, and opinion. It was also that decency had become "common," morality had become "general," religion had become a popular "duty," and opinion had become "public." The respectability that supported and was supported by the state was rendered, in other words, normative. Universality, generality, and uniformity became of far more importance than they had ever been before in this context, and as a result, legal terminology was expressing the uniform as essentially "good" and the idiosyncratic as essentially "bad."

The individual indeed was replaced completely in this ideological shift by the collective, nationalist "people," a concept far removed from the civic notion of "citizen" highlighted in the Gülhane decree.[13] If anything, the individual had become a threat—by definition not "general" or "universal," and by definition, therefore, a likely source of the "defect" that the law was now targeting. Insults to public opinion and the corruption of the universal had become the primary crimes that the law was seeking to prevent—a situation that merely reinforces the extent to which law had been re-imagined as the normative protector of a collective "general will." The positivist advocacy of a pure, uncontaminated social organism had indeed taken hold in these decrees to such a degree that it had become necessary to police any and every individual deviation from what was defined as an increasingly universal common good.

The invocation of the universal, the common, the general, and the respectable was one side of the new legal terminology. The other side involved the growing insistence on scientific and empirical knowledge in reforming criminal law. The defect that threatened the social organism was not just a moral defect, that is, but a scientifically determined one. In general, for example, the new laws were far more interested in getting at the "essential nature" of both the crime and the criminal than earlier laws had been. Variations on the word "*mahiyet*," or "reality," "true nature," or "essence" of a thing recur in post 1908 legislation, whereas they did not in legislation from before. In a decree of February 1912, for example, the primary goal of the text is to determine not just the "nature" of the crime, but the social "identity" (*hüviyet*) and "capability" (*istitaat*), as opposed to the "name of," the criminal.[14] The increasingly frequent use of such words in Young Turk legislation was not an accident. Their understanding of sociological positivism and legal transformation demanded an accurate and empirical description of both the crime and the criminal's position in relation to the social organism. The essence and nature of criminality, rather than, say, the environmental causes, personal respon sibility, or moral implications of crime, were key components of the legal edifice they were constructing in support of their political philosophy.

It is also not an accident that this scientific approach appeared most blatantly in legislation having to do with Islamic law. The target of this particular decree, for example—those whose identity, capability, and position within a social hierarchy had to be determined—was once again Albanians acting out and implementing a local rather than a central form of *şeriat.*[15] Their criminal act was thus twofold. On the one hand, they were flying in the face of central authority writ large, disobeying the laws of those whose power rested solely on the ability to command and to legislate. On the other hand, the *nature* of their disobedience was particularly insidious. Islamic law had to be centrally administered, uniform, and normative for it to serve its sociological purpose—for it to be a manifestation of the twentieth century "general will." The concept of "local Islamic law," that is, had to become a contradiction in terms, or if nothing else at least deviant or misguided. That the Albanians were refusing to implement a centrally sanctioned form of religious law therefore also undermined the moral foundation on which the new collective identity was being built.

The Young Turks, however, managed to mobilize positivist notions of criminality against this threat, and indeed to turn it into something of an ideological support. By identifying these local jurists as deviant, by measuring and then dismissing the "capability" of local law, they were also reasserting the power of the social whole. Once identified, once placed within a hierarchy of criminal types, the Albanian jurists, along with their decisions, would no longer be a danger; they would instead help in the definition of collective morality—defining the norm by their deviance. In this way, Young Turk legislators were able both to co-opt religion and morality for the purposes of their own nation building, and to use the two as tools in the strengthening of the "organism" along scientific lines.

The Young Turks, that is, were certainly not averse to incorporating Islamic law and its institutions into their new philosophical framework. But religion had to conform to the scientific orientation of their ideology. In 1889, when İbrahim Temo, Abdullah Cevdet, and Mehmed Reşid first formed the secret society that became the CUP, they did so, again, in the Ottoman medical school.[16] From the beginning, therefore, it was biology that was both explanatory for and analogous to politics and law.[17] All organizations functioned as biological bodies did, and they could be cured and administered in the same way. Religion, however, was not antithetical to this approach, even as many members of the organization took pride in their "atheism."[18] A "universal" religious morality, as well as the basic concept of the *ummah* (Muslim community) remained appealing to Young Turk reformers.[19] Both concepts underlined the individual's duty to society and not to himself—both emphasized, like the biological model, the social whole.[20]

COMBATING THREATS AND ELIMINATING DEFECTS

Unsurprisingly, however, once the social organism had become an actor in the legislation of criminal law, countless threats immediately appeared to attack it. These attacks, though, came from a direction one might not expect. The Young Turks, for example, had something of an obsession with sexual crime. Rape, indecent assault, and abduction receive far more attention in post 1908 legislation than they had in earlier Ottoman law. But this interest in sexual deviance and sexual crime was merely the logical conclusion to the positivist fascination with progress and modernity, the emphasis on a biologically determined collectivity that defined their broader philosophical position. Rape, indecent assault, and abduction became threats not to the individual, in other words, not to any social or religious morality in and of itself, but to the abstract notion of a social whole.

If the purpose of criminal law was to protect the purity of the social organism from defect, that is, it was crimes that struck at this purity that were the most dangerous. Yes, murder was violent, but in the end it destroyed only individuals. Sexual deviancy, and especially violent sexual deviancy, however, tarnished society as a whole. These acts were acts against "common decency" far more than they were acts against people. That this was the case in turn meant that crimes like rape were no longer imagined as relevant to individual women—or if they were, women were only secondary victims. They were crimes instead against the social organism and against the state. Especially in the later years, as women were co-opted into the nationalist discourse, and become the asexual "mothers" or "daughters" of the nation, sexual attacks on them became attacks on the nation. To the extent that women fulfilled their nationalist roles, therefore, sexual attacks against them were punished severely. When they did not, the legal system was simply not interested.

Between 1908 and 1918, for example, a number of new regulations came out addressing rape and indecent assault. But most of these regulations were not directly—or at least solely—concerned with the crime and its punishment. Instead they attempted to define the act for the purposes of social or national progress and then, more importantly, to differentiate rapists from other, "normal" criminals. The first of these regulations was the most straightforward. In it, we see discussed a variety of different scenarios in which children or women might be kidnapped and how the perpetrator of each crime ought to be punished. The regulation notes especially that if the kidnapper also commits indecent assault (*fiil-i şeni*), his penalty will be increased and will include hard labor.[21] If the kidnapper marries his victim, however, the penalty is less severe—a distinct departure from earlier Ottoman legislation, which focused on the damage done to the woman or to her family regardless of a possible future marriage.[22] After 1908, in other words, marriage could change the deviant act into a decent one, could eliminate completely the social threat (and thus any threat) posed by the crime.

The purifying effect of marriage was in fact highlighted in the law. An additional article, seemingly unrelated to the larger question of kidnapping, for instance, noted that people who got married without state permission were subject to imprisonment, as were those who knowingly performed a marriage ceremony for such a couple. Marriage, therefore, did have a salutary effect, and could transform a deviant into a normal member of society. But this could occur only if the marriage was state sanctioned. The issue at stake, that is, was not the issue of individual or religious sin—a secret marriage performed by an Islamic law judge without the bureaucracy's permission would easily have eradicated that problem. Instead the issue was the social and political sanctioning of a sexual relationship. With this law, both rape and marriage had become issues at the heart of the progressive Young Turk state and society.

The later references to rape get at this issue more obviously. Three laws from 1913 and 1914 having to do with forgiveness and amnesty mention sexual crime prominently. The first states simply that those who commit rape (*hetk-i irz*) or indecent assault cannot be pardoned or given commuted sentences.[23] The second is a more detailed law discussing convicts who have been called upon to go to war. In it, any convict (largely defined) who wants to go to the front, will be allowed to do so. The one exception is those who have committed rape or indecent assault—such criminals will not "profit by" the new law.[24] Finally, the third law refers to a general amnesty granted on the part of the Sultan. All convicts except, in this case, those who have been sentenced to death and hard labor or those who have committed rape or indecent assault, will be pardoned.[25]

Neither the Sultan nor the state, neither the nation nor the military, that is, could forgive a sexual deviant. Murderers, thieves, and brigands could be called upon to defend the nation against attack—to be purified through military service. Political criminals and corrupt officials could be pardoned by the Sultan and become functioning members of society again. Sexual deviants, however, were too much of a threat to the moral and physical health of the whole to benefit from any of these exceptions to the law. They were impurities that had to be expunged at all costs. Once the state and its legislators had co-opted the language of public health and morality, in other words, once abstract threats to collective purity had become the target of legislation, it was the deviant rather than the criminal who lost out. A murderer committed a crime against an individual and could be forgiven. A rapist, however, attacked the very heart of national respectability; he infected the purity of the progressive social organism.

But it was not just in laws against sexual crime that this fear of a contaminated society played out. Any crime that threatened notions of general heath, universal security, or public decency became increasingly serious after 1908. In 1911, for example, a decree was issued announcing that the 99th article of the criminal code was to be broadened to target those who publicly (*alenen*) broke their Ramazan fast. The new article noted that, first, the Istanbul police, the office of the *Şeyhülislam,* the interior ministry, and the legal establishment would all work together to deal with this new criminal threat. Second, it argued that since the criminal law as it stood was not explicit enough, there would be an amendment to the code to protect general morality and decency as well as encourage safety and discipline. Third, it stated that a decree to that effect would be issued on the part of the state (*devletçe*), and that those who did not obey it would be fined one to five lira or be imprisoned from 24 hours to one month. And finally, it noted that those who deliberately and without excuse or apology broke the fast were both sinners and criminals, and that those who did so publicly were violating general Muslim decency, as well as Muslim public opinion.[26]

The first point to note about this decree is the hierarchy of criminal behavior. Most reprehensible were those who *publicly* broke the fast, because they violated general (non religious) decency and threatened universal safety and discipline. Above all else, this act was criminal because it corrupted the moral health of the social whole. Interestingly, it also threatened "safety and discipline." How exactly breaking the Ramazan fast would have created an unsafe or undisciplined environment is a bit of a question, but it is not answered in the text. Presumably, again, any deviant act was a socially dangerous one. It was only *after* these issues were presented that the religious aspect of the crime—the sin of breaking the fast—came up. This does not, of course, mean that the issue was not a religious one. Fundamentally, that is all it was. It does mean, however, that religious morality was supporting the health of the social whole at this point, that it was reinforcing normative notions of respectability, rather than the other way around. Moreover, the bureaucracy, as represented by the interior ministry, the police, the legal establishment, the religious establishment and, above all of these, the state, acted as the enforcer of the new ideology. Sexual decency, religious decency, and social decency had all become key, and indeed primary, concerns of the state, the social organism, and the new laws set into place to define and protect them.

Obviously, however, if threatening behavior is going to be redefined, the means of dealing with it must also be redefined. And this the Young Turks did in a classically positivist way. Instead of playing up the punitive or moral nature of the new punishments, Ottoman legislation after 1908 saw punishment as an increasingly scientific or medical affair. If the criminal was not to be eliminated completely, for instance, he was to be "cured" in a clean, scientific, and medical fashion. For example, although those convicts who might be sent to the front were those who were undergoing "deterrent punishment" (*mücazat-ı terhibiyye*),[27] a concept wed to liberal criminology, the idea of purification by means of national military service—and the fact that rapists were excluded from such a purification—is positivist. Purification could happen only if a subject was scientifically determined to be capable of such treatment. Sexual deviants fell outside of that category.

Likewise, a regulation from May 1911, initiating an investigation and reorganization of the prison system,[28] insisted upon detailed reports of the "reformatory measures" or "treatments" (*tedabir-i ıslahiyye*) undergone by prisoners in jails and houses of detention. These reports, the regulation continues, should be compiled into dossiers for inspection. The scientific approach to punishment in this case is obvious—the medical, rather than moral, coloration of the "treatments" is at the heart of the investigation. At the same time, however, once again, only those who *could* be cured would be treated in this way. Those who represented a more nefarious and incurable threat were simply eliminated. This includes not just rapists, but also, for example, disobedient soldiers. A decree from 1912, for instance, is particularly concerned with soldiers who incite others to "deviate from discipline" (*inzibattan inhiraf*), who publicly speak disobedient words or make disobedient speeches, who "seduce" (*ilkaat*) or "corrupt" (*ifsad*) through such speeches, and especially who incite "the people" in general (*halk*), and thus endanger the discipline and security of the state as a whole.[29] Seducing the population through turbulent roadside speeches was, it seems, incorrigible and incurable behavior in the same way that sexual deviancy was, and its punishment was therefore indefinite detention as a state prisoner (*kalebend*).[30]

RELIGION AND THE MILITARIZATION OF LAW

We have, therefore, the creation of the social organism, the determination of those who weaken it, and the elaboration of punishments to deal with such deviants—the construction of a scientific, biologically based criminal law system. As time passed, however, Young Turk criminal law became not just increasingly scientific, but increasingly military; there is in it a growing fascination with war, discipline, and military strength. Post 1908, that is, the Ottoman legal establishment became basically militaristic in its regimentation, proto-fascist in its reliance upon military ideology and institutions to reinforce "domestic" state power, and extreme in its desire to protect the social and eventually the national whole.[31]

Prior to 1908, criminal law in the military context had operated according to a separate military code. This code existed parallel to the civilian code and regulated the behavior of soldiers and to some extent the police. After 1908, although the two codes remained distinct, the civilian code started gradually taking on military facets. This trend appeared most obviously in the legislation on banditry. It is true that prior to the Young Turk period, bandits had not been simply "criminals," but also representatives of a far more nefarious external and internal aggression—the epitome of the collective threat to the state's self definition.[32] Even before 1908, that is, bandits represented a distinct internal "military" threat to Ottoman power. By December 1910, however, this blurring of the lines had become institutionalized—bandits were targeted not just by the legal establishment, but by the War Ministry.[33] The self consciousness of being in a state of both ordinary war against outside aggressors, and extraordinary war against internal enemies pervaded nearly all aspects of criminal law and legal reform following the Young Turk revolution.

The regulation of September 1912,[34] for instance—concerning the soldiers who incited the population to disobedience—plays on both of these themes. First, it needs to be emphasized that this discussion of the behavior of both soldiers and sailors occurred not in the military code, but in the civilian one. Second, although the text begins with a straightforward discussion of the threats posed to the state by military disobedience in "a time of war," it soon is discussing the less immediate threats to the security of the country as a whole (*emniyet-i memleket*) posed by disobedient or corrupting speech. In the end, we come to a passage about the dangers of inciting "various classes of the population" (*sunuf-ı muhtelif-i ahali*) against one another. So in this new article of the civilian criminal code, military disobedience and social disobedience have become to a large extent synonymous. "Corrupting speech" that might cause social or political unrest has become just as dangerous as straightforward military disobedience. Both are simultaneously abstract and concrete attacks on the notion of a strong, uniform social whole. Similarly, the active crime of "inciting," "corrupting," or "seducing" the civilian or military population to revolt has been conflated with the passive crime of disobedience in general. All were re-imagined as threats to society, all undermined the security of the nation as a whole, and all made clear the necessity of a strong state whose job it was to protect them both from attack.

But the militarization of the law was not just about protecting civilian populations from corruption by the inappropriate behavior of soldiers. The military could also purify those civilians who had transgressed social norms. Convicts, again, could be sent to the front as soldiers, their sentences postponed or commuted. More interesting, the commission formed to decide who might take advantage of (literally "profit from") this rule was a joint commission composed of functionaries from the Ministry of War, the Ministry of the Navy, and the Ministry of Justice.[35] The military establishment and the legal establishment would work together, that is, to highlight war—and the participation in war—as a cure for anti-social behavior. By committing violence on behalf of the state, a criminal could erase the violence that he had already committed against the social whole.

The militarization of the law, that is, affected both the civilian population and convicted criminals. But what effect did it have on the relationship between the population as a whole and the state? Essentially, it created a situation in which the state consolidated its power and extended its social control far more effectively than it had before. Two laws from 1912 and 1913, granting amnesty to those who had committed political or military crimes, demonstrate this new relationship clearly. In the first, the War, Justice, and Interior Ministries worked together in decreeing that those who participated in counter state movements in Albania in 1910/1328 would be granted a general amnesty.[36] The second grants a similar general amnesty for those convicted of the "political crimes" (*ceraim-i siyasiyye*) of having participated in various "crushing military defeats" (*hezimet*).[37] A defeated commander, that is, someone who presumably tried to fight on behalf of the nation and state, was rendered just as criminal as those who actively took up arms against the government. In other words, intent and personal circumstance—to the extent that they ever had existed—fell completely by the wayside here. The source of any contamination of the health of the collective was equally guilty and equally subject to punishment. At the same time, however, all of these criminals were likewise equally likely to be granted amnesty—a seemingly strange situation given the authoritarian trends in Young Turk legislation.

If we consider the political and psychological effects of amnesty, however—the idea that the act of personally granting mercy creates a far more intimate and secure bond between transgressor and judge than following an abstract and "rational" legal procedure does[38]—this situation begins to make sense. By placing vague issues like responsibility for military defeat under the civilian legal system, Young Turk legislators were doing two things. First, they were creating a situation in which virtually any act that apparently hurt the state or the society could be legally, if not rationally, considered "criminal." Second, they were opening up an arena for widespread acts of amnesty and mercy on the part of the state. They were erasing any specific formulation of "crime," "punishment," "circumstances," or "intent" and were creating a situation in which the only the only way a judge and transgressor could operate was by means of an intimate, personal relationship. Conflating the military and the civilian in this way, as well as granting the state this personal power, emphasized the emotional and psychological bond between the forgiving progressive nation and the contrite deviant citizen. This final aspect of Young Turk legislation thereby cemented the universality of political and social power. It was emotionally and biologically—as well as legally—impossible for individual consciousness to override collective national consciousness. This new legislation helped the CUP to create a militarized society in which the security of regimentation and the emotional bond of political amnesty worked together to maintain a pure, protected social whole.

Indeed, when war became a key part of Young Turk legal ideology, military concepts seeped into other aspects of Ottoman legal culture as well. Among a number of extensive new regulations governing the behavior of judges, legal secretaries, and other legal functionaries, for example, one in particular stands out. In July 1915, the Young Turk government issued a regulation that not only defined the ranks and roles of various employees of the legal establishment, but also their behavior. "Social interaction" (*ihtilat*) while on the job was forbidden—especially such interaction in the hallways (*koridorlarda*) with "people on official business" (*eshab-ı mesalih*). Moreover, those who did come "on official business" to the court or to an institution associated with the Justice Ministry had to behave according to carefully established rules, and could speak only with the head secretary.[39] Most likely "social interaction" in the hallways continued despite the new regulation. It is easy to imagine, however, the ideal situation envisioned by the drafter of this law. Each functionary would define himself according to his rank, his role and nothing else. The only relationship he would have would be to the court or to the institutional hierarchy broadly defined. In the end, unnecessary or irrelevant social relationships would be eliminated and a new military efficiency would be introduced into the administration of law and justice.

This militarization of the law and legal establishment occurred with good reason. Positivists saw the social whole as a biological organism constantly under threat of both internal and external attack. In the same way that early twentieth century medical terminology began taking on a militaristic coloration, in which parasites or viruses were equated with foreign aggression,[40] legal terminology conflated internal deviance with external attack. Under the Young Turks, this positivist take on law and society came head to head with earlier authoritarian ideas about the role of the state in the political relationship. The result was a very strong legal foundation on which the more overtly authoritarian structures of the Turkish Republic could eventually be built.

But before going in that direction, we need to consider one last aspect of Young Turk criminology—and that is the role of the religious establishment. Up until now, we have seen a gradual incorporation of both religious legal functionaries and Islamic law ideology into the regular system. Given, however, the vocal insistence by various Young Turk ideologues on a scientific rather than religious basis for social interaction, we might expect this trend to reverse itself after 1908. In fact, the opposite occurs. Between 1908 and 1918, religion became one of the most important pillars of Ottoman criminal law. Between 1908 and 1918, that is, the final piece of a proto-totalitarian legal system was set into place.

The appointment of *ulema* to positions within the hierarchy of criminal law courts continued unabated after the Young Turks came to power, for example. Far from being stalled by the 1908 Revolution, the careers of those who had been attached to the religious establishment were even given a push by the new administration.[41] Similarly, many *ulema* worked as functionaries in the Justice Ministry under Young Turk rule,[42] especially after the Islamic law courts were placed under its purview.[43]

Education for *ulema* also seemed to aim at creating judges to fill the new roles. In 1914, the regulations for the *kadı*'s school were reformed. The goal of the school became at this point, among other things, to train court secretaries and public defenders.[44] Teachers of international law (*hukuk-i düvel*) were also hired to train judges for their work in the Islamic law courts.[45] Finally, according to article 20,

> the teachers of legal and criminal writs will teach the preparation and rules of regular (*nizamî* and *kanunî*) writs and documents which are to be prepared by first instance, appeal, and cassation, according to the degree of the courts and the procedure and rules and the legal issues at hand,[46]

meaning that by 1914, *kadı*s had to show proficiency in the functioning and administration of all levels of the regular criminal court hierarchy.

*Kadı*s, and especially their position vis à vis the regular legal system, seem in fact to have been a subject of fascination for Young Turk legislators. A law of April 1913, for instance, discusses what happens when a *kadı* transgresses various personal and professional boundaries.[47] In essence, even though the *kadı* was attached to an Islamic law court, any time he went to trial, he would be tried under regular auspices by a regular judge. The office of the *Şeyhülislam* would be kept informed of the process, but in general, a *kadı*'s behavior was overseen by the regular bureaucracy.

The law of August 1913, discussing the punishment of those who conducted marriage ceremonies for couples without certificates of permission[48] similarly, if not explicitly, aimed to control the irregular behavior of Islamic law judges. It is, after all, only a *kadı* who would make such a slip, or be called upon to perform such a ceremony. Less directly, a law of March 1915 required that professional legal representatives in Islamic law courts met certain educational and bureaucratic requirements. Fundamentally they had to demonstrate a specific sort of "capability" as it was defined by the state.[49] Religious functionaries were thus tied tightly to the state apparatus as the Young Turk period progressed. By no means were they undercut, sidelined, or marginalized—indeed their power over the population and their central role in the regular system are institutionalized in these laws. They simply became supports of the increasingly modern, increasingly positivist, soon to be fascist system.

That the maintenance of the Ramazan fast in 1911/1329 would become a self conscious prerogative of the state—that indeed it would be maintained "*devletçe*"—makes a great deal of sense given the legal environment created by the Young Turk government. Under the scientific, positivist, self proclaimed atheist CUP, religion and state had become unified as they had never been before. It is true that there was a hierarchy—religion acted as a support for state power. But such a redefinition merely reinforced the moral authority of the Islamic legal establishment. By the advent of the First World War, it was in fact the religious establishment and the military alone that had a monopoly on purifying Ottoman Turkish society. Religion and violence would work in concert to create the eventual Turkish Republic.

The positivist Young Turks may have been intrigued by sexual deviancy, but their interest was nothing compared to the fascist obsession with it nearly everywhere following the First World War. Social and sexual threats to the nation as well as pseudo biological understandings of social parasitism became the focus of criminal law in virtually every fascist state.[50] Fascist law was, after all, largely positivist law with a twist.

Alfredo Rocco, Mussolini's Justice Minister, for example, had a great deal to say about such issues. After insisting first on the criminality of those who knowingly spread syphilis or engaged in other unhygienic activities, after including important positivists such as Enrico Ferri on the commission responsible for drafting Mussolini's new criminal law, Rocco argued that a self consciously fascist law had above all else to discard the fetish of the individual in legal culture in favor of the overriding personality of the state.[51] Second, it had to protect and incorporate religious sentiment but not religious freedom into legal culture.[52] And finally, fascist legislators had to realize that the nation and society did not exist on their own, but were the creation of an overriding and generative state.[53] The Ottoman CUP found all of these ideas intriguing. It was only under the Republican Turks, however, that such concepts realized their full expression.

Chapter Eight

1920 and Beyond: Modern or Fascist?

The previous chapters of this book have all flirted to a greater or lesser degree with comparative history. What was happening in the Ottoman Empire and Turkey in the nineteenth and twentieth centuries was happening all over the world, and this needed to be emphasized. When we get to the Turkish Republic circa the 1930s, however, this sort of general comparison becomes insufficient. It was in the 1930s that the Turkish government adopted Italy's fascist criminal code, and therefore Italy, the Italian fascist context, and how both were understood in Turkey deserve some detailed attention.

But first we need a definition of fascism. Fascism, for the purposes of this chapter, will be the specific form of government run by Mussolini in Italy. This may seem like something of an evasion, but given the political similarities between Italy and Turkey in the early part of the twentieth century, it should make at least some sense. The trends in Italy toward a fascist legal situation mirror the trends we have seen in the Ottoman Empire. Religion, nationalism, and the abstraction of criminality all played key and remarkably familiar roles in the creation of both Italian fascism and Italian fascist law. This does not mean, of course, that authoritarianism and totalitarianism, as well as the institutions and ideologies associated with them did not exist elsewhere. In Italy and Turkey, however, they came together in remarkably similar forms.

FASCISM IN ITALY: STATE, SOCIETY, RELIGION, AND LAW

Most scholars agree that the First World War was the catalyst that brought fascism into being in Italy. Many also note that dissatisfaction with the peace was an equally important impetus.[1] At the same time, although fascism as such did not exist before the war, the antecedents of what would become fascism, inchoate and confused as they may have been, did.[2] The following few paragraphs will bring together four overreaching elements which most see as the defining characteristics of fascism and proto-fascism in Italy: its anti-liberal and anti-socialist nature, its adherence to an extreme nationalism, its syndicalism, and its reliance upon authoritarian power structures.

In practice and propaganda, Italian fascist leaders waged political battles with their liberal counterparts and engaged in violent street fighting with their socialist counterparts—underscoring the ideological differences among the three, while downplaying their points of unity.[3] The fascists rejected, for example, the ideology of class conflict[4] and economic determinism that were at the heart of socialist theory, while adopting, at least in part, socialism's anti-capitalism and syndicalism. They similarly rejected the individualism,[5] capitalism, materialism, and rationalism valorized by liberal[6] theory, adopting instead its anti-socialism, the idea of a social hierarchy based upon bourgeois predominance,[7] and nationalism. Finally, one element of both socialism and liberalism that occupied a rather complex position in fascist thinking was secularism. Although this concept will be examined in greater detail later on, for now it suffices to say that although Mussolini himself was an atheist and many early Italian fascist thinkers were staunch secularists, the extreme secularism and anti-clericalism practiced by both contemporary liberals and contemporary socialists was not taken up by Italian fascists in practice, and to a large extent not in theory either.[8]

Fascism, that is, was above all an anti-liberal and anti-socialist movement. Almost more so, however, it was a radically nationalist movement.[9] Although fascist style nationalism in Italy did not immediately take on the racist elements inherent to German national socialism, Mussolini's government did begin to look both backward and forward to a mythical imperial glory. A number of theories attempt to account for the importance of nationalism to fascism in the 1920s and 1930s. Some cite as a causal factor the search for a new value system following the partially successful attack made by liberalism on traditional systems which had held sway before.[10] Others see fascist nationalism as the culmination of the international competition for empire prior to the First World War.[11] Still others highlight the incorporation of many former conservative nationalists into the fascist movement as it gained momentum.[12] And finally, many argue that the sentiment created by Italian unification[13] and the position of Catholicism in Italian politics led to an extreme form of nationalist thought later on.[14] Another possible explanation is simply that nationalism was, again, very popular everywhere in the early part of the twentieth century.

At the same time, fascism has also been seen by many as the logical conclusion to modern, nineteenth century trends in authoritarian politics. Although most scholars do not attempt to look for antecedents to the "leadership principle" in fascist philosophy per se, they do attempt to find a historical basis for the appeal of an authoritarian government. One explanation advanced for the importance of the charismatic leader, however, is the entry of the masses into electoral politics following the First World War.[15] The fascists, it is argued, simply were the most successful in exploiting the new dynamic during the 1920s. A second explanation looks further back to the conservative authoritarian reaction to liberalism prior to the war. This explanation sees in the alliance made between post-war fascists and the threatened pre-war conservative element, the seeds of a new form of political manipulation[16]—in other words, largely what we saw with Louis Napoleon in mid nineteenth century France. In general, then, it is the combination of the authoritarian principle inherited from conservative politics and the entry of the masses into this equation following the war, which most see as the primary impetus for Mussolini's construction of the uniquely fascist leader/population relationship developed after the First World War.[17]

The role of the religious establishment—the Catholic Church in this case—in the rise of Italian fascism is an issue which lies at the heart of this study. It is also an issue with roots a number of decades prior to Mussolini's coming to power. First of all, the unification of Italy was not simply a territorial blow to the Vatican, with the wholesale confiscation of church properties by the new Italian government, but also an ideological disaster, with the emergence of a new and attractive ideology in Italian politics. The post-unification leaders of Italy were self-described moderate liberals, and this they demonstrated energetically, by abolishing Church control over education, civil law, religious minorities, and other institutions and groups.[18] Although, therefore, they were by far more conservative than their French counterparts, Italian liberals became the enemy par excellence to Vatican leaders.

Most scholarship on the relationship between the Church and fascism thus begins with a discussion of the fight between the Vatican and the liberal establishment in post-unification Italy, but then quickly moves on to ask the larger questions: to what extent did the Catholic Church seek to be allied with the fascists after the "failure of liberalism"? To what extent was such an alliance political and to what extent ideological? And how much did the higher clergy approve of Mussolini's policies? Since the Vatican was such a powerful institution, this sort of analysis makes a great deal of sense. In order to make a comparison with the Ottoman and Turkish scenarios, however, the opposite sort of argument is necessary. The religious establishment in the Ottoman Empire and especially Turkey was not nearly as strong vis-à-vis the state as its Italian counterpart,[19] and so what is of interest when examining the relationship there, is the extent to which the state wanted to be allied with the religious establishment. In the Italian context, that is, our question is how much Mussolini sought to ally himself with the Vatican.

Historical events would seem to indicate that Mussolini wanted to quite a bit. The relationship he sought, however, was one in which religion would support the state and act especially as a catalyst for the fascist party's nationalist aims. Mussolini may have been an atheist, but he never believed in secularism in the liberal sense of "separation of religion and state."[20] In fact once he had moved beyond his socialist beliefs, and until he fell under the influence of the German national socialists after 1938, his goal, never successfully realized, was the subordination of the church to political power.

Mussolini's desire to promote this sort of relationship is clearly evidenced in his appointment of pro-clerical figures to important positions within the state infrastructure. In 1924, the anti-clerical Minister of Education was replaced with Pietro Fedele, a pro-clerical fascist who would have little problem with the introduction of religious instruction into state schools.[21] Likewise, in 1926, the "secularist" Fascist Party Secretary, Roberto Farinacci, was replaced by the pro-clerical Agusto Turati.[22] Finally, Alfredo Rocco, whose ideas will be discussed in more detail later on, replaced the earlier, anti-clerical Minister of Justice in 1925. Rocco and the pro-clerical elements of the fascist party all believed to some extent in the repudiation of liberal secularism and the creation of a "more actively Catholic" Italian state.[23] By 1938, it is true, this pro-clerical element of Italian fascism had been rooted out,[24] but for an important fifteen year period, during which Italian fascist thought and practice were developing in earnest, the more powerful political trend was toward a merging of religion and state, even if an incorporation of the former by the latter was not possible.

As early as 1920, in fact, Mussolini himself had argued that Catholicism could play a meaningful role both in the creation of a strong, state-based, morally upright society, and in the furthering of Italy's national and imperial aims.[25] His brother Arnaldo was even more vehement and "saw the Catholic Church as the essential element of historical continuity between the values of ancient Rome—order, discipline, hierarchy—and their modern reincarnation in fascism . . ."[26]

And practice followed ideology. Indeed, as long as pro-clerical fascists such as Alfredo Rocco and Arnaldo Mussolini remained in positions of influence, the Vatican had every right to see nationalization as a threat. But it had no need to fear a complete destruction along the lines of what the German national socialists attempted under Hitler. To emphasize, Italian fascists between 1924 and 1938,[27] and especially between 1924 and 1931, did not seek the destruction of the religious establishment, but its incorporation into the state structure as a means of strengthening fascist power. Destruction of institutionalized religion in Italy would merely have meant the elimination of a potentially useful tool in the unification of the Italian people—an elimination that would have been both unnecessary and dangerous.[28]

At the same time, although the Italian fascist state tended toward a more pro-clerical stance between 1922 and 1938, there was nonetheless a great deal of discord between the pro-clerical and the anti-clerical elements within the party itself. The anti-clerical elements in fact never lost power altogether, and they even enjoyed something of a resurgence after 1938. Alfredo Rocco, however, the Justice Minister and architect of the fascist criminal code was very much in the pro-clerical camp. Moreover, his support of traditional nationalism,[29] and indeed his personification of a pro-clerical "conservative fascism" shaped all of the laws that he enacted. Rocco's career path and personality, his beliefs and how they influenced the Italian legal transition, in fact helped to set the religious and conservative foundations on which fascist criminal law would later be built.

Alfredo Rocco became Minister of Justice in January of 1925 when the former minister, Oviglio, refused to support Mussolini's growing pro-clerical and pro-Vatican stance.[30] It was with Rocco's appointment in particular that the pro-clerical components of the fascist party began to gain influence,[31] and until his dismissal in 1932[32] and his death in 1935,[33] Rocco's twin goals of total state authority and the transformation of religion into a pillar of this authority were also the goals of fascist legal reform. Rocco believed that the protection of state interests was the primary objective of legal culture, and that it was only after the primacy of this objective had been guaranteed that the state might "[limit] its own power in order to strengthen itself by conceding individual liberties."[34] The importance of state authority was stressed to such a degree in Rocco's philosophy that, unlike the German national socialists, he in fact advocated the subordinate role of even the fascist party to state interests.[35] It is noteworthy that in these beliefs, Rocco has been considered by at least one scholar as "more than the philosopher Gentile . . . the true ideologist of the regime."[36]

The origins of Rocco's ideology, as of much fascist ideology in general, can be found in what was perceived as the failure of liberalism in Italy and the resurgence of a new form of conservative authoritarianism. In 1913, Rocco had argued that liberalism and socialism, with their doctrines of class conflict and their inherent corruption, had brought about the decline of Italian culture. The solution he proposed to this decline was,

> a replacement of the liberal system by a corporativist order in which a powerful industrial class would control sectors of the economy under the auspices of a strong state under which the authority of the monarchy, the military, and the church had been restored.[37]

By 1918, Rocco was even more unambiguously supportive of the dominant position of Catholicism in a new Italian nationalism. In 1922 he claimed that,

> the Italian State must become more openly and more actively Catholic, promoting and defending the Catholic religion in return for the Church's loyal support of the social and political order in Italy—nothing less than the restoration of the 19th century alliance of 'throne and altar'...[38]

Although, therefore, some have seen the 1929 alliance between the Vatican and the Fascist Party as a blow to the totalitarian ideology Rocco had developed,[39] this blow occurred not so much because of the influential position the church adopted in state affairs—that is, not so much because the church had not been destroyed completely—but because of the still not subordinate position of the Church to state interests.

Rocco's conservative and fascist beliefs are also reflected in numerous aspects of the criminal law which he created. It is, for example, not an accident that the committee Rocco brought together to draft the fascist criminal code was composed not only of newly legitimized fascist thinkers, but also of legal specialists from the previous age.[40] Moreover, after Rocco had commissioned the committee to draft the law, the new Justice Minister also emphasized that their goal should not be to replace completely the liberal/conservative 1889 code, as had been the aim of the abortive 1919 positivist commission, but to amend it. In his decree announcing the formation of the committee, Rocco stated that the objective of the project was to "integrate and complete the norms of the pre-existing code, and not of course to suppress them or modify them radically."[41] The earlier code, he held, had been hindered by its interest in protecting the individual alone, whereas the new law would protect the state and its personality instead.[42]

In the decree introducing the code as well, Rocco's entire rhetorical structure revolves around a comparison of the 1889 law and the 1930 one which followed—in what areas the 1889 code had fallen short (such as protection of the state, the political economy, and religious practice)—and how the new text would be remedying these shortcomings. The idea, in other words, that emerges from the introduction to the Rocco text is that although the 1930 code is in revolutionary opposition to its predecessor, it also comes unquestionably out of the same conservative tradition. It in fact would not exist without this code as its foundation.

Rocco also contends in this explication of his philosophy first, that a cult of the state and a cult of the divine are not in any way incompatible; second, that the state recognizes religious sentiment as an essential element in the moral elevation of the individual and society; and third, that the protection or incorporation of religious sentiment, although not necessarily religious freedom, would likewise be a prerogative of the state and of criminal law.[43] By doing so, he makes quite clear the extent to which he was attempting both to incorporate previous elements of the conservative and religious systems into Italy's new legal structure, and to use these elements as pillars of the fascist state itself. The question that now arises, therefore, is to what extent Rocco's law, as the culmination of pre-fascist and early fascist legal development, was relevant to the situation which had arisen in the contemporary Turkish Republic.

"HARSH AND SCIENTIFIC": REPUBLICAN TURKISH LEGAL REFORM

It need hardly be noted that Turkey, like Italy, was hugely affected by the First World War. Mustafa Kemal's successful rejection of the Treaty of Sèvres was in fact something of an encouragement to contemporary political leaders who had felt similarly outraged by an unjust peace,[44] if also something of a discouragement to their imperial aspirations.[45] But other elements of Ottoman and Turkish legal development, including the way in which legal scholars understood "liberal reform," the increasingly nationalist nature of criminal law, and the presence of authoritarian ideologies in legal discourse appear to have followed the Italian model as well.

The ways in which liberalism and authoritarianism interacted in the Ottoman context, for example, were quite similar to the ways in which they interacted in Italy. Ottoman reformers rejected liberal individualism as a basis for their new legal culture, both by subordinating personal law to political law and also by eventually "adopting" the authoritarian Napoleonic code as their first import. Liberal secularism also received very little attention from Ottoman legal scholars. The religious establishment and its ideology formed a key component of modern Ottoman criminal law, and never was there a moment at which a secular separation of the two realms made any sense. Ottoman reformers were similarly indifferent to liberalism's reliance upon revolutionary change. In the Ottoman Empire, we see gradual, top down "conservative modernization" just as we saw in Italy. Indeed, even the purity of radical Republican reform comes into question when we consider the leftover Ottoman functionaries who were in charge of implementing it.

The government did, therefore, see the reform of criminal law as a route toward a radical, progressive modernity, especially to the extent that modernity would strengthen state authority. But they also, like their Italian counterparts, opposed the introduction of a culture of individual rights as opposed to responsibilities[46] into their new system. Whenever a hint of liberal individualism does appear in the Ottoman codes, in fact, it is always in reference to the absolutist and eventually authoritarian state surrounding these individuals. Certain liberal structural elements thus did find their way into the Ottoman criminal law system—elements such as a specific and limited definition of the ruler/ruled relationship, the invocation of "rationality" or "organization" in creating the bureaucratic hierarchy of courts, and a circumscribing of some of the powers of traditional elites. But these liberal structures did not grow "deep roots" in the Ottoman Empire for the very logical reason that nobody had ever intended them to. The trajectory taken by Ottoman legal ideology, from the earliest Tanzimat era codes to the final 1938 text indeed involved the repeated acknowledgement of certain liberal concepts, and then the eventual rejection of these concepts in favor of a state-centered form of authoritarian nationalism.

This transformation of legal ideology could not have happened, however, without the support of the religious establishment. Once again, the primary difference between the Italian state/religion relationship and the Ottoman and Turkish state/religion relationship was the relative power and autonomy on the "religion" side of the former equation. Whereas Mussolini, despite protestations to the contrary, was not successful in bringing the Vatican under the control of the fascist state, Mustafa Kemal Atatürk was quite successful—in the beginning, at least—in defining and subordinating a normative "Islam" in Turkey to the political organs of the Republic. There are, however, numerous similarities in the roads taken toward these two eventualities which are quite alike in their intent, if not in their outcome.

In the same way that Italian unification brought about a crisis in the relationship between state and religion in Italy, for example, the Tanzimat brought about a crisis in the same relationship in the Ottoman Empire. After 1839, Ottoman intellectuals began to question the social and political position of the religious establishment. Although the redefinition of religion during the Tanzimat was certainly not "secular," therefore, it did force an eventual reinterpretation of the balance between state and religion. In the end, religion and religious morality were essentialized, centralized, tied to the Ottoman state apparatus, and then made key elements in the Ottoman state's movement toward modernity. In the same way that Mussolini deliberately appointed pro-clerical elements to his political ministries, attempted to infiltrate ecclesiastical legal structures with (pro-clerical) state elements, and tried to merge the two systems into a fascist whole, the Ottoman government repeatedly appointed *ulema* as well as civil servants to both courts and commissions, made the Law School curriculum "more religious," and used *ulema* as tools in its centralizing policies.

This did not all come to a halt with the rise of the Turkish Republic. Despite much Republican rhetoric to the contrary, the religious establishment continued to play a role in the transformation of criminal law. Yes, some *ulema* became victims of the Republican Turkish revolution. The functionaries in the office of the *Şeyhülislam,* for example, had no such powerful institution under which to continue working. Teachers at the religious schools found themselves in a similar situation. But in general it appears that even functionaries from these two areas did find employment—and quite similar employment to that which they had held before. Again, a number of Ottoman *ulema* did end badly—some unemployed, some committing suicide, some fleeing the country, and some executed by the Independence Tribunals.[47] But the majority, it appears—and in particular those who had worked as judges and legal functionaries earlier on—made the transition into the Republican period quite easily, continued to hold positions in the Republican equivalents of the Ottoman Justice and Religious Ministries, and continued to take advantage of the Ottoman and Turkish incorporation of "traditional" elements into the new framework.

Out of a sample of eighty *ulema* who transitioned from the Ottoman period into the Republican period,[48] for example, fourteen found post-Republican teaching positions, either at the local level or in universities. Twenty-two went into the Republican Religious Ministry. Twenty-four went into to the Justice Ministry, and two found jobs in other Republican government ministries. On the other side of the equation, eleven remained unemployed after the fall of the Ottoman Empire, five were convicted by the Independence Tribunals and either executed or imprisoned, one fled the country, and one committed suicide. Overall, therefore, over three quarters of these Ottoman religious functionaries maintained their positions under the new Republican government.

And these positions were by no means low-level ones. Although a number of those who remained in the "religious establishment" became local *müftü*s or mosque functionaries,[49] the majority secured managerial positions within the newly conceived Ministry of Religion.[50] More interesting, of the fourteen who took teaching positions,[51] those who had held professorships and higher teaching positions under Ottoman rule did not lose status or position under the new administration. Of the five who had been professors during the Ottoman period, one became a professor of literature at Istanbul University,[52] one continued to teach religious studies at the same university,[53] one taught civil law on the Istanbul University Law Faculty until 1957,[54] one taught hadith and Islamic history in the Theology Faculty of Istanbul University until his retirement,[55] and the last taught on the Theology and Literature Faculties of Istanbul University.[56]

But Ottoman *ulema* became functionaries in the Republican Justice Ministry more often than they did anything else. One of these, Mahmut Aziz Efendi, for example, had held various positions in both the Ottoman religious and regular systems. After briefly losing his job at the Ministry of Justice in 1919, he was reinstated in this position in 1920, where he remained—despite various new ministerial names—until his retirement.[57] Another, Mehmet Burhaeddin Efendi, after holding both bureaucratic and legal positions, joined the Republican Justice Ministry in 1924 following the dissolution of the office of the *Şeyhülislam*, and then took a job as a public prosecutor in Istanbul.[58] Finally, Mehmet Emin Ali Efendi, after serving as a *naib* in various local and higher courts, became a member of the highest Imperial regular court in 1917 and then became the Republican equivalent following the dissolution of the office of the *Şeyhülislam* in 1924.[59] These three examples are just a few of many. The point is simply that the Turkish Republican government, much like the Ottoman government before it, needed the religious establishment. Ideologically, it was indispensable to the continuing redefinition of criminality in the new Republican context.

But what was this ideology? As set forth in the speeches by Turkish parliamentarians, it is, first of all, a strikingly familiar one—indeed echoing[60] remarkably well the ideologies set forth by Rocco in contemporary speeches of his own. The majority of these speeches begin by referring to the earlier Ottoman Napoleonic code, and how this code, although admirable, was old fashioned and not in keeping with the requirements of the age.[61] In particular, it lacked all of the elements necessary to a code of law promulgated by a modern and modernizing government—specifically, articles guaranteeing the protection of the state, the protection of the nation, and the protection of the revolution, all at the expense of the individual.

One speaker, for example, deplores the fact that the French code lacked the power to punish a number of important state crimes.[62] He continues by stating that whereas before, only the rights of the sultan and the individual were taken into consideration, now the rights of the state, the revolution, and the people, in that order, would be emphasized.[63] In a similar manner, the Turkish Justice Minister, Mahmut Esat, noted that

> our criminal code is very harsh because the revolution is very jealous. But it is both harsh and scientific. Those who will be afraid of it, and those who have need to be afraid of it are those who are against the interests of the Turkish nation, against the rights of the Turkish nation, and against the revolution, and these people ought to be afraid. [applause] . . .[64]

Other parliamentarians emphasized the inappropriately central position of the individual and individual rights in Islamic Law. One speaker notes, for example, that the greatest problem with the old religious law was not so much its religious nature, as its indifference toward the security and the inviolability of the nation.[65] A member of the legal reform committee itself, Yusuf Kemal, further argued that the old law was "harnessed" to the personal rights protected and determined by Islamic law—a situation not in keeping with the mentality of the Turkish nation,[66] which was to be both statist and secular.

At the same time, however, nearly all of the speakers re-affirm the fact that the legal reform, the adoption of the new law, and its implementation would not have been possible without the participation of specialists held over from the old system. The leader of the committee, for example, is respected for his years of experience as a former Ottoman cassation court president.[67] Likewise, older scholars are seen as personally responsible—given their years of (wrong thinking, it is true) Ottoman legal knowledge—for the creation of new judges to implement the codes.[68] More to the point, the composition of the committee responsible for drafting and translating the Republican code reflects an astonishingly accurate balance between Ottoman and Republican, conservative and radical. Of the ten committee members, three were administrators who had had no previous experience in Ottoman courts, four had graduated from the Ottoman Law School and had been employed as functionaries in both the civil and the criminal courts, one had been appointed to various Justice Ministry commissions, without apparently having entered the Law School, and one was an Islamist nationalist philosopher.[69]

This amalgam of administrators and scholars, of holdovers from the Ottoman legal system and people who had never held clear positions within it, of older conservative elites and relatively radical nationalists can account to a large extent for the direction in which the reform of Republican criminal law later went. The insistence upon a harsh system that would uphold state, nation, and revolution, the claim that the greatest problem with the earlier, quasi-religious law was its emphasis on crimes against the individual, and the implicit acknowledgment of the importance of the previous system in the new revolutionary framework are all eminently logical when considering the individuals responsible for them.

In the final analysis, in fact, it seems that Republican Turkish legal scholars and their predecessors took the same road that Rocco and his predecessors were following. Their emphasis upon a conservative foundation for the law, their authoritarian interest in the primacy of the state and the leader, and their new, radicalized ideas about nation and revolution were all very much a part of early twentieth century fascist ideology. Given the historical context of legal reform in the Ottoman period, however, this coincidence of ideology and practice should hardly be surprising. Nor, for that matter, should the comments of one visitor to the Turkish Republic in 1935. This visitor noted in particular that Turkey resembled Italy in its "one party system with aggressive leadership," its tendencies toward "economic nationalism," and, more to the point, the fact that the government advocated "worshipping the state in place of Islam." He continued, though, that whereas "the state still retains the right to interfere in religious matters, the regime has practiced tolerance to some degree ... Islam must conform to the nationalist program."[70]

Chapter Nine

Turkey Adopts a Fascist Law

In 1958, a committee of Turkish members of parliament proposed a project to reassess and reform the thirty-two year old Turkish Republican criminal code. The project was soon contested and defeated by its opponents, however, the reason[1] being that the suggested revised code was to be a complete translation of the 1930 Italian fascist criminal law.[2] A question arises: if the Turkish government had already adopted Mussolini's code of law, why would they need to do so again? It is here that things become complex. Yes, in 1927 the Italian criminal code, in effect under Mussolini, had been promulgated in Turkey. The actual text of the law, however, was the text of the 1889 Royal code, which bore little or no resemblance to its 1930 counterpart. So what happened between 1927 and 1958?

Some scholars argue that Mustafa Kemal admired Mussolini's style of government and therefore adopted throughout the 1920s various aspects of Italian fascist rule, including the Italian criminal law.[3] This would indeed help to explain the later interest in a fascist as opposed to liberal law. It nonetheless, however, leaves something to be desired: in 1927, the Turkish government did not adopt Mussolini's fascist criminal code for the very simple reason that it had not yet been composed. Turkish legal reformers instead adopted the, again, 1889 royal Italian code, which happened to be still in place under Mussolini's government.

The view of a number of other scholars may therefore be of more use. It goes as follows: in 1927, the Turkish government adopted the 1889 Italian Royal code, but then altered it to such an extent over the next ten years that it became a purely national law, born out of Republican Turkish sensibilities and legal philosophy and no outside source whatsoever.[4] Chronologically, this approach makes sense. It is true that between 1927 and 1938 the majority of the original 1889 text was completely altered with a view to creating a code more in keeping with the ideals of contemporary Turkish society. But there does still remain one problem. It does not explain why, then, in 1958, anyone in Turkish parliament would care to look back at the 1930 Italian fascist criminal law—a law which would, according to the above at least, be completely irrelevant to the Turkish situation.

When examining what exactly was changed in the text of the 1889/1927 law, and where these changes came from, however, it becomes clear that the fascist law did indeed play a prominent role. Yes, it was the 1889 code that was adopted, and yes, over the next ten years it was drastically altered to conform to Turkish values. But the changes that were implemented came, often word for word, straight from Mussolini's newly promulgated 1930 fascist code of criminal law.

The real question, therefore, is why and how did this situation arise? It is to answering this question that the rest of this chapter will be devoted. In 1926/7, the government of the Republic of Turkey set about adopting the Kingdom of Italy's 1889 royal criminal code for its own use. In the report which introduced the new code, the Justice Minister, Mahmut Esat, argued that,

> the Republican Turkish regime is the result of systems established by the Turkish revolution; it is based upon the most democratic and secular of principles. Without question it could not adapt itself to penal codifications from the era of absolutism and of the sultanate, [codifications] which have no rapport with the [democratic and secular] principles to which they were even diametrically opposed. For laws are a forcible expression of the eras and times and regimes which have given them life.[5]

In other words, in order to rid itself in particular of the absolutist ideology represented by the 1859 Ottoman (Napoleonic) code, the Turkish government chose to adopt "the most secular and democratic" text around at the time.

Between 1931 and 1938, however—in three separate stages (1931–33, 1936, 1937–38)—more than half of the articles of the original text were changed,[6] creating a law quite different from the 1927 original. So different was this law, in fact, that by 1939 the French/Turkish publishing house responsible for translating many of the new Republic's legal texts into European languages had printed a new edition of the Turkish criminal code. In it, the same Justice Ministry report from the 1927 edition was faithfully reproduced. And although the changes, abrogations, and additions were noted in a table at the beginning of the text, the source of these changes was not elaborated.

In general, therefore, the implication was that although the text was to a large extent altered, it still conformed to the democratic and secular principles elaborated earlier. The idea that the 1939 version of the Turkish code might bear more of a resemblance to the certainly not democratic, and only questionably secular 1930 Italian fascist code was not advanced. When comparing the changes made to the Turkish code between 1931 and 1938 to the 1930 Italian text, however, the source of many of the new and modern ideas becomes obvious. In particular as they relate to crimes against the state, the nation, and race, the elements of the Republican code which were changed came almost exclusively from the new fascist law.

Between 1933 and 1938, Book Three of the original code, on misdemeanors, was of very little renewed interest on the part of Turkish legal scholars. Contrarily, more than half of Book One, on general legal philosophy, and more than one third of Book Two, on serious crime, were altered—indicating that the government paid a much more obvious attention to them than to Book One. Similarly, of the ten titles in the second book, the four that received the most scrutiny were those relating to the state and political structure: state security, public trust, administration of justice, and public order. Of the nine chapters in Book Two that received the most attention,[7] all but two relate to crimes against the state or the nation/race.

That is, early Republican law makers, just like their Ottoman counterparts, focused not on protecting the individual from criminal attack or society from moral contravention, but instead on protecting the state and eventually the nation or race from threats to their self definition. In general, for example, the reformed Turkish code is far less interested in criminal intent and individual culpability, and far more interested in extending and toughening existing punishments.[8] Moreover, the idea that an individual must repent for what he has done is gradually replaced in the reformed text by the positivist/fascist idea that the individual must be removed to protect the whole. In article 68 of the original 1927 text, for instance, if an individual commits multiple serious crimes, he is subject to an extended, but fixed, period of cellular isolation.[9] In the 1938 text, the period of cellular isolation is reduced, but the death penalty is recommended for those who commit multiple serious crimes.[10] In comparison, the Italian fascist text lowers the period of isolation to not more than four years and not less than six months, and stipulates that anyone committing more than one serious crime be put to death.[11]

The idea here then in both the Italian fascist and the reformed Turkish codes is that whereas cellular isolation is not going to change a socially and morally insane individual incapable of reform, putting that individual to death will help, in the sense that it will rid the social organism and state of a dangerous element. This concept did not exist in the original 1927 Turkish version. The other changed articles in the section tend to follow the same pattern—raising severe punishments to the levels of the Italian text, and lowering those which aim more at rehabilitation than removal.[12]

It is in Book Two of the reformed Turkish code, though, that we start to see direct translations from the fascist text. Again, the nine chapters of the second book which changed the most include: crimes against the nation, crimes against state powers, crimes against state security, resisting arrest, crimes related to money, counterfeiting, abduction/seduction, rape and attack, abortion, and damages to others. The first of these, on crimes against the nation, changed completely between 1931 and 1938, and is, for all intents and purposes, a word for word translation of the 1930 Italian fascist chapter on the same.

At the same time, the disparate titles given to this chapter in each code indicate slightly different attitudes in each context. The 1927 Turkish code, for example, calls the chapter "Crimes against the Nation," the 1930 Italian code calls it "Crimes against the International Personality of the State," and the 1938 Turkish code calls it "Crimes against the International Existence of the State." The Republican Turkish government as of 1938, that is, had still not quite personified the state to the degree that the Italian fascists had.

Similarly, whereas this chapter in the 1927 Turkish code is made up of 21 articles,[13] five of which carry the possibility of a death sentence,[14] in the 1930 Italian code, it consists of 35 articles, 13 of which carry the death sentence. [15] In the 1938 Turkish code, the chapter contains 21 articles just like its 1927 predecessor, but into these 21 articles, with four exceptions, are transposed word for word all 35 articles from the 1930 Italian text.[16] The four exceptions are: 1) the designation "national" in the Italian text is replaced by the more liberal "citizen," in the Turkish version, 2) the order of the articles differs between the two texts, 3) the articles on political and economic defeatism and instigating soldiers to disobey are moved out of the "international existence" section and placed in the "state powers" section, and 4) in two cases, the period of penal servitude is slightly shorter in the Turkish version. Aside from these discrepancies, 1930 Italian fascist philosophy and practice on crimes against the international existence (if not personality) of the state were adopted totally by the Republican Turkish government.[17]

Later sections[18] of the 1938 Turkish version of the text go in similar directions. In effect, these changes involve broadening the definition of state crime to include those who "encourage," instead of those who "excite" others to bear arms, legislating against those who have hidden arms with the intent of fomenting an insurrection, and raising the punishment for these crimes from not more than fifteen years of penal servitude, to not less than twenty.[19] What we see here, then, is once more a Turkish Republican attempt to place Italian fascist ideas about state security and personality into an earlier, more liberal framework.

Four other articles inserted directly from the Italian fascist code offer much more straightforward evidence of this particular attitude. First of all, the original version of these articles—on provoking soldiers, insulting the Republic, judicial authority in such cases, and publishing anti-state propaganda—were simply expunged from the 1927 Turkish text. They were then replaced with much more draconian, and often unrelated combinations of articles[20] from the 1930 Italian fascist law. The result was a situation in which before, these crimes were narrowly defined and punished accordingly. After, they were broadly and vaguely defined and much more seriously punished.

The next chapter of the Turkish code which underwent a great deal of change between 1927 and 1938 concerned a related issue, anti state associations or bands. Between 1927 and 1938, the definition of what constituted such a band broadened considerably and the punishment for participating in such an organization went from ten years or less to ten years or more of penal servitude.[21] It is true that this is more a positivist than a fascist outlook—with the open-ended as opposed to simply harsh sentence and the focus on collective criminality. Nonetheless, we can still make a relatively convincing argument that in this case the line between positivism and fascism was not a particularly distinct one.

The final article of this chapter, which defines "penal servitude," was lifted entirely out of the later Turkish text. It was then replaced by a combination of articles 310 and 313 of the 1930 Italian fascist law. These articles define in detail "time of war" (but not penal servitude) for the purposes of criminal law and the overriding authority of the Justice Ministry in all such issues.[22] First of all, removing an article that defines "penal servitude" obviously places that much more definitional power into the hands of the bureaucracy. Moreover, the fact that this article was replaced by a definition of "time of war" underlines the activist and militaristic turn that the code was taking. Even if these definitional and procedural transformations do not indicate any drastic practical change to overall criminal law philosophy, that is, the fact that they were taken into consideration at all and then adopted as the most reasonable around, indicates the extent at least to which the legal thinkers at the time were attempting to militarize further the Turkish legal environment.

The next section, "crimes against public faith," contains two chapters—on paper money and on counterfeiting stamps and seals. The first of these contains eleven articles, all except one of which were transplanted from the Italian fascist code. The second contains twelve articles, all except two of which came from the same source. As a result of these transplants, what had once been a section prescribing twelve years of penal servitude for only the most serious of a number of straightforward counterfeiting crimes,[23] became a section prescribing sentences of twelve years of penal servitude for a variety of crimes and accessory crimes relating to all aspects of the counterfeiting process.[24] Attacking the state's "honor" via counterfeiting had become an issue of interest as early as the Tanzimat reforms. Here, however, it was resurrected and reconfigured—of similar interest to Republican Turkish (and Italian fascist) scholars, who believed above all that the honor the state had to be protected at any cost.

Almost as important as the honor of the state, however, was the honor and purity of the social body, and the next major section of the code to attract attention covered crimes against morality and the family. The most important chapter within this section discussed abduction. All six articles of this chapter—on abducting women for the purpose of rape or marriage, on the same crime committed against a minor, and on extenuating circumstances—were altered completely, inspired by if not translated from the 1930 Italian fascist criminal law. All likewise follow the more stringent fascist standards rather than the slightly less extreme penalties from the earlier code. The purpose for which the abduction was undertaken also receives more attention in both the fascist Italian and the later Turkish code (although the former separates the two into different articles, whereas the latter treats them in the same one). It receives slightly less in the 1927 law.[25]

More to the point, though, we see a great deal of interest in the question of abortion and how it relates to "the health of the race" in the reformed Turkish code. The fascist understanding of crime against the "integrity and health of the race" indeed seems to have appealed quite powerfully to Turkish legal reformers, and although there are a few other instances of entire chapters being taken from the 1930 Italian law and placed into the 1938 Turkish one,[26] the chapter on the health of the race is preserved almost[27] completely intact. Moreover, along with the chapter on crimes against the state, it is one of the most indicative of the new fascist character of Turkish law. In addition to the prohibition against abortion, for example, this chapter also includes articles penalizing "procured impotence to procreate," and "incitement to practices against procreation." These crimes are then rearticulated as direct threats to the health of the social and political whole. Whereas before, that is, sexual crime was either a moral or an individual issue—part of a more classical "crimes against the person" section—with the revised law, these articles took up where Young Turk legislators had left off, and became crimes against the state, nation and race. They were thus placed into an extreme version of the Young Turk philosophical framework—a framework in which the role of the individual was a deviant and threatening one, in which sexuality especially had to be regulated in the name of political uniformity.

By 1938, that is, Turkish legal specialists had revised or completely altered more than half of their original 1927 criminal law. The law ceased to be a relatively faithful translation of the 1889 Italian royal code, and instead became a code in keeping with the needs of the Turkish nation at the time. It is true, and it ought to be emphasized, that many of the changed aspects of the code were indeed newly conceived by the Turkish legal community. At the same time, however, many more of these were simply a second wave of transplants from the same source, this time with a fascist as opposed to "liberal" philosophy. Yes, the framework of the code remained as it had always been. But the particular sections that were changed the most—on crimes against the nation/state, on counterfeiting, on the race, on money, and on abduction—were also, those that were the most relevant to creating a fascist state. Indeed, they were those elements of criminal law that the Italian fascist Justice Minister, Alfredo Rocco himself listed as the most important to the new regime[28]—the protection of the personality of the state, religion, the economy, the race, and familial organization.[29] These were not only changed, but distinctly and deliberately brought into line with contemporary Italian philosophy.

The final 1938 Turkish code, however, was also nothing more nor less than the culmination of a Turkish and Ottoman legal transformation that had begun with the advent of the Tanzimat. Once again, when the original 1927 Turkish/Italian criminal law was promulgated, Mahmut Esat, the Justice Minister, wrote that this particular text was chosen in order to further the democratic and secular aims of the new Turkish Republic. In 1938, when the revised version of the Turkish/Italian law came out, the same statement was appended to the text as an introduction. Never mind that the democratic ideals had to a large extent fallen by the wayside with the authoritarian exaltation of the personality of the state. Never mind that the secular aims had never been particularly well articulated to begin with. The primary goal of the adoption of both codes had been indeed the needs of the Turkish state. And these needs would not be met by a liberal law. The aims of the 1938 Turkish code were identical to those of every other Tanzimat and post-Tanzimat Ottoman law: to strengthen the state and eventually the "race" at the expense of the individual, to extend state control and the concept of criminality over areas hitherto untouched, to combine and to merge criminal law and political law, and to leave those areas of law concerned with the individual to a large extent isolated—of interest only for the moral value they could lend to the more important arena of political crime.

Mussolini's experiment with fascist thought and practice ended badly—both for himself and for Italy. Mustafa Kemal, contrarily, is still in death a hugely respected figure in Turkey, and the reforms which he instituted are defended vigorously. But a number of years have passed since the promulgation of the 1938 Turkish Republican code of criminal law. Throughout this period Turkey's identity—as a "European" or "Middle Eastern," "secular" or "religious" state—has been the subject of much discussion. If the text of Turkey's criminal law is any indication, this aspect of Turkish society, at least, is indeed "European"—fascism as a political philosophy has been almost exclusively connected with modern European history. But this connection does not necessarily mean that such thinking could not have developed in an Islamic context. Ottoman religious functionaries and the infrastructure under which they worked were as meaningful in legitimizing the eventual adoption of a fascist code of criminal law as Italian religious leaders and sentiment were in supporting Alfredo Rocco's vision. Both provided a normative "traditional" foundation from which the new and eventually radical philosophy might operate.

The result was a Turkish Republican system of criminal law very much in keeping with the dominant European political/legal philosophy of the time. That this system of criminal law remained in place and was elaborated as years passed is the problematic issue facing the Turkish legal establishment today. In a continuing effort to attain their goal of membership in the European Union, the center left and center right parties in the Turkish parliament have been sponsoring endless re-evaluations and reforms of all aspects of Turkey's legal system, especially in the spheres of political and criminal law. It ought to be emphasized once again, however, that although the process which led up to the adoption of these apparently inappropriate legal codes and mores came out of a nineteenth century merging of religious and regular systems of law, the product was every bit as European as the Republican Turkish establishment might have wished.

Conclusion

Invoking Dostoevsky is tempting when writing about crime and criminality in the modern period. This is not just because "Crime and Punishment" in x or y context makes for an evocative chapter title. In most of his works, at some point, Dostoevsky grapples with the ongoing transformation of nineteenth century criminal law or at least with changing notions of and attitudes toward criminality. Gary Morson, for example, argues in his analysis of *Notes from Underground* that,

> If nature reduces our most willful acts to so many chemical reactions governed by mathematical laws then it has deprived us of our very selves; and it is this deprivation that insults the man from underground. Or to rephrase this parody: he takes personally his absence of personhood.[1]

Morson continues by noting that all his life, the underground man "has been offended by the laws of nature"—"a strange and self destructive reaction." "It is paradoxical," Morson notes "to take offence at the laws of nature, but not at laws passed by congress."[2]

Arguably, however, the trend in late nineteenth and early twentieth century legal reform everywhere was toward a unification of these two sets of rules. Liberals, "liberal" authoritarians, positivists, and fascists all wanted to turn both the state and its legal system into a force of nature—as "inevitable" as mathematics or biology. In the Ottoman and Turkish context, they to some extent succeeded. Why they succeeded is a question that can be answered by turning to a second theme that occurs quite frequently in Dostoevsky. It is paradoxical to take offence at the laws of nature, it is not paradoxical to take offence at laws passed by congress—what about laws revealed by God?

In both *Crime and Punishment* and *The Brothers Karamazov,* religion is a redemptive force that tempers both civilization and its laws—irrational but purifying and essential. This to some extent holds true in the Ottoman Empire and Turkey, but we would be hard pressed to find an analogy for the angelic monks and cleansing whores who populate the pages of Dostoevsky's work. Indeed, rather than representing individual salvation against an uncaring system, religion and its moral authority instead shaped the system, provided the normative framework for the creation of the uncaring violence of the criminalizing state. It is true that Mustafa Kemal Atatürk was able to enact widespread and sweeping reforms largely because the system of checks and balances had broken down when he took power. But the earlier incorporation of the religious establishment into the larger state structure certainly did not hurt matters. By the advent of the Turkish Republic, administrative purity, legal purity, and moral or religious purity had all come together in their contemporary and authoritarian form.

The third chapter of this book argued that Ottoman criminal law in the 1840s became increasingly a tool of bureaucratic self-definition, in which local, popular practice was of little or no interest. The law concerned itself not with what was, but with what ought to be, and bureaucratic purity became the first priority of penal legislation. Chapters Four and Five examined the repercussions of this transformation. Once the concept of "criminal" had been co-opted by the bureaucracy, those who fell into that category began to play vastly different roles. Instead of oppressing "victims," criminals threatened an administrative ideal. In the 1851 Ottoman criminal code, in fact, crimes against "life" were more frequently crimes against the state or its administration than against any one individual. The state was thereby eventually imbued with a personality that was far more real than that of any single person—by 1876, political law and criminal law had become largely synonymous.

Chapter Six looked in detail at the incorporation of the Ottoman and Turkish religious establishments into the newly defined legal system. Over the course of the late nineteenth and early twentieth centuries, Ottoman *ulema* were trained, paid, and politicized. They became the representatives of a legal system in which deviance from the administrative norm became religiously "reprehensible." Although the rhetoric of the Turkish Republican period may have undermined the concept of a state "religious hierarchy," therefore, the moral and religious tone of bureaucratic purity remained alive and well. The Turkish Republican legal and moral environment would not have been possible, that is, without the Ottoman historical context.

Finally, Chapters Seven, Eight, and Nine brought all of these trends into focus. The positivism of the Young Turks—at least in the legal sphere—led eventually to fascism on the part of early Republican reformers. In the same way that Enrico Ferri found it simple to shift from a positivist to a fascist framework in Italy, Turkish legal scholars also had little difficulty replacing "social body" with "state" in their intellectual discourse. Deviance had already been defined both religiously and bureaucratically, and if the Young Turks focused more on sexual deviance, whereas the Republican Turks focused more on political deviance, this was hardly problematic. The motivation behind the two stances was the same—the creation of an abstract whole, a "general will," that could overcome any individual threat to its self definition.

Scholarship on nineteenth and twentieth century Ottoman legal reform has focused for the most part on the concrete. To what extent were the new legal codes secular? To what extent were they modern? To what extent were they genuine codes? And most important, to what extent were they authentic? All of these questions are excellent ones and deserve a great deal of attention. They also lead, however, to further, more theoretical quandaries. One result of the uneasy relationship between late Ottoman religion and late Ottoman state, between the idea of authenticity and the idea of reform, between the "transparency" and the "rigidity" of codification is the fluid position that criminality began to occupy in the Ottoman imagination. As Ottoman criminal law was repeatedly reinterpreted over the course of the nineteenth and early twentieth centuries, what could be defined as "criminal" also changed. In particular, as we have seen, there was a blurring of the lines over these years between religious or moral crime and political or bureaucratic crime.

By the beginning of the twentieth century, that is, criminality had become a political rather than a moral category. The abstract concept most in need of legal protection had become not "the individual," "God," or even "society," but "the state." A corrupt bureaucratic functionary began to pose more of a threat to Ottoman self definition than a murderer, an apostate, or a sexual deviant. The culmination of this trend was the eventual Turkish Republican adoption of Mussolini's fascist code of criminal law in 1938—a key moment in the development of Turkey's intrusive state structure.

At the same time, although the Turkish Republican government was relatively unique in adopting an explicitly fascist code of criminal law, the tendencies that led to this adoption had corollaries in a variety of other contexts. In nineteenth century China and Argentina, there was a similar fascination with the purity of bureaucratic function, leading in the end to legal systems and bureaucracies focused for the most part on policing themselves. In France and England—both "at home" and in the colonies—political crime, and especially collective political crime, likewise became the primary focus of new legislation. In general, that is, this authoritarian understanding of crime in the Ottoman Empire is one case study in a broader international phenomenon. Indeed, legal change in the Ottoman Empire was nothing if not "normal," and arguably, we are still for the most part subject to states that continually reinterpret criminality as a deviant threat to the themselves—and that base their legislation squarely upon an authoritarian, and occasionally totalitarian, logic.

At the end of *Crime and Punishment,* Rodion Raskolnikov turns himself in.[3] For the careful reader, this is not much of a shock. The entire text, in fact, leads to this, again, "inevitable" conclusion. What is interesting is the reasoning behind Raskolnikov's decision. He does not turn himself in because having murdered the woman he murdered is wrong. He does not turn himself in because murder is against the law. Instead, there is on the one hand the inexorable force of the bureaucracy—the apparatus of criminal law. The civil servants, investigators, police officers, and bureaucrats with whom Raskolnikov interacts may not have been unduly interested in him, but Raskolnikov himself is obsessively and even self destructively interested in them—as well as with the institutions they represent. On the other hand there is religious redemption in the form of Sonya, the prostitute. In the end, Raskolnikov does not mind having been "caught" by the criminal law apparatus, given that at the beginning of his penal servitude "a new story begins, the story of a man's gradual renewal, his gradual rebirth, his gradual transition from one world to another, of his growing acquaintance with a new, hitherto completely unknown reality."[4]

Dostoevsky was likely not writing a story about the coming together of religious and bureaucratic morality, and how these lead to an inherently authoritarian situation. At the same time, however, the way in which this theme plays out—in this work that was written just as these massive transformations in criminal law and the concept of "criminality" were occurring—is worth noting. The Ottoman Empire and Turkey certainly were unique environments—and the Ottoman and Turkish governments undoubtedly made use of these more general processes for their own purposes. But overall, what happened to Ottoman and Turkish criminal law happened everywhere, with greater or lesser degrees of "success."

Notes

NOTES TO INTRODUCTION

1. Among many others, see for example D. Ergil, "Secularization of Islamic Law and Institutions in Turkey," *Studies in Islam* 15 (1978): 71–142.
2. Starting with Max Weber, who argued that codifications undertaken by "patrimonial monarchs," like the Ottoman sultan, were not true codifications, but merely "mechanical arrangements" of pre-existing and specific principles. A true codification, in his opinion, would arise from the needs of a rational bureaucracy and would be total, all-inclusive, uniform, and general. He did not see these conditions existing outside of Europe. *Economy and Society*. New York: Bedminster Press, 1968. Vol. 2, pp. 848–850.
3. An excellent example of this trope is Scot Lehigh's "analysis" of apostasy in Islamic Law in "Islam's Critic from Within," *Boston Globe* July 23, 2003. A19.
4. See Joseph Schacht, *An Introduction to Islamic Law*. Oxford: Clarendon Press, 1964. pp. 69–76; Wael B. Hallaq, "Was the Gate of Ijtihad Closed?" *International Journal of Middle East Studies* 16 (1984): 3–41; L.A. Mansurnour, "Shawkani and the Closed Door of Ijtihad: Did Shawkani Possess the Key to the Reopening of the Closed Door of Ijtihad?" *Hamdard Islamicus* 11 (1988): 57–65; and others.
5. I borrow this term from David Streckfuss, "Kings in the Age of Nations: The Paradox of Lèse Majesté as Political Crime in Thailand," *Comparative Studies in Society and History* 37 (1995): 445–475.
6. James M. Donovan, "Magistrates and Juries in France, 1791–1952," *French Historical Studies* 22 (1999): 379–420. p. 388
7. Xu Xiaoqun, "The Fate of Judicial Independence in Republican China, 1912–1937," *China Quarterly* 149 (1997): 1–28. p. 3.
8. Mark D. Szuchman, "Disorder and Social Control in Buenos Aires," *Journal of Interdisciplinary History* 15 (9184): 83–110. p. 90.
9. See, for example, Elizabeth Thompson, "Ottoman Political Reform in the Provinces: The Damascus Advisory Council in 1844–45," *International Journal of Middle East Studies* 25 (1993): 457–475. and Halil İnalcık, "Application of the Tanzimat and its Social Effects," *Archivum Ottomanicum* 5 (1973): 97–128.
10. For example, Bernard Lewis, *The Emergence of Modern Turkey*. New York: Oxford University Press, 1967.

11. For example, Benjamin J. Fortna, *Imperial Classroom: Islam, The State and Education in the Late Ottoman Empire.* New York: Oxford University Press, 2002, who argues that the Hamidian period especially was not a time of "secularization." *passim.*
12. For example, Erik J. Zurcher, *Turkey: A Modern History.* London: I.B.Tauris, 1993. pp. 70–71.
13. For example, M. Şükrü Hanioğlu, *The Young Turks in Opposition.* New York: Oxford University Press, 1995.
14. Haim Gerber, *State, Society, and Law in Islam: Ottoman Law in Comparative Perspective.* Albany: State University of New York Press, 1994. p. 68.
15. The first half of this book will be devoted to showing that the reform of Ottoman criminal law went in this direction in the Tanzimat and post-Tanzimat periods. As for evidence of this attitude in general among the architects of the Tanzimat, the best place to look is at Reşid Paşa, the author of the Edict of Gülhane. Reşid Paşa actually began setting the groundwork for the proclamation of the Tanzimat a number of months before he prepared the edict. The British military had just helped the Ottoman military to put down the threat to Ottoman sovereignty posed by Mehmet Ali, the governor of Egypt. With this event in mind, Reşid Paşa wrote to his British counterpart, Lord Palmerston on August 12, 1839, discussing his plan to promulgate the new law.

    From the very beginning, that is, the Tanzimat reforms were performed first for the benefit of Ottoman civil servants, and second for that of their bureaucratic counterparts in other states. One of the very first arguments that Reşid Paşa makes in his memorandum is that "trouver une solution [à la quéstion d'Egypte] ne suffirait pas pour obtenir un résultat satisfaisant et définitif." (Frank Bailey. British Policy and the Turkish Reform Movement. Cambridge: Harvard University Press, 1942. Appendix III, p. 272.) Egypt, the obvious, straightforward, practical military threat is definitely one obstacle in the path of re-imagining the state. But it is certainly not the primary obstacle. Instead, what is important is the re-creation and re-definition of the bureaucracy—"internal reform"—and the elimination of any "fanatics" who might block this self redefinition. It is only after establishing this foundation, that Reşid goes on to explain how important such a reform would be to the survival of the Ottoman state, and what role various European bureaucracies might play in supporting that movement.

    With reference to the new Sultan, for example, Reşid Pasha writes that "pour [sic] son jeune âge et son inexpérience, le nouvel émpereur sera plus facilement accéssible aux machinations de l'intérieur et du déhors . . ." (in Bailey, p. 273.) It is worth pausing here to look at what exactly this statement implies. Upon first glance, "inside" seems to refer to inside the Ottoman state, whereas "outside" refers to European or other non-Ottoman powers. But the inside/outside dichotomy is also a reference to those civil servants within the bureaucracy who understand the importance of creating a rational bureaucratic ideal versus those outside of the state, who are too influenced by their connections to the population. It is extremely important that those on the "inside" win out in the competition for the Sultan's ear. Indeed, Reşid Paşa immediately continues by blaming the apparent failure of past reforms on the previous Sultan, Mahmud II's, inability to understand what an ideal bureaucracy ought to be. He writes that although during Mahmud II's reign "le fanatisme de la nation Mosulman," and "la force des ulémas" (in Bailey, p. 274.)

had been weakened, Mahmud II simply "n'avait aucunement des connaissances à l'administration des affaires." (in Bailey, p. 272.)

The "Muslim nation" refers to the majority of the population of the Ottoman state at the time. The people for whom, in a "liberal" context, these reforms would have been undertaken. The population could not, however, in Reşid's view, understand the importance of bureaucratic redefinition, and so they represented a threat. The "force of the ulema" is a bit trickier. The key role that the Ottoman *ulema* eventually play in the Tanzimat and post Tanzimat reforms—in reforming both the educational system and the legal system—leads one to wonder what Reşid Paşa was getting at. But when we recall that this memorandum was written in 1839, things begin to make more sense. The "force" of the *ulema* at this point is presumably their connection to the "Muslim nation"—their role as intermediaries between the bureaucracy and the population. The disjuncture, then, is between the population and their fanaticism on the one hand, and the "administration of affairs" on the other.

Which brings us to the final part of Reşid Paşa's criticism of Mahmud II. The former Sultan simply had no idea whatsoever about the administration of affairs. Arguably, Mahmud II did understand the administration of affairs. He began the process of institutional centralization, he reorganized the army, many scholars see his policies as essentially proto-Tanzimat ones. But if we define "administration of affairs" as the creation of a uniform, self-referential bureaucratic ideal, then no, Mahmud II did not have any idea. His reforms were undertaken in response to social and military problems that arose on the ground. He never managed to disassociate the Ottoman bureaucracy completely from the Ottoman population, and in this way, he was every bit as much of a failure as Reşid Paşa claims that he was.

This situation would be remedied with Mahmud II's successor, Abdülmecid I. It is in fact remarkable the extent to which Reşid Paşa aligns the Ottoman bureaucracy with the bureaucracies of other states, rather than with other segments of the Ottoman state. He and his bureaucracy can relate easily to Palmerston and Palmerston's bureaucracy. He cannot relate to the Ottoman Sultan, to the Ottoman population, or—at this point—to the Ottoman religious establishment. He even goes as far as to note to Palmerston that:

> [l]es propositions qui lui seraient faites ne venant pas d'une seule nation, mais bien de l'alliance de toutes les grandes puissances; par la suite, ce cas excéptionnel ne pourrait servir ni de prétexte ni d'antecédent à aucune d'entre elles pour s'ingérer seule dans les affaires intérieures de la Sublime Porte. (in Bailey, p. 274)

It is a given that some foreign bureaucracy or another will interfere in the internal affairs of the Ottoman state. Reşid Paşa does not seem to have an issue with that. What is important is that even this interference be general rather than specific, abstract rather than personal, and that the "propositions" of those who interfere match the "propositions" of their internal counterparts, the Ottoman bureaucracy. He continues:

> Il faudrait dire à la Porte que . . . si [elle] suit désormais une meilleure route, si elle place la sureté des personnes et des fortunes sous la garantie de sages

> règlements et des lois fidèlement exécutées en délivrant complètement sa population au juge de la tyrannie; qu'en retour de cette conduite, le secours des puissances ne lui faillira pas.... Lui faire entendre ces représentations sévères et d'autres semblable serait un acte de la plus haute importance. (in Bailey, p. 276)

Although there is mention of "delivering the population from the yoke of tyranny," the majority of this statement is vague. The Ottoman state must follow "a better route," it must enact and execute "wise regulations and laws." The statement highlights once again the connection that Reşid Paşa, as an Ottoman bureaucrat, feels to the bureaucracies of outside states, rather than to the "fanatics" within his own. He wants the representations to be "severe" so that it is not just from within, but from without that the re-creation of the bureaucracy will come. Reşid Paşa is asking Palmerston to join him in redefining and abstracting Ottoman functions. Palmerston, however, made no reply to the memorandum, and Reşid Paşa returned to Istanbul shortly after sending it. (Bailey, p. 190)

16. Weber, vol. 2, p. 604.
17. Michel Foucault, *Discipline and Punish: The Birth of the Prison.* New York: Vintage Books, 1977. pp. 300–301.
18. Schacht, pp. 90–91.
19. The Marquis de Sade, "Philosophy in the Bedroom," in *The Marquis de Sade: Justine, Philosophy in the Bedroom, and Other Writings.* trans: Richard Seaver and Austryn Wainhouse. New York: Grover Press, 1965. pp. 311–313.
20. Donna T. Andrew, "Debate: The Secularization of Suicide in England 1660–1800," *Past and Present* 119 (1988): 158–165., p. 159.
21. For example, Lewis, p. 40.
22. M. Patricia Dougherty, "The Rise and Fall of L'ami de la religion: History, Purpose and Readership of a French Catholic Newspaper," *Catholic Historical Review* 77 (1991): 21–41.
23. S.J. Woolfe, *Fascism in Europe.* London: Methuen, 1968, 1981. p. 5.
24. Xiaoqun, p. 3.
25. Gerber, pp. 67, 76.
26. Uriel Heyd, *Studies in Old Ottoman Criminal Law.* Oxford, Clarendon Press, 1973. p. 174.
27. Streckfuss, pp. 448–453.
28. Actually, the fascist code was not adopted. Instead, the 1889 liberal Italian criminal code came into use, but between 1933 and 1938 it was "reformed" itself, such that large chunks of the newer 1930 fascist code replaced the older text. For a detailed discussion of this process, see below, Chapters Eight and Nine.
29. I should emphasize here that when I refer to "positivism" I am referring to the sociological movement and not to the more narrowly defined "legal positivism." See below, Chapter Seven, for an elaboration.
30. Enrico Ferri, *Sociologie criminelle.* Paris: A. Rousseau, 1893. p. 27.
31. Jacob Landau, *Pan Turkism in Turkey: A Study in Irredentism.* Hamden CT: Archon Books, 1981.
32. See, for example, Ehud R. Toledano, "The Legislative Process in the Ottoman Empire in the Early Tanzimat Period," *International Journal of Turkish Studies* 1, no. 2 (1980): 99–106. p. 99. T. Miras, "Le tanzimat et son système legislatif,"

Annales de la Faculté de Droit d'Istanbul 17 (1967). pp. 26–28. Köksal Bayraktar, "Influence du droit française sur les tentatives du mode juridique turc pour s'occidentaliser," *Annales de la Faculté de Droit d'Istanbul* 42 (1979). pp. 321–2. And many others.

33. For example, Feroz Ahmad, *The Making of Modern Turkey*. New York: Routledge, 1993.
34. For example, Nathan J. Brown, "Shari'a and State in the Modern Middle East," *International Journal of Middle East Studies* 29 (1992): 359–376.
35. For example, Timothy Mitchell, *Colonising Egypt*. New York: Cambridge University Press, 1991.

NOTES TO CHAPTER ONE

1. See, for example, Zurcher, pp. 23, 54. And others.
2. For example, Jonathan Grant, "Rethinking Ottoman 'Decline': Military Technology Diffusion in the Ottoman Empire, the Fifteenth to the Eighteenth Century," *Journal of World History* 10 (1999): 179–201. And many others.
3. "The Hatti Şerif of Gülhane, 3 November 1839," in J.C. Hurewitz, *Diplomacy in the Near and Middle East*. New York: D. Van Nostrand Company, 1956. p. 113.
4. Ibid. There is debate about the extent to which the references to Islamic law and jurisprudence in the edict are "genuine." I shall address this debate in more detail below, in Chapters Three and Four.
5. Talat Miras, "Le conseil d'état et la jurisdiction administrative en Turquie," *Revue du Droit Public et de la Science Politique en France et à l'Étranger* 55 (1938): 693–701. p. 691.
6. Lewis, p. 122.
7. The word that I am translating here as "regular" is "*nizamî*." The *nizamî* courts were the courts set up to administer the codes and procedure put into place over the course of the Tanzimat. Scholars tend to leave the word un-translated, although when it is translated, it often appears as "secular." Given any reasonable definition of the word "secular," however, this is a bit problematic. Throughout the course of this book, I shall be calling the courts and the law that they administered "regular," which is a far closer translation of the original and also gets more to the heart of what the Tanzimat was about.
8. Fortna, p. 241. Also, Lewis, pp. 178–9.
9. Hanioğlu, pp. 203–211
10. Hugh Poulton, *Top Hat, Grey Wolf and Crescent*. New York: New York University Press, 1997. p.93.
11. See below.
12. Or, again, series of "regulations."
13. Fortna has made this point quite convincingly in his work.

NOTES TO CHAPTER TWO

1. This argument is contrary to conventional wisdom about the Tanzimat. Most scholars see a separation of the two spheres over the nineteenth century. Please see below for an elaboration of my argument.

2. See below for an elaboration of this argument.
3. E. Tyan, "Kadi," *Encyclopedia of Islam*. Vol. 4. Leiden: Brill, 1997. p. 373.
4. F.E. Vogel, "Siyasa Shar'iyya," *Encyclopedia of Islam*. Vol. 6. Leiden: Brill, 1997. pp. 695–696
5. Ekinci, E. "Osmanlı Hukukunda Mahkeme Kararlarının Kontrolü," *Belletin* 65 (2001): 959–1005. p. 962. I should pause here and also say something about the education of the *kadı*s. In general, Ottoman *ulema* became *kadı*s by following an established and relatively transparent route. After having been educated in local or provincial religious schools (*medreses*) attached to mosques, *ulema* would enter "one of the eight famous *medreses* attached to the Mosque of Sultan Mehmed the Conqueror" in Istanbul. From there, by making combined use of patronage and the prestige of his *medrese,* an *alım* would be appointed as a *kadı,* or he would wait for such an appointment, teaching in one of the schools. Suraiya Faroghi, "Social Mobility Among Ottoman 'Ulema in the Late Sixteenth Century," *International Journal of Middle East Studies* 4 (1973): 204–218. p. 212.
6. Ibid. p. 961.
7. Ibid. p. 962.
8. Ibid. p. 971.
9. Ibid. p. 971.
10. Heyd, p. 202.
11. Ibid, p. 176. Akgündüz also notes the relatively political, rather than personal, character of the early codes. vol. 1, p. 75.
12. C.V. Findley, "Mahkama," *Encyclopedia of Islam*. Vol. 5. Leiden: Brill, 1997. p. 5. Findley points out that in general the Ottoman administration tried to keep the line between the *kadı* court and *mazalim* "indistinct."
13. Ekinci, pp. 971–2.
14. I ought to note here that I shall be working within the framework of the Hanafi school of law—the school followed for the most part by Ottoman jurists.
15. Rudolph Peters, "The Islamization of Criminal Law: A Comparative Analysis," *Die Welt Des Islams* 34 (1994): 246–260. p. 251. Faizan Mustafa, "Islamic Law of Confession—A Comparison with Western and Indian Laws," *Islamic and Comparative Law Review* 131 (1993): 27–37, p. 31.
16. Mustafa, pp. 34–5.
17. It was on this doctrine—"public benefit," "public welfare," or *maslaha*—that the legitimacy of the *mazalim* courts rested, given the absence of any explicit textual support upon which it could rely. J.S. Neilsen, "Mazalim," and Madjid Khadduri, "Maslaha" *Encyclopedia of Islam*. Leiden: Brill, 1989. pp. 933–935; 738–740.
18. The concept of public welfare also protected the defendant in *mazalim* trials. Since the procedure in these trials was about defining the public and its rights as a whole, it could equally limit the plaintiff's room for maneuver. Once the judge had identified the plaintiff and the defendant, for example, the burden of proof rested with the plaintiff. Not only did the plaintiff have to bring evidence and witnesses of relatively trustworthy—if not perfect—character, he had to show that the injuries done to him or his property were indeed analogous to injuries done to the public at large. In cases of negligence, for instance, there could be no liability if the harm done to the individual was more than counterbalanced by the benefits to the public at large; if the individual suffered damages because his neighbor was exercising

his rights of ownership; or if a greater injury was prevented by the lesser injury. (Muhammad Ghauth, "Torts due to Negligence: Burden of Proof," *Islamic Culture* 32 (1958), pp. 153–163. p. 161.)

19. "Maslaha," *Encyclopedia of Islam.*
20. If we assume that one defining characteristic of the "modern mindset" is a belief in the value of "progress."
21. "Maslaha"
22. J.N.D. Anderson, "Homicide in Islamic Law," *School of Oriental and African Studies Bulletin* 13 (1951): 811–828. p. 812.
23. Ibid, p. 820.

NOTES TO CHAPTER THREE

1. Michael John, "The Peculiarities of the German State: Bourgeois Law and Society in the Imperial Era," *Past and Present* 119 (1988): 105–131. p. 106.
2. Desmond Brown, "Abortive Attempts to Codify English Criminal Law," *Parliamentary History* 11 (1992): 1–39. pp. 2–4. Lindsay Farmer, "Reconstructing the English Codification Debate," *Law and History Review* 18 (2000): 397–444. p. 398.
3. Farmer, p. 425.
4. Heyd, p. 176. This is despite the fact that the two well-known codes were divided, first, into chapters on a) adultery, b) cursing and quarrelling, and c) drinking alcohol, theft, seizure, and rape, and second, into chapters on a) suspicion, b) crimes related to craftsmen, and c) police. Ahmet Akgündüz follows Heyd's line with regard to the relatively unimportant position occupied by private and personal crime in these codes. He argues that judgments in classical Ottoman criminal law were legitimized for the most part according to the doctrine of *tazir.* That is, they were seen as crimes related to the temporal authority, not covered explicitly by Islamic law. He continues by stating that even the 1859 criminal code was formulated using this doctrine of legitimacy. Ahmet Akgündüz, *Osmanlı Kanunnâmeleri ve Hukukî Tahlilleri.* Istanbul: Hilâl Matbaası, 1990. vol. 1, p. 75.
5. Heyd, p. 151.
6. See above, Ekinci.
7. Gabriel Baer, "The Transition from Traditional to Western Criminal Law in Turkey and Egypt," *Studia Islamica,* 45 (1977): 139–158. likewise makes this point, arguing that "the general purpose of all the early criminal codes of the Tanzimat period was similar to that of the old Ottoman *qanun.* It was the chief object of the *qanun* to safeguard public order, provide for smooth administration and to protect the common people against oppressive officials and fief-holders, not so much to safeguard the rights of the individual against a criminal." pp. 143–4.
8. Ömer Turan, "Legal Adjustments of the Tanzimat and 'Mecelle,'" *Études Balkaniques* 35 (1999): 213–221. p. 215.
9. Crimes such as treason, excitation to revolt, corruption, tax fraud, and others. Articles 1, 2, 5, 6, 9, 12. In Heidborn, p. 366.
10. Ahmed Lütfi, *Mirat-ı Adalet, yahud Tarihçe-i Adliye-yi Devlet-i Aliyye.* Istanbul: Kitapçı Ohannes, 1304 (1888) p. 128. (1840 code) "Gülhane'de kıra'at olunan hatt-ı hümayun-i ma'delet-makrun-i hazret-i şahane mucibince kaffe-i teba'a-i

Devlet-i Aliyye bila-istisna emniyet-i can ve mal ve mahfuziyet-i ırz ve namus hukuk-i mefruzasına ez-ser-i nev nail olmuş ve ber-mukteza-yı hürriyet-i şer'iye huzur-i şer' ve kanunda ve mevadd-ı hukukiyede herkesin yeksan ve siyyan olması . . ." "According to the imperial decree read at Gülhane, to which justice is joined, without exception, all subjects of the Sublime State have attained the obligatory rights of security of life and property and protection of chastity and honor by the decree of Providence and everybody has become alike and equal before the *şeriat* and law according to the liberties [granted by] the *şeriat.*"

11. ". . . bu hususun dahi icra-yı iktizasına ibtidar olunsun ve bazı zeyl ve ilavesi muktaza olan şeyler oldukça onun dahi icabına bakılsın." Ibid, p. 128.
12. Ibid, (1840 code), chap. 1, art. 1, pp. 129–130. "bila-istisna teba'a-i Devlet-i Aliyye'den olanların metbu'-i şer'isi olan padişahına ihanet ve Devlet-i Aliyye aleyhine ikaz-ı fitneye cesaret ve katl-i nefse cür'et misillu bir hareket-i sarihası vuku'bulup da şer'an ve kanunen ve alenen ve tahkikat-ı lazıma ve tedkikat-ı muktaziye ile kerraren ve miraren da'vası görülerek bila-garaz cünhası ba'd'el-sübut hükm terettüp etmeksizin hafi ve celi ve katilen ve tesmimen ve hiç kimsenin canına kasd olunmamasına taraf-ı eşref-i hazret-i şahaneden ahd ü misak buyurulmuş olduğundan Devlet-i Aliyye memurlarından ve ale-l-ıtlak sair eşhastan hiç kimse diğer birisinin canına kast edemeyeceğine binaen faraza vüzeradan birisi tarafından bir çobanın bile canına kast vuku'unda ol vezirin hakkında dahi kısas-ı şer'i icra oluna." "His Imperial Majesty has solemnly promised and sworn that without exception the life of no subject of the Sublime State may be deliberately targeted, either secretly or publicly, by execution or poisoning. But those who openly venture to commit such acts as treachery against the Sultan, the *şer'i* sovereign of their allegiance, inciting rebellion against the Sublime State, or murdering humans [may be subject to execution] only after the necessary investigation and required inquiries are made, their cases have been heard many times, and a verdict has been pronounced upon the establishment of their guilt without prejudice; [aside from these situations] without exception, no functionary of the Sublime State or any other person may attempt to kill another person; for instance, should a vezir murder a shepherd, let *kısas* (*lex talionis*) be inflicted upon that vezir."
13. For example, Ibid, (1840 code), chap. 3, art. 1, pp. 132–133. "Irz ve namus dahi kişinin canı gibi aziz ve muhterem olarak muhafaza ve vikayesi mükteza-yı hamiyet ve mütebegga-yı insaniyetten olup faraza bir ademin itibarına dokunacak söz söylemek ve bir ademi döğmek ve bir şahsa söğmek onun namusunu hetk etmek demek olduğundan ve bundan böyle zabıta-i askeriye ve neferat ve kavas ve sair umur-i zabtiye ve rabtiye memurları hod be hod kimseyi döğemeyip ve kimseye bed lakırdı söylemeyip fakat onların memuriyetleri sokaklarda gavga ve niza' vuku'unda ve bazı erbab-ı töhmetin zuhurunda tutup hiç bir şey yapmaksızın doğruca iktiza eden zabıta mahalline götürüp teslim etmekten ibaret olacağından fi-ma'bad gerek umur-i zabtiyye ve rabtiyeye memur olan asakir ve kavaslardan ve ale-l-ıtlak her hangi rütbe ve sınıftan olur ise olsun her kim bir gayrısına söğecek ve itibarına dokunur bir söz söyleyecek olur ise faraza bu keyfiyet Dersaadet'te vuku'bulup da buna mütecasir olan dahi ya Devlet-i Aliyye'nin eshab ü meratibinden veyahud ulemadan olur ise da'vası mutlaka Meclis-i Ahkam-ı Adliye'de görülerek cünhasının cesametine ve derecesine göre zabıta tarafından beş günden yirmi beş güne kadar mahbus ola ve cünhası gayet hafif olduğu tebeyyün ettiği

takdirde Meclisce kendisini tekdir ve takbih ile iktifa oluna." "Chastity and honor are as sacred and dear to a person as his life, and the safety and protection of these are among the necessities of patriotism and humanity. For instance, to dishonor a person with words, to beat a man, or to curse a person, mean violating that person's honor. Therefore, from now on, military and other law enforcement personnel such as soldiers, guards, and others shall not beat and swear at anyone as they wish. Thus, in the event of a fight or a quarrel in the streets, the duty [of law enforcement personnel] will be to apprehend the accused people and bring them directly to the appropriate police station without doing anything to them. From now on, regardless of his rank, whoever, whether he is a soldier or guard working in the service of law enforcement, swears at any other person or dishonors a person with words [will be punished]. If, for instance, such an event takes place in Istanbul and the person who dares to commit such an act happens to be a functionary of the Sublime State or a member of the *ulema,* let his case be heard at the Meclis-i Ahkam-ı Adliye, and let him be imprisoned for five to twenty five days, according to the importance and degree of his offence, and if it is established that his offense is very light, let the Meclis [-i Akham-ı Adliye] reprimand and scold him."

14. Ibid, (1840 code), chap. 1, art. 1–4, p. 129–130. art. 1: see footnote above. art. 2: "ve'l-hasıl işbu katl-i nefs maddesinde büyük ve küçük müsavi tutula." [incorporated into chap. 1, art. 1 of the 1851 text] art. 3: "bu makule katl maddeleri Dersaadet'te olur ise mutlaka huzur-i fetvapenahide görülerek tevatüren sabit olup şahidler dahi kemal-i dikkat ile tezkiye-berle hakikat-ı hal tahakkuk etmedikçe ve ba'dehu hakipa-yı hümayuna arz ile ferman-ı âli sadır olmadıkca icrası caiz olmaya." "If these sorts of murders occur in Istanbul, they will, absolutely, be heard in the audience of the *Şeyhülislam,* and the implementation [of verdicts of execution] may not be permitted unless a consensus on the validity of various reports is reached and an investigation on the antecedents of the witnesses—in order to know whether they and their testimony are receivable—is carried out; then an imperial decree [approving the execution] will be issued upon submitting the [verdict] to His Imperial Majesty." art. 4: Taşralarda dahi vuku'buldukta memleket meclis-i meşveretinde marifet-i şer'le şeriat-i muharrereye tatbikan da'vası görülüp ba'dehu ilam-ı şer'isi ve meclis mazbatası Dersaadet'e irsal ve taraf-ı fetvapenahiye takdim ile tasdik olunup ondan sonra dahi kezalik hakipa-yı hümayuna arz ile ferman-ı âli sadır olmadıkça icrası caiz olmaya." "When [murders] occur in the provinces, the implementation [of verdicts of execution] may not be permitted unless such cases are heard at provincial councils by means of the *şeriat* and other written rules; a *şer'î* verdict and a memorandum by the [provincial] council are then sent to Istanbul to be submitted to the *Şeyhülislam,* and upon his approval, they are submitted to His Imperial Majesty and an imperial decree is issued in the same manner."

15. Ibid, (1840 code), chap. 2, art. 1–4, esp. art. 2, pp. 130–131. art. 1: "Sai-i bi'l-fesad olanlar iki suretten hali olmayıp birisi kavlen ve diğeri fi'len olacağından mesela bir adem diğer bir ademi veyahud bir takım ademleri Devlet-i Aliyyeye ve kavanin ve nizamata mugayir harekata tergip vadisinde fesadlı sözler söyleyecek olursa bir seneden beş seneye kadar fesadının derecesine göre vaz'-ı kürek oluna." "those endeavoring to rebellion are of two types: those who rebel verbally and those who rebel in deed. For instance, if a man encourages another man or a group of men

with rebellious words to actions against the Sublime State or its laws and regulations ("kavanin ve nizamat"), let him be sentenced to one to five years of hard labor depending on the degree of his conspiracy." art. 2: fi'len olduğu halde bir kimseyi veya bir takım ademleri bağı ve isyana davet etmek ve onlara eslaha ve barut vermek gibi şeylere tasaddi edecek olduğu takdirde bu makule ademlerin cünhası pek azim olacağından katl ve idam kılına. Şu kadar ki, bu makule siyseten katl olunacakların idamına hükm olunduktan sonra taraf-ı eşref hazret-i padişahiye arz ü istizan olundukta sahib-i cünhanın katle bedel müebbeden küreğe vaz'ı irade-i merahim'ade-i hazret-i şahaneye müfevviz ola." "If someone endeavors to invite a man or a group of men to act rebelliously or to revolt and give them things such as weapons and gunpowder, let that person be killed by execution, since the guilt of such men will be a substantial one. However, once verdicts of execution have been pronounced for such men, these [verdicts] will be submitted to His Imperial Majesty and the sentencing of a guilty person to a life sentence of hard labor [rather than execution] is up to His Imperial Majesty's merciful discretion." art. 3: "bu misillu fesad-ı kavli ve fi'liye cesaret edenler Dersaadet'te oldukları halde da'valarının rü'yeti ve tevatüren isbatı mutlaka Meclis-i Ahkam-ı Adliye'ye mahsus ve münhasır buluna." "In case those who dare to commit conspiracy by word or act happen to be in Istanbul, the hearing of their cases and the establishment of their [guilt] must fall specifically under the jurisdiction of the Council of Judicial Ordinances." art. 4: "taşralarda vuku'bulduğu takdirde dahi evvel-emirde memleket meclisinde görülüp ba'dehu meclis mazbatasıyla beraber ol adem ve iktiza eden şahidler Dersaadet'e celb ile kezalik Meclis-i Ahkam-ı Adliye'de tekrar da'vası görüle." "should [it] occur in the provinces, [the case] will initially be heard in the provincial council, and then the [accused] person will be summoned to Istanbul, along with the necessary witnesses and a memorandum by the [provincial] council, for a second hearing in the Council of Judicial Ordinances."

16. Sandria B. Freitag, "Crime in the Social Order of Colonial North India," *Modern Asian Studies* 25 (1991): 227–261. p. 230.
17. A similar situation occurred in Thailand, where prior to the seventeenth century legislation against political crime (in this case lèse majesté) was directed toward elites who threatened monarchical power. It was only after the "desacrilization" of the king that "the public" started committing this political crime. Streckfuss, p. 447.
18. An argument is often made that legal codification of any kind is at heart purely secular. By throwing out centuries of religious interpretation of texts in favor of a simple, transparent statement of what these texts "actually" say, a code is undermining both the duty and the function of any religious establishment. But if we define "secular" in a basic way as the separation of religious institutions from state institutions, the Ottoman system became less, not more, secular over the Tanzimat period. Never had the Ottoman government been so self conscious about the relationship between religion and the state. Never had the government been so intent upon incorporating religious institutions and structures into the state apparatus. Again, one primary purpose of the 1840 criminal code was to define religion and to define its relationship to the state. The code that followed it a decade later in 1851 went one step further, and explicitly incorporated religion into the state apparatus. It is absolutely true, therefore, that the nature of the Ottoman religious

establishment changed throughout the nineteenth century. But this changing nature did not necessarily lead to a marginalization or sidelining of religion during the Tanzimat and post-Tanzimat reforms. Religion instead became an integral element of the nascent modern understanding of criminal law and criminality.

19. Ahmed Lütfi, p. 128. (1840 code) "Gülhane'de kıra'at olunan hatt-ı hümayun-i ma'delet-makrun-i hazret-i şahane mucibince kaffe-i teba'a-i Devlet-i Aliyye bila-istisna emniyet-i can ve mal ve mahfuziyet-i ırz ve namus hukuk-i mefruzasına ez-ser-i nev nail olmuş ve ber-mukteza-yı hürriyet-i şer'iye huzur-i şer' ve kanunda ve mevadd-ı hukukiyede herkesin yeksan ve siyyan olması . . ." "According to the imperial decree read at Gülhane, to which justice is joined, without exception, all subjects of the Sublime State have attained the obligatory rights of security of life and property and protection of chastity and honor by the decree of Providence and everybody has become alike and equal before Islamic law (*şeriat*) and law according to the liberties [granted by] Islamic law (*şeriat*)."
20. Ibid: "kaffe-i teba'a-i Devlet-i Aliyye bila-istisna emniyet-i can ve mal ve mahfuziyet-i ırz ve namus hukuk-i mefruzasına ez-ser-i nev nail olmuş ve ber-mukteza-yı hürriyet-i şer'iye huzur-i şer' ve kanunda ve mevadd-ı hukukiyede . . ."
21. Ibid, (1840 code), chap. 1, art. 1, pp. 129–130. "bila-istisna teba'a-i Devlet-i Aliyye'den olanların metbu'-i şer'isi olan padişahına ihanet ve Devlet-i Aliyye aleyhine ikaz-ı fitneye cesaret ve katl-i nefse cür'et misillu bir hareket-i sarihası vuku'bulup da şer'an ve kanunen ve alenen ve tahkikat-ı lazıma ve tedkikat-ı muktaziye ile kerraren ve miraren da'vası görülerek bila-garaz cünhası ba'd'el-sübut hükm terettüp etmeksizin hafi ve celi ve katilen ve tesmimen ve hiç kimsenin canına kasd olunmamasına taraf-ı eşref-i hazret-i şahaneden ahd ü misak buyurulmuş olduğundan Devlet-i Aliyye memurlarından ve ale-l-ıtlak sair eşhastan hiç kimse diğer birisinin canına kast edemeyeceğine binaen faraza vüzer-adan birisi tarafından bir çobanın bile canına kast vuku'unda ol vezirin hakkında dahi kısas-ı şer'i icra oluna." "His Imperial Majesty has solemnly promised and sworn that without exception the life of no subject of the Sublime State may be deliberately targeted, either secretly or publicly, by execution or poisoning. But those who openly venture to commit such acts as treachery against the Sultan, the Islamic legal (*şer'i*) sovereign of their allegiance, inciting rebellion against the Sublime State, or murdering humans [may be subject to execution] only after the necessary investigation and required inquiries are made, their cases have been heard many times, and a verdict has been pronounced upon the establishment of their guilt without prejudice; [aside from these situations] without exception, no functionary of the Sublime State or any other person may attempt to kill another person; for instance, should a vezir murder a shepherd, let *lex talionis* (*kısas*) be inflicted upon that vezir."
22. Ibid, (1840 code), chap. 1, art. 1–4, p. 129–130. art. 1: see footnote above. art. 2: "ve'l-hasıl işbu katl-i nefs maddesinde büyük ve küçük müsavi tutula." [incorporated into chap. 1, art. 1 of the 1851 text] art. 3: "bu makule katl maddeleri Dersaadet'te olur ise mutlaka huzur-i fetvapenahide görülerek tevatüren sabit olup şahidler dahi kemal-i dikkat ile tezkiye-berle hakikat-ı hal tahakkuk etmedikçe ve ba'dehu hakipa-yı hümayuna arz ile ferman-ı âli sadır olmadıkca icrası caiz olmaya." "If these sorts of murders occur in Istanbul, they will, absolutely, be heard in the audience of the *Şeyhülislam,* and the implementation [of verdicts of

execution] may not be permitted unless a consensus on the validity of various reports is reached and an investigation on the antecedents of the witnesses—in order to know whether they and their testimony are receivable—is carried out; then an imperial decree [approving the execution] will be issued upon submitting the [verdict] to His Imperial Majesty." art. 4: Taşralarda dahi vuku'buldukta memleket meclis-i meşveretinde marifet-i şer'le şeriat-i muharrereye tatbikan da'vası görülüp ba'dehu ilam-ı şer'isi ve meclis mazbatası Dersaadet'e irsal ve taraf-ı fetvapenahiye takdim ile tasdik olunup ondan sonra dahi kezalik hakipa-yı hümayuna arz ile ferman-ı âli sadır olmadıkça icrası caiz olmaya." "When [murders] occur in the provinces, the implementation [of verdicts of execution] may not be permitted unless such cases are heard at provincial councils by means of the *şeriat* and other written rules; a *şer'î* verdict and a memorandum by the [provincial] council are then sent to Istanbul to be submitted to the *Şeyhülislam,* and upon his approval, they are submitted to His Imperial Majesty and an imperial decree is issued in the same manner."

23. And eventually codification. This aspect of legal reform will be addressed in the next chapter, however. Weber, vol. 2, pp. 650, 848.
24. Weber argues that codifications undertaken by many "patrimonial monarchs," like the Ottoman sultan, are not true codifications, but merely "mechanical arrangements" of pre-existing and specific principles. A true codification, in his opinion, would arise from the needs of a rational bureaucracy rather than those of a monarch and, more important, would be total, all-inclusive, uniform, and general. Vol. 2, pp. 848–850.
25. Ibid, vol. 2, pp. 792, 847. See also the description of "khadi justice," in vol. 3, pp. 976–8.
26. Ibid, vol. 2, p. 848.
27. "Patrimonial power" is defined as traditional personal domination. This definition is in opposition to "Sultanism," which is a personal authority based upon arbitrary discretion, rather than tradition. Halil İnalcık, "Comments on 'Sultanism' in Max Weber's Typification of the Ottoman Polity," *Princeton Papers in Near Eastern Studies* 1 (1992): 49–72. p. 49.
28. Ibid, p. 50.
29. Ibid.
30. Ibid, p. 51.
31. Further evidence that such was the case might be supplied by Robertson's discussion of the alarm with which the Ottoman government met nineteenth century European demands for a separate criminal law system for Egypt. pp. 112, 125, 129, 131. In the end it was agreed that the sultan would maintain his nominal control over an autonomous Egyptian criminal legal system, especially with regard to the confirmation of death sentences. Gabriel Baer, *Studies in the Social History of Modern Egypt.* Chicago: University of Chicago Press, 1969. p. 114. Later on, Baer also cites the Ottoman view that the Egyptian claims for a separate criminal law system were groundless, given that "the population of Baghdad, Kurdistan, Hijaz, and Tripoli lived under conditions similar to those of Egypt and farther away from the central government." p. 117. Many of these areas will be discussed in more detail below.
32. İnalcık, p. 99.

33. Ibid, p 104.
34. Ibid, p. 101.
35. That is, the proportion of capital cases to a region's population. My analysis is based upon cases collected in the Ottoman Prime Ministry archives. For a more detailed collection of tables and graphs produced from this data, please see: Ruth A. Miller, *From Fikh to Fascism: The Turkish Republican Adoption of Mussolini's Criminal Code in the Context of Late Ottoman Legal Reform.* Unpublished Dissertation, Princeton University, June 2003. pp. 53–58. For a number of alternative tables and statistical analyses of criminal case distribution, see Tevfik Güran, ed. *Osmanlı Devleti'nin ilk istatistik yıllığı, 1897.* Ankara: Devlet İstatistik Enstitüsü Matbaası, 1997. With one or two exceptions (notably the numbers for Istanbul itself), my conclusions appear to match those of the Ottoman government ca. 1897. The discrepancies in my findings may have to do with the fact that my analysis of criminal case distribution was undertaken according to *sancak,* whereas the Ottoman Statistical Yearbook was undertaken according to *vilayet.* Also, my analysis covers a thirty-five year period, whereas the far more detailed and complete Ottoman Yearbook covers only the year 1897.
36. The provinces of Prizren, Yanya, Kütahya, Diyar-i Bekir, and Bolu had a higher than average proportion of these cases tried over the years, for instance. The provinces of Drama, Manastır, Üsküp, İzmir, Cezayir-i Bahr-i Sefid, Muş, Mamuretül-aziz, Saruhan, Mosul, Tırhala, Berat, Kıbrıs, Bursa, Karesi, Karahisar-ı Sahib, Aydın, Menteşe, Hamit, and Urfa likewise saw a greater than average amount of activity.
37. The areas of least activity were the eastern Balkans including the provinces of Sofya, Tuna, Edirne and Selanik; central Anatolia including the provinces of Ankara, Adana, Sivas Trabzon, Erzurum, and to some extent Konya; and the Arab provinces of Bağdad, Suriye, and to some extent Halep.
38. Almost exclusively the 1840s and 1850s, with the four exceptions of 1866, 1874, 1876, and 1896.
39. Roderic Davison, *Essays in Ottoman and Turkish History, 1774–1923.* Austin: University of Texas Press. 1990. p. 164.
40. In Tuncer Baykara, ed. *İzmir ve Batı Anadolu.* İzmir: Akademi Kitabevi, 1994. p. 81.
41. *İslam Ansiklopedisi.* Ankara: Türkiye Diyanet Vakfı, 1988. vol. 2. pp. 61–2.
42. In 1841, for example, Hüdavendigar became its own *eyalet,* in 1845 Karesi was detached and then later re-attached. *İslam Ansiklopedisi,* "Karesi." Between 1849 and 1851, it might be added, Hungarian refugees were settled in the Kütahya region. In Hakkı Yıldız, *Kütahya'nın Tarihçesi,* Istanbul: Formül Matbaası, 1981. p. 47.
43. Abdülmecit Mutaf, *Salnamelerde Karesi Sancağı: 1847–1922.* Istanbul, 1997. p. 14.
44. *İslam Ansiklopedisi,* vol. 8. p.
45. Sinan Marufoğlu, *Osmanlı Döneminde Kuzey Irak.* Istanbul: Evren, 1998. p. 164.
46. Evangelos Kofos, *National Heritage and Identity in Nineteenth and Twentieth Century Macedonia.* Athens: Hellenic Foundation for Defense and Foreign Policy, 1991. pp. 5–6.
47. Ioannes Chasiotes, *Landmarks and Principal Phases in the History of Modern and Contemporary Macedonia.* Thessaloniki: Parateretes, 1992. p. 34.

48. Kofos, p. 5.
49. Miranda Vickers, *The Albanians: A Modern History*. London: I.B. Tauris, 1999. p. 24.
50. Anton Logoreci, *The Albanians*. Boulder: Westview Press, 1977. p. 37. Stefanaq Pollo and Arben Puto, *The History of Albania*. London: Routledge, 1981. p. 110.
51. The area was divided up into three separate *vilayets* in an attempt to stabilize the region. Vickers, p. 26.
52. Guangyuan Zhou, "Illusion and Reality in the Law of the Late Qing: A Sichuan Case Study," *Modern China* 19 (1993): 427–456. p. 430.
53. And it is also worth pointing out that this tension between local practice and abstract bureaucratic practice is not unique to the Ottoman Empire in the nineteenth century. In Germany, for example, we can see a similar situation in which "the stress on certainty and generality did not exclude the possibility of legislation to meet local and sectional needs; it merely means that the code was an inappropriate vehicle for the satisfaction of such demands." Michael John, p. 118. It is not that local needs necessarily undermine bureaucratic needs (although occasionally they do). It is simply that local needs are irrelevant to the larger system.
54. In a sample of twenty-five documents and thirty-five capital or banishment cases spanning the years 1840–1850, 59% contain Islamic legal writs and 41% do not. When it comes to the legitimization of decisions—that is, a decision that is taken by "the requirements of Islamic law (*şeriat*)," a decision taken by "the requirements of the imperial legal code," or a decision that rests upon a combination of the two—24% were decided by the requirements of Islamic law, 30% were decided by the requirements of the code, 35% were decided by a combination of both, and 12% referenced neither. As for the proof forwarded during the trials, it should first be noted that many reports will note that the case was "tespit" or "rü'yet" "şer'iyyan," "kanunen," or both. If the defendant confessed, that particular case was left out of the sample. 58% were proved by Islamic law rules, 16% were proved according to the rules set out in the code, 16% were proved using a combination of the two, and 11% referenced neither. Finally, of the sentences imposed, 39% were Islamic law sentences, 45% were sentences taken from the code, and 16% were *siyasî* (discretionary political/administrative) sentences—that is, for example, banishment or execution legitimized solely by the will of the padişah or the political authority. For a more detailed analysis of this data, please see Miller, *From Fikh to Fascism*, pp. 123–125.
55. İradeler—MV 188, 8 L 1256. "ber mukteza-yı şeriat . . ."
56. İradeler—MV 299, 11 S 1257. MV 299, 11 S 1257. "Meclis-i Vâlâ'ya celb ile bi'l-istintak ifadat-ı vakı'aları zabt olunarak madde-i katl ve hukuka dair mevadd ber-nehc-i şer'î rü'yet olunmak üzere huzur-i fetvapenahide mümaileyh Yahya Ağa ile merkum Osman ve eşhas-ı merkume bi-t-terafu mümaileyh Yahya Ağa ikame-i beyyine ile isbat-ı müdde'aya muktedir olamamasıyla muarazadan men' ilamı verilmiş ve merkumların haklarında dahi bir gûna hükm-i şer'î lahik olamamış olduğundan merkumların hin-i istintakta vaki' olan ifadeleri üzerine icabat-ı kanuniye ve nizamiyenin icrası hususuna dair Meclis-i Ahkam-ı Adliye'den kaleme alınan bir kıt'a mazbata mah-ı Safer'ül-hayr'ın sekizinci Çarşanba günü Meclis-i Umumi'de led'il-kıra'a merkum muytabl Halil ber-mucib-i irade-i seniyye beş sene müddet için küreğe vaz' olunmuş olduğundan merkumun müddet-i

mezkure tekmiline kadar kürekde ibka[sı]." "[They were] summoned to the Meclis-i Vâlâ where they were interrogated and their statements were recorded. Then the case [was moved to the offices of the] *Şeyhülislam,* who was present at the trial to see those parts of it which related to murder and common law in the context of *şeriat.* The aforementioned Yahya Ağa and Osman, and the other people mentioned above appealed mutually to the judge. Yahya Ağa could not exhibit proof to verify his claim. Thus a verdict of interdiction of dispute was pronounced and a report was prepared by the Council of Judicial Ordinances, which discussed the legal measures to be applied in this case after taking into consideration the testimonies of the aforementioned people. This report was read in the general council on Wednesday, the eighth day of the month of Safer. [In conclusion], it was decided that since the hair rope maker Halil had been sentenced to hard labor with exile for a period of five years, he should continue serving this sentence until the end of the aforementioned period."

57. İradeler—MV 294, 7 S 1257. "Ve bir kıt'asında dahi Bazarcık Kazası ahalisinden Yovan nam zımmi mukaddema haydudluk töhmetiyle tutuldukta kabul-i İslam etmiş ise de bu defa mürted olmuş ve mersum dahi Dersaadet'e gönderilmiş olduğu beyanıyla iktizasını istizan ve canib-i fetvahaneden dahi merkumun şübhesi var ise keşf olunarak üzerine İslam arz olundukta kabulden imtina ile irtidadına israr ederse şer'an katli lazım geleceği zahr-ı ilama tahrir ve beyan olunmuş olmakla bu surette merkumun huzur-i hazret-i fetvapenahide istintakıyla şübhe var ise keşf ü hall olunarak ber-mukteza-yı şer'-i şerif merkuma İslam arz olunup onun üzerine ne merkezde bulunur ise iktiza-yı şer'isini ilam eylemek üzere bu hususun ba-buyuruldu-i sami İstanbul Kadısı Faziletlu Efendi Hazretleri'ne havalesi icabından olduğu." Another document states that a non-Muslim named Yovan from the district of Bazarcık had converted to Islam upon being arrested on the charge of banditry. He then, however, apostatized and was sent to Istanbul. The document requests that the necessary measures be taken and states that if the *Meşihat* had doubts about this person, the necessary investigation should be conducted and he should be interrogated at the *Meşihat.* A marginal note is written on the back of the judicial decree stating that if he refuses to acknowledge that he was a Muslim and insists upon his apostasy, he should be executed. Thus the aforementioned person should be interrogated at the *Meşihat* and all doubts should be removed. During this process, he should be asked if he is a Muslim, as required by *şeriat,* and his response should be forwarded to His Honor, the Kadı of Istanbul, by the Grand Vezir's Office for a judicial decree.

58. İradeler—MV 915, 7 S 1259. "Prlepe kazası sakinlerinden Feyzullah nam şahs el-iyazu billah-ı te'ala küfrü mü'eddi bir takım kelimat tefevvühüne ve hilaf-ı şer'-i şerif rafiziyâne harekata ibtidar etmekte olduğundan kendisi Manastır'a celb ile her ne kadar keşf-i şübhe edecek ve itminan-ı kalb hasıl olacak suretle nesayih-i lazıma icra olunmuş ise de itikad-ı batılından bir vechile rücu' etmemekle zuhur-u irade-i seniyyeye kadar merkum mahbese ilka." "A certain Feyzullah, an inhabitant of the sub-province of Prlepe dared, Heavens forefend, to utter some blasphemous words and heretical actions against *şeriat.* He was, therefore, summoned to Manastır and given the necessary advice to provide tranquility of heart and to remove doubts. But he did not retract at all from his superstitious beliefs and therefore he was put into prison until the issuance of an imperial decree. "siyaseten

katli meşru idüğü canib-i fetvahaneden zahr-ı ilama tahrir ve inba kılınmış . . ." "It is written and communicated in the judicial decree issued by the *fetvahane* that his punishment by death (*siyaseten katli*) is legitimate . . ." "Meclis-i Umumi'de kıra'at olunan bir kıt'a mazbatada istizan ve iş'ar vermeyip mazbata iktiza-yı şer'isinin icrası meclis-i umumide dahi bittezekkür menzur-u âli buyurulmak için . . ." "A memorandum that has been read at the general council does not request an authorization and make any communication for the application of the necessary *şer'î* measures. This memorandum has been discussed at the grand council in order to submit it to the Sultan."

NOTES TO CHAPTER FOUR

1. Kristin Ruggiero, "The Devil and Modernity in Late Nineteenth-Century Buenos Aires," *Americas* 59 (2000): 221–233. p. 221.
2. Ibid, p. 222.
3. Ibid, p. 222.
4. E.R. Toledano, "Legislative Process in the Ottoman Empire in the Early Tanzimat," *International Journal of Turkish Studies* 1 (1980): 99–106. p. 106.
5. Ibid.
6. Ibid, p. 100.
7. Ahmed Lütfi, (1840 code), chap. 1, art. 1, pp. 129–130.
8. Ibid, (1840 code), chap. 1, art. 2, p. 130.
9. Ibid, (1851 code), chap. 1, art. 1, pp. 152–3.
10. For example, Ibid, (1851 code), chap. 1, art. 1 discusses rebellion, conspiracy against the state, and homicide (as, however, does the corresponding article of the same chapter of the 1840 code), art. 4 discusses the duty of state functionaries in homicide trials (not in the 1840 code), art. 5 discusses sedition (this article falls into a separate chapter on the state in the 1840 code), art. 6 discusses revolt (also in a separate chapter on the state in the 1840 code), art. 7 discusses sedition in more detail (not in the 1840 code), art. 8 discusses homicide occurring as a result of state duty (not in the 1840 code), art. 9 discusses the sacking of railways and homicide occurring as a result (not in the 1840 code), art. 10 discusses armed insurrection, the sacking of railways and homicide occurring as a result of both or either (not in the 1840 code), art. 11 discusses the position of heirs in homicide cases (not in the 1840 code), art. 12 discusses homicide in cases where the heirs are absent or far away (not in the 1840 code), art. 13 discusses manslaughter (not in the 1840 code), art. 14 discusses homicide through intermediaries (not in the 1840 code), art. 15 discusses homicide committed by women or against women (not in the 1840 code), art. 16 discusses bearing arms against police, officials, or ordinary people (not in the 1840 code), and art. 17 discusses wounds inflicted with drawn weapons (not in the 1840 code). Again, however, the point is that with the exception of the first article, homicide/wounding and state crimes are analytically separate in the 1840 text, whereas in the 1851 text, of the fourteen articles from Chapter One mentioned above, six refer to homicide or wounding alone, three refer to state crimes alone, and five refer to both.
11. This fascination on the part of Tanzimat era legal reformers with honor and slander is also very much a part of the modern understanding of criminal law. If we

return briefly to Buenos Aires, for example, we see that by 1831, the second most common crime after theft was "offending and insulting one's social superiors." (Mark D. Szuchman. p. 87.) Moreover, as early as the 1820s, slander against the social hierarchy in Buenos Aires had started to become conflated with slander against the administrative hierarchy. Soon, "corruption" became an issue of key importance to both the population and the government. (Szuchman. pp. 92, 102–3.) The social hierarchy, that is, began to give way to the administrative hierarchy.

12. The first begins with a definition of the crime, goes into great detail about what happens when the police or other officials are involved in a slander case, notes that if *ulema* or other unnamed high ranking officials are involved, the case should be sent to the Council of Judicial Ordinances (*Meclis-i Ahkam-ı Adliye*), and ends with the stipulation that a typical sentence for more serious slander cases is five to twenty-five days in jail, and less serious slander, a reprimand. (Lütfi, (1840 Code) chap. 3, art. 1, pp. 132–133). So following the definition, we see a reference to all segments of Ottoman society within the context of the crime and a discussion of what the punishment for said crime ought to be. The second article in the 1840 text further discusses *ulema* and army officers. Any cases involving an *'alim* and an officer, it states, should be sent to the Council of Judicial Ordinances, and a punishment of the officer based on the military code should be given by the military authorities. The third article focuses on members of Ottoman society who do not have any special rank. Finally, the fourth article mentions briefly that slander cases in the provinces may be tried by the representative assemblies. (Lütfi, 1840 Code), chap. 3, art. 2–4, pp. 133–134). These articles all show a definite consciousness of rank—in particular military or police rank—and hierarchy. There is arguably, however, no obsession with it.
13. Ibid, (1851 code), chap. 2, art. 1. pp. 159–60. Cont. : "... ırz ve namusu dahi kişinin canı gibi aziz ve muhterem olarak muhafaza ve vikayesi mukteza-yı insaniyetten olmakla faraza bir ademin itibarına dokunacak söz söylemek ve bila-mucip döğmek veya söğmek onun namusunu hetk etmek olduğundan o makule hetk-i namusa mütecasir olan kesanın cünhası şer'an sabıt olup hadd-ı şer'i lazım geldiği halde hadd-ı şerisi icra oluna." "let the crime of he who dares to dishonor another thus be proved by Islamic law/*şeriat* and if *hadd* is necessary let *hadd* be enforced."
14. Ibid, (1851 code), chap. 2, art. 2, for example notes "bu misillu madde Dersaadet'te vuku'bulduğu ve cünhası yalnız tazirde kaldığı surette tazir dahi herkesin hal ü şanına göre olduğundan ol kimesne ulema-yı fihamdan ve sadat-ı kiramdan ve zi-rütbe zevattan ise Meclis-i Vâlâ'ya celb ile tazir kılına ve evsat nas ve ehl sevk olup burada olanlar iktizasına göre ihzar haps ve nefy oluna ..." "If such a crime should occur in Istanbul, and if the offense should merit only a reprimand, let social status be taken into consideration, since the correction should be in accordance with this. If a [guilty] person happens to be a member of the illustrious ulema or a noble seyyid or a rank possessing personality, let him be summoned to the Meclis-i Vâlâ and reprimanded there; average people will be dispatched [to courts] and imprisoned or banished."
15. Article six of the second chapter of the 1851 text also notes that social status is of importance, in this case in the determination of a punishment or lack thereof for abducting girls. This interest, granted, is arguably a more traditional than

modern one, but it is an attempt to preserve the social hierarchy nonetheless. Ibid, (1851 code), chap. 2, art. 6: "... ve o misillulerden birisi kaçırdığı kızı kaza-yı aher mahkemesine götürür ise kefaet maddesi bilinemeyeceğinden hükkam efendiler tarafından akdi hususuna mesağ gösterilmeyerek mülkiye memuru tarafından bi'l-ihbar tutturulup mahalli mahkemesine götürtüle." "... And if one of these people takes a girl abducted by him to a court in another district, the judges should not permit a marriage since they may not know whether they are socially equal and the civil authorities ought to be asked to apprehend them and send them to their own local court."

16. Wim Mellaerts, "Criminal Justice in Provincial England, France, and the Netherlands, c. 1880–1905: Some Comparative Perspectives," *Crime, Histoire, et Sociétés* 4 (2000): 19–52. p. 45.
17. Which corresponds to chapter 4, articles 1–2 of the 1840 text
18. Ahmed Lütfi, (1851 code), chap. 3, art. 1: "Taraf-ı Devlet-i Aliyye'den kimsenin mal ve emlakine vaz'-ı yed olunmaya ve büyük ve küçük bir kimse diğer birisinin mal ve emlakine bi-gayr-ı hak taarruz ve tasallut ve müdahale etmek veyahud cebren almak veya sattırmak için bizzat veyahud bi'l-vasıta icbar eylemek misillu şeyler vechen min-el-vücuh caiz olmaya ve eğer bu misillu madde-i memnu'a ve makruheye cesaret eden olur ise faraza birinin mal ve emlakine tasallutu vuku'unda men' ve ref' olunup şayed bir takrip ile zabt etmiş bulunursa mazbut olan mal ve emlak mevcud ise aynen değil ise semenen sahib oluna redd ettirildikten sonra ol şahsın hilaf-ı kanun harekete cesaretine binaen erbab-ı manasıb ve memuriyetten ise hidmetten tard ve ihrac olunup bu takımdan olmadığı halde memleketinden aher bir mahalle bir sene durmak üzere nefy ve tagrip kılına." "Let the property and lands of no one be seized by the Sublime State and let acts such as the unlawful attack against, the exercising of sovereignty over, and the occupation, usurpation, or selling by force of the property or lands of another, either by important or by lesser people, be absolutely not permissible; and if a person dares to commit such a prohibited and reprehensible act—for example, should someone attempt to exercise sovereignty over another person's property or land—let him be suppressed, and should he usurp the land by some means, let the usurped property and land be [returned to its] owner, if they still exist. Let the [perpetrator] who dared to commit this unlawful act be expelled and dismissed from his position if he is a functionary of the state; if he is not, then let him be banished and exiled to a region outside of his own for one year."
19. Ahmed Lütfi, (1840 code), chap. 4, art. 1, p. 135: "Taraf-ı Devlet-i Aliyye'den kimsenin mal ve emlakine vaz'-ı yed olunmayacağına canib-i mu'alla-yı menakıb-ı hazret şahaneden kezalik ahd ü misak buyurulmuş olduğundan büyük ve küçük bir kimse diğer birisinin mal ve emlakine bi-gayr-ı hak taarruz..." "Since his Imperial Majesty also promised and swore that nobody's property and land would be seized by the Sublime State, nobody, either important or lesser, may unlawfully attack the property and land of another."
20. Ibid, (1851 code), chap. 3, art. 1, p. 163: "Taraf Devlet-i Aliyye'den kimsenin mal ve emlakine vaz'-ı yed olunmaya ve büyük ve küçük bir kimse diğer birisinin mal ve emlakine bi-gayr-ı hak taarruz ve ..." See above for translation.
21. Based on chap. 6, articles 1–3; chap. 7, articles 1–2; chap. 7, article 3; and chap. 7, article 4 of the 1840 text respectively. Ahmed Lütfi, pp. 138–141.

22. Ibid, (1840 code), chap. 6, art. 2, p. 139.
23. Ibid, (1851 code), chap. 3, art. 2, "mücazata müstahak olacağından şahsına ve derece-i cünhasına göre . . ." "since he deserves punishment, [he will be punished] according to the degree of his offense and his social status . . ."
24. Based on chap. 5, art. 2; and chap. 5, art. 5–7 of the 1840 text respectively. Ibid, pp. 136–138.
25. Ibid, (1851 code), chap. 3, art. 8: "İrtişa maddesi şer'an ve kanunen emr-i münker olmakla fi-ma'bad işbu irtişa fi'l-i mekruhuna hiç kimse tarafından cesaret olunmaya eğer cesaret eden olur ise aldığı rüşvet beyt'ül-mala teslim olunmak üzere alınıp mürteşi bulunan adem dahi erbab-ı menasıp ve memuriyetten bulunduğu halde ba'dezin menasıp ve memuriyet-i Devlet-i Aliyye'de kullanılmamak üzere bulunduğu hidmetten azl ve ihraç ve rütbesinden hatt ü tenzil ile şahsına göre te'dip kılına ve bir gûna memuriyet ve hidmet erbabından bulunmadığı surette hiç mesalih-i Devlet-i Aliyye'de istihdam olunmamak üzere kezalik te'dip oluna." "Receiving a bribe is prohibited both by Islamic law/*şeriat* and regular law/***kanun;*** thus let no one dare to commit this disgusting act. If someone dares to commit it, then let the bribe that he received be taken from him and given to the treasury. If the person who received the bribe happens to be a functionary of the state, let him be expelled and dismissed from his post and never be allowed to work in government service, let him be stripped of his rank, and let him be punished according to his social status. If he is not a functionary, then let him similarly be punished and never hired for official services by the Sublime State."
26. In the 1851 version of the article, the situations in which gift giving, as distinct from bribery, are also elaborated in much more detail. The four lines on this subject from the 1840 text are expanded into seven in the 1851 text, for instance.
27. Ahmed Lütfi, (1840 code) "Gülhane'de kıra'at olunan hatt-ı hümayun-i ma'delet-makrun-i hazret-i şahane mucibince kaffe-i teba'a-i Devlet-i Aliyye bila-istisna emniyet-i can ve mal ve mahfuziyet-i ırz ve namus hukuk-i mefruzasına ez-ser-i nev nail olmuş ve ber-mukteza-yı hürriyet-i şer'iye huzur-i şer' ve kanunda ve mevadd-ı hukukiyede herkesin yeksan ve siyyan olması . . ." "According to the imperial decree read at Gülhane, to which justice is joined, without exception, all subjects of the Sublime State have attained the obligatory rights of security of life and property and protection of chastity and honor by the decree of Providence and everybody has become alike and equal before Islamic law/*şeriat* and regular law according to the liberties [granted by] Islamic law/*şeriat.*" It also implies the legitimacy of the continuing existence of the Council of Judicial Ordinances. The code, it notes, is incomplete because of its rushed promulgation, and thus additions to it will continue to be made, (". . . bu hususun dahi icra-yı iktizasına ibtidar olunsun ve bazı zeyl ve ilavesi muktaza olan şeyler oldukça onun dahi icabına bakılsın." Ahmed Lütfi, p. 128.), presumably by the newly formed committee.
28. Ahmed Lütfi, p. 128 (1840 code): "kaffe-i teba'a-i Devlet-i Aliyye bila-istisna emniyet-i can ve mal ve mahfuziyet-i ırz ve namus hukuk-i mefruzasına ez-ser-i nev nail olmuş ve ber-mukteza-yı hürriyet-i şer'iye huzur-i şer' ve kanunda ve mevadd-ı hukukiyede . . ."
29. "The three matters exhibited in the imperial decree read at Gülhane, to which imperial majesty is a companion, are security of life and property, and the protection of chastity and honor. It is an obvious fact that these are based upon *şer'î*

principles that may not be obliterated, and therefore, they may not be altered or convulsed by the change of time ..." Ibid, pp. 150–1. (1851 code) "Gülhane'de kıra'at olunan hatt-ı hümayun-i şevket-makrun-i hazret-i şahanede mansus olan mevadd-ı selase ki emniyet-i can ve mal ve mahfuziyet-i ırz ve namusdur. Bunlar esas-ı adim'ül-indiras-ı şer'-i şerif üzerine mebni olarak takallübat-ı dehriyye ile kabil-i tağyir ve tezelzül olamayacağı derkardır ..." "The three matters exhibited in the imperial decree read at Gülhane, to which imperial majesty is a companion, are security of life and property, and the protection of chastity and honor. It is an obvious fact that these are based upon Islamic law/*şer'î* principles that may not be obliterated, and therefore, they may not be altered or convulsed by the change of time ..." The following [directly after "derkardır" above] does not appear in any form in the 1840 introduction: "fakat bunlara müteferri' olub ittifak-ı ara ile vaz' ü te'sis buyurulmuş olan kavanin-i cezaiyenin havadisat-ı kevniyeye tatbikan ve mizac-ı mülk ve millete tevfikan vakt-be-vakt tahfif ve teşdidi ve teshil ve tatbik ve tevsi' ve taklil ile ta'dili icab edeceği kazaya-yı müsellemeden olmak ve kanunname-i hümayun hatimesinden tezyil ve ilaveye gösterilmiş olan mesağ dahi buna binaen kayd ü tezkir olunmak hasebiyle mua'ahharan vücuda gelen bazı hadisenin asıl cezası namevcud ve cezası mevcud olan bazı hadise-i ahiranın dahi takallubat-ı dehriyenin mümana'atıyla icra-yı cezasında ta'assür ve belki ta'azzür ru-nümun olduğundan led'il-iktiza tahdiş-i ezhan ve efkar ve usul-i haliye ve kevniyeye sarf-ı im'an ve enzar olunarak bu hususlara dair halen ve istikbalen kesb-i taassür ve taazzür etmeyecek." "However, it is an incontestable judicial decision that the criminal laws that were derived from these [principles] and were issued with a conformity of opinions should, from time to time, be reduced, intensified, facilitated, compared, extended, and diminished in accordance with new developments and the requirements of the country and the people. Thus the permission granted for adding and appending in the concluding chapter of the imperial law should be noted and understood accordingly. Since there does not exist an explicit punishment for some issues that arose after [the issuance of the imperial decree], and difficulties and even impossibilities have been faced in hearing some criminal cases as a result of the changes in time, it has become necessary to [make addenda to the penal code] related to these subjects and to prevent present and future difficulties and impossibilities by making a meticulous investigation, taking [various] opinions into consideration, and paying attention to present practice and new developments." Ahmed Lütfi, p. 150–1. (1851).

30. See footnote above for translation.
31. Ahmed Lütfi, p. 151 (1851 code): [mention of 1839 hatt-ı humayun and its concepts] "[b]unlar esas-ı adim'ül-indiras-ı şer'-i şerif üzerine mebni olarak takallübat-ı dehriyye ile ..."
32. Although Islamic law (*şeriat*) is mentioned far more often in, for example, Süleyman I's sixteenth century code than it is in the 1840 criminal code, it is actually less prominently mentioned in the sixteenth century text than it is in the 1851 text. Of the 126 article sixteenth century code, Islamic law/*şer'î* concepts or *lex talionis/kısas* are mentioned in only fourteen articles (11%) (compare the 1851 text of forty-two articles, of which twenty-four (57%) mention Islamic law/*şeriat* prominently). In addition, the conflation of *kanun* (regular/*nizamî*) and Islamic law/*şer'î* concepts that occurs in the 1851 text almost never appears in the sixteenth century

one. The two ideologies are kept completely separate. At the same time, it is true, as Gerber notes (p. 63), that any inclusion at all of *şer'î* concepts in a supposedly fully temporal sixteenth century document is odd. When one looks at the areas in which Islamic law/*şeriat* or those concepts related to Islamic law/*şeriat* are explicitly mentioned in the sixteenth century text, however, one sees that of these fourteen articles, at least nine merely refer to Islamic law in a symbolic, perfunctory manner, noting at some point that some element of the article is "in accordance with the sharia." (See Heyd, "OCC," art. 46, 85, 86, 91, 103, 109, 126) They do not elaborate any further. Although the concepts codified in articles 10 through 12 of the 1851 text, on the liability of functionaries to *lex talionis/kısas* and the right of the state to step in as a representative heir in cases of homicide, were in practice throughout the classical period, therefore, the fact that they were actually codified in 1851, along with an explicit conflation of Islamic law/*şeriat* and regular/*nizamî* punishments, shows the extent to which theory as well as practice was moving toward a modern incorporation of Islamic law/*şer'î* ideas into the temporal infrastructure.

33. Ibid, (1851 code), chap. 1, art. 1, p. 152: "bila-istisna teba'a-i Devlet-i Aliyyeden olanların metbu'-i şer'isi olan Devlet-i Aliyye aleyhine ikaz-ı fitneye cesaret ve katl-i nefse cür'et misillu bir hareket vuku'bulup da şer'an ve kanunen ve alenen ve tahkikat-ı lazıma ve tedkikat-ı muktaziye ile kerraren ve miraren da'vası görülerek bila-garaz cünhası ba'd-el-sübut hükm-i şer'i tertip etmeksizin hafi ve celi ve katilen ve tesmimen ve gerek suver-i mümkine ile hiç kimsenin canına kast olunmaya ve kast vuku'unda bizzat etsin veya ettirsin her kim olur ise olsun hakkında kısas ve hükm-i şer'i icra oluna velev ol maktulün veresesi diyet ahzıyla razı olmak veyahud ol katili bütün bütün afv etmek suretinde olsalar bile işbu idam madde-i kabihasına cesaret iden memur beher hal siyaseten ve nizamen idam kılına ve'l-hasıl işbu katl-i nefs maddesinde büyük küçük müsavi tutula." [The last sentence is art. 2 of the 1840 text.] "Without exception, the life of no subject of the Sublime State may be deliberately targeted, either secretly or publicly, by execution or poisoning or any other possible means. But those who openly undertake acts such as inciting rebellion against the Sublime State, the Islamic law/*şer'î* sovereign of their allegiance, or killing humans may be subject to execution, only after the necessary Islamic law/*şer'î* and regular/*kanunî* investigation and required inquiries have been made, their cases have been heard many times, and an Islamic law/*şer'î* verdict has been pronounced upon the establishment of their guilt without prejudice. Should such an act occur, let *lex talionis/kısas* and Islamic law/*şer'î* judgments be inflicted upon he who carried out the act, whether directly or through an intermediary; even if the slain person's heirs accept "blood money"/*diyet* or completely forgive the murderer, let the functionary who dared to commit this shameful crime of murder be executed for the sake of order. In this issue of killing humans, let the important and lesser individuals be treated equally."

34. It ought to be pointed out here that the concept of executing a punishment *siyaseten* seems to be undergoing a change in these texts. Throughout the classical period, *siyaset* was defined as the ruler's discretionary punishment. According to İnalcık, "if confiscation of property or capital punishment was carried out against the *re'aya* (common people) without due process of law in the religious court, the act was regarded as religiously wrong and a flagrant injustice (*zulm*), injurious to

the reputation of the ruler. In the classical mirror-for-princes literature, the ruler was admonished to avoid such acts and to prevent them in his subordinates. The ruler's discretionary punishment (*siyaset*) was legitimate in principle only against his *kul*s ['slaves'/Janissaries]." İnalcık, p. 58. By 1851, however, we are seeing a transformation of *siyaset* from completely discretionary punishment inflicted by the sultan, to state punishment, partially discretionary and partially legitimized by its placement into the criminal code.

35. Ahmed Lütfi, (1840 code), chap. 1, art. 1, p. 129: "cünhası ba'd-el-sübut hüküm terettüp etmeksizin . . ." "without a guilty verdict having been pronounced . . ."
36. Ibid, (1840 code), chap. 1, art. 1–4, p. 129–130. art. 1: see footnote above. art. 2: "ve'l-hasıl işbu katl-i nefs maddesinde büyük ve küçük müsavi tutula." [incorporated into chap. 1, art. 1 of the 1851 text] art. 3: "bu makule katl maddeleri Dersaadet'te olur ise mutlaka huzur-i fetvapenahide görülerek tevatüren sabit olup şahidler dahi kemal-i dikkat ile tezkiye-berle hakikat-ı hal tahakkuk etmedikçe ve ba'dehu hakipa-yı hümayuna arz ile ferman-ı âli sadır olmadıkca icrası caiz olmaya." "If these sorts of murders occur in Istanbul, they will, absolutely, be heard in the audience of the *Şeyhülislam,* and the implementation [of verdicts of execution] may not be permitted unless a consensus on the validity of various reports is reached and an investigation on the antecedents of the witnesses—in order to know whether they and their testimony are receivable—is carried out; then an imperial decree [approving the execution] will be issued upon submitting the [verdict] to His Imperial Majesty." art. 4: Taşralarda dahi vuku'buldukta memleket meclis-i meşveretinde marifet-i şer'le şeriat-i muharrereye tatbikan da'vası görülüp ba'dehu ilam-ı şer'isi ve meclis mazbatası Dersaadet'e irsal ve taraf-ı fetvapenahiye takdim ile tasdik olunup ondan sonra dahi kezalik hakipa-yı hümayuna arz ile ferman-ı âli sadır olmadıkça icrası caiz olmaya." "When [murders] occur in the provinces, the implementation [of verdicts of execution] may not be permitted unless such cases are heard at provincial councils by means of the *şeriat* and other written rules; an Islamic law/*şer'î* verdict and a memorandum by the [provincial] council are then sent to Istanbul to be submitted to the *Şeyhülislam,* and upon his approval, they are submitted to His Imperial Majesty and an imperial decree is issued in the same manner."
37. Ibid, (1840 code), chap. 2, art. 1–4, esp. art. 2, pp. 130–131. art. 1: "Sai-i bi'l-fesad olanlar iki suretten hali olmayıp birisi kavlen ve diğeri fi'len olacağından mesela bir adem diğer bir ademi veyahud bir takım ademleri Devlet-i Aliyyeye ve kavanin ve nizamata mugayir harekata tergip vadisinde fesadlı sözler söyleyecek olursa bir seneden beş seneye kadar fesadının derecesine göre vaz'-ı kürek oluna." "those endeavoring to rebellion are of two types: those who rebel verbally and those who rebel in deed. For instance, if a man encourages another man or a group of men with rebellious words to actions against the Sublime State or its laws and regulations ("kavanin ve nizamat"), let him be sentenced to one to five years of hard labor depending on the degree of his conspiracy." art. 2: fi'len olduğu halde bir kimseyi veya bir takım ademleri bağî ve isyana davet etmek ve onlara eslaha ve barut vermek gibi şeylere tasaddi edecek olduğu takdirde bu makule ademlerin cünhası pek azim olacağından katl ve idam kılına. Şu kadar ki, bu makule siyseten katl olunacakların idamına hükm olunduktan sonra taraf-ı eşref hazret-i padişahiye arz ü istizan olundukta sahib-i cünhanın katle bedel müebbeden küreğe vaz'ı irade-i

merahim'ade-i hazret-i şahaneye müfevviz ola." "If someone endeavors to invite a man or a group of men to act rebelliously or to revolt and give them things such as weapons and gunpowder, let that person be killed by execution, since the guilt of such men will be a substantial one. However, once verdicts of execution have been pronounced for such men, these [verdicts] will be submitted to His Imperial Majesty and the sentencing of a guilty person to a life sentence of hard labor [rather than execution] is up to His Imperial Majesty's merciful discretion." art. 3: "bu misillu fesad-ı kavli ve fi'liye cesaret edenler Dersaadet'te oldukları halde da'valarının rü'yeti ve tevatüren isbatı mutlaka Meclis-i Ahkam-ı Adliye'ye mahsus ve münhasır buluna." "In case those who dare to commit conspiracy by word or act happen to be in Istanbul, the hearing of their cases and the establishment of their [guilt] must fall specifically under the jurisdiction of the Council of Judicial Ordinances." art. 4: "taşralarda vuku'bulduğu takdirde dahi evvel-emirde memleket meclisinde görülüp ba'dehu meclis mazbatasıyla beraber ol adem ve iktiza eden şahidler Dersaadet'e celb ile kezalik Meclis-i Ahkam-ı Adliye'de tekrar da'vası görüle." "should [it] occur in the provinces, [the case] will initially be heard in the provincial council, and then the [accused] person will be summoned to Istanbul, along with the necessary witnesses and a memorandum by the [provincial] council, for a second hearing in the Council of Judicial Ordinances."

38. A "memur" and not "naib," "kadı," or "reis".
39. Ahmed Lütfi, (1851 code), chap. 1, art. 4, p. 153. "Devlet-i Aliyye'nin her sınıfında bulunan memurlarından birisi ber-vech-i meşruh muhakemesi memleket meclisinde sebkat ve mürafa'ası marifet-i şer'le rü'yet olunarak katl madde-i fazihasına ictisarı sabit ve kısasına hükm-i şer'i lahik olan şahs hakkında suret-i muhakemeyi mutazammın tuğralı ferman-ı âli sarih bulunmaksızın icra-yı kazası hususu kanunen men' olunmuş olduğundan usul-i meşruhaya riayet ve itina etmeyen memur hilaf-ı kanun harekete cesaret etmiş olacağından hakkında nizamen mücazat-ı layıka icra kılına." "the trial of any functionary of the Sublime State, regardless of his rank, who is tried in a provincial court in the manner described above, whose case is heard by means of Islamic law/*şeriat,* whose guilt in committing a shameful act of murder is established, and who receives an Islamic law/*şer'i* writ ordering *lex talionis*/*kısas,* is prohibited by law without an imperial decree that contains the trial order and that bears a genuine imperial monogram at the top. Therefore, any functionary who does not follow the aforementioned practice and does not pay attention to it will commit an unlawful act. Let him receive the necessary regular (*nizamî*) punishment as ordered by the regulations."
40. Ibid, (1851 code), chap. 1, art. 9, specifically, "adem telef ettikleri halde bi't-tahkik sabit olduktan sonra iktiza-yı şer'isi vechile idam kılına . . ." article as whole: "kutta'-ı tarik olanlar eğer itlaf-ı nüfus beşer'iye etmeyerek fakat adem soymak fazihasına cesaret etmiş ise yedi sene müddet içün vaz'-ı kürek oluna ve o misillu adem telef ettikleri halde bi't-tahkik sabıt olduktan sonra iktiza-yı şer'isi vechile idam kılına." "let highway robbers be sentenced to hard labor for seven years if they did not kill humans but committed a shameful act of robbery; in the event that such men dared to kill humans, if this fact is established through investigation, let them be executed in accordance with the requirements of Islamic law/*şeriat.*"
41. For example, Ahmed Lütfi, (1851 code), chap. 1, art. 16: "Umur-i zabtiye ve rabtiye memurlarına karşı durup silah çekmek misillu halat-ı reddiyeye cesaret

edenler işbu kabahatten ma'ada zabıta adem-i ita'at töhmetiyle dahi mütehhim olacağından derece-i cünhasına göre iki aydan iki sene ve silah boşaltmış olduğu halde üç aydan üç sene ve gerek kurşun ve sair alat-ı carihe ile cerh etmiş olduğu surette iltiyamına kadar mesarifi ondan alınıp kendisi beş aydan beş seneye kadar ta'yin-i müddetle vaz'-ı pranga olunarak hidemat-ı süfliyede istihdam oluna ve mecruh olan adem carihan vefat ettiği halde artık madde katl meselesine intikal edeceğinden iktiza-yı şer'i ve kanunisi icra oluna." "let those who dare to defy law enforcement personnel by acts such as resisting and drawing arms be further accused of disobeying the police; thus let them receive, according to the degree of their offense, from two months to two years of hard labor, and if they discharge any weapons, let them receive from three months to three years of hard labor, and if they injure [a law enforcement official] by a bullet or other hazardous instrument, let them pay the [medical] expenses until the wounded person is healed, and let them be put in fetters and used in low quality services from five months to five years; and should the matter will become an issue of manslaughter, with the wounded person dying as a result of his wounds, let the [perpetrator] be punished according to the requirements of Islamic law/*şeriat* and regular law."

42. Ibid, (1851 code), chap. 1, art. 10, "... maktul olanlar içün kısası lazım gelinmez ise de hayyen tutulan eşhasın bila-muhakeme idamı caiz olmayacağından buna cesaret edenler hakkında dahi hükm-i kısas icra kılına." "*kısas* (*lex talionis*) is not appropriate for those who are killed [during a clash with law enforcement personnel]. Since the execution without trial of individuals [different individuals] who are caught alive may not be lawful, however, let *lex talionis*/*kısas* be inflicted upon those who dare to carry out such an act." [for example, if law enforcement personnel catch brigands alive and kill them on the spot, the former will be held accountable.]

43. Ibid, (1851 code), chap. 1, art. 11–12, p. 156–7. art. 11: "Mucib-i kısas olup sonradan bazı veresenin afvı veyahud sulh ile deyne ve mala münkalip olan ve mucibi ibtida diyet bulunan madde-i katlin iktiza-yı şer'isi icra olunduktan sonra Dersaadet'te ise bu makule şahs-ı katil derecesine göre bir seneden beş seneye kadar küreğe ve taşrada ise bulunduğu mahallin mensup olduğu şehr-i muazzam neresi ise anda prangaya konularak süfli hidmetlerde kullanıla." "If a murder case that requires the application of *lex talionis*/*kısas* and the payment of "blood money"/*diyet* becomes an issue of debt and [transfer of] property because of an agreement [reached between the perpetrator and the heirs of the victim] or if [the perpetrator] is forgiven by the heirs [of the victim], then let the [perpetrator], if he is in Istanbul, receive one to five years of hard labor according to the degree of his [crime], and if he happens to be in the provinces, let him be put in fetters and used in low quality services in the biggest town in his region, upon the application of the necessary Islamic law/*şer'î* requirements." art. 12: "maktul diyar-ı aherde olur veya veresesi taşrada bulunur ise zuhuru melhuz olan veresenin vüruduna kadar şahs-ı katil mahbusan tevkif olunup fakat veresesi bulunmayan maktulün da'vası taraf-ı saltanat-i seniyyeye isabet edeceğinden ba'd'ül-terfi sabit olduktan sonra o misillu katilin kısasan idam veyahud beyt'ül-malı için diyet ahzıyle mücazat olmasını re'y-i ulu'l-ül-emr müfevvaz bulunduğundan olvechile icra oluna." "should the murdered person be in another land, or should the heirs be in the provinces, until the arrival of the expected heir is manifest, let the murderer be

placed under arrest, but in case the heirs of the murdered cannot be found, let the case be brought by the sultanate, and after it has been proved, let the murderer thus be executed or pay the "blood money"/*diyet* into the treasury."

44. Ibid, (1851 code), chap. 1, art. 14, pp. 157–9. art. 14: "bir adem diğer ademin canına kasd ile fakat bizzat icra etmeyerek başka bir şahsı akçe veyahud sair cihetle ıtma' ve iğfal edip de onun vesatetiyle idam ettirecek olur ise asıl katil hakkında şer'an ve kanunen iktiza eden hükm icra olunacağından madde-i katli amir olan şahıs derecesine göre bir seneden beş seneye ve katil mu'ini bulunan kimse kezalik bir seneden üç seneye kadar vaz'-ı kürek ve pranga kılına." "If a man makes an attempt on the life of another man, and has the latter murdered through the assistance of an intermediary, either by paying [the intermediary] money or by deceiving him, let the necessary requirements of the Islamic law (*şeriat*) and regular law be applied to the actual murderer. Therefore, let the person who ordered the murder receive, according to the degree of his [crime] one to five years of hard labor, and similarly let the individual who assisted the murderer receive one to three years of hard labor and be put into fetters."
45. all except the last on assault and false accusation of assault.
46. Indeed, only the third article, which focuses on members of Ottoman society who do not have any special rank, refers to Islamic legal principles.
47. For example, Ahmed Lütfi, (1840 code), chap. 3, art. 1, pp. 132–133. "Irz ve namus dahi kişinin canı gibi aziz ve muhterem olarak muhafaza ve vikayesi mükteza-yı hamiyet ve mütebegga-yı insaniyetten olup faraza bir ademin itibarına dokunacak söz söylemek ve bir ademi döğmek ve bir şahsa söğmek onun namusunu hetk etmek demek olduğundan ve bundan böyle zabıta-i askeriye ve neferat ve kavas ve sair umur-i zabtiye ve rabtiye memurları hod be hod kimseyi döğemeyip ve kimseye bed lakırdı söylemeyip fakat onların memuriyetleri sokaklarda gavga ve niza' vuku'unda ve bazı erbab-ı töhmetin zuhurunda tutup hiç bir şey yapmaksızın doğruca iktiza eden zabıta mahalline götürüp teslim etmekten ibaret olacağından fi-ma'bad gerek umur-i zabtiyye ve rabtiyeye memur olan asakir ve kavaslardan ve ale-l-ıtlak her hangi rütbe ve sınıftan olur ise olsun her kim bir gayrısına söğecek ve itibarına dokunur bir söz söyleyecek olur ise faraza bu keyfiyet Dersaadet'te vuku'bulup da buna mütecasir olan dahi ya Devlet-i Aliyye'nin eshab ü merati-binden veyahud ulemadan olur ise da'vası mutlaka Meclis-i Ahkam-ı Adliye'de görülerek cünhasının cesametine ve derecesine göre zabıta tarafından beş günden yirmi beş güne kadar mahbus ola ve cünhası gayet hafif olduğu tebeyyün ettiği takdirde Meclisce kendisini tekdir ve takbih ile iktifa oluna." "Chastity and honor are as sacred and dear to a person as his life, and the safety and protection of these are among the necessities of patriotism and humanity. For instance, to dishonor a person with words, to beat a man, or to curse a person, mean violating that person's honor. Therefore, from now on, military and other law enforcement personnel such as soldiers, guards, and others shall not beat and swear at anyone as they wish. Thus, in the event of a fight or a quarrel in the streets, the duty [of law enforcement personnel] will be to apprehend the accused people and bring them directly to the appropriate police station without doing anything to them. From now on, regardless of his rank, whoever, whether he is a soldier or guard working in the service of law enforcement, swears at any other person or dishonors a person with words [will be punished]. If, for instance, such an event takes place in Istanbul

and the person who dares to commit such an act happens to be a functionary of the Sublime State or a member of the ulema, let his case be heard at the *Meclis-i Ahkam-ı Adliye,* and let him be imprisoned for five to twenty five days, according to the importance and degree of his offence, and if it is established that his offense is very light, let the *Meclis* [*-i Akham-ı Adliye*] reprimand and scold him."

48. Of the nineteen articles in this chapter, the first nine were pulled from various disparate parts of the earlier code, and the last ten are completely new.
49. Ibid, (1851 code), chap. 3, art. 11, pp. 169. art. 11: "Teba'adan şer'i bulunmayan madde-i sirkatte nisab-ı sirkat bulunup da bir kaç yüz guruşluk şey ahz edenlere ziyade müddet tahsisle mücazat oluması usul-i adle tevafuk etmeyeceğinden ahz olunan eşyanın kıymetine nazaran ahz eden şahs üç aydan bi't-tefavüt nihayet üç seneye kadar prangabend olarak hidemat-ı süfliyede istihdam oluna" "in a matter of theft that does not produce an Islamic law/*şer'î* consequence, creating a certain degree of theft and imposing more than the deserved punishment on a thief who has seized something worth a few hundred piasters would not be in accordance with justice; therefore, let the person who seizes [something] be put into fetters and used in low quality services from three months to three years, in view of the value of the goods stolen."
50. Based on chap. 5, art. 2; and chap. 5, art. 5–7 of the 1840 text respectively. Ahmed Lütfi, pp. 136–138.
51. Ibid, "irtişa maddesi şer'an ve kanunen emr-i münker işbu irtişa fi'l-i mekruhuna hiç kimse tarafından cesaret olunmaya ..." "with corruption being unlawful by Islamic law/*şeriat* and regular law/*kanun,* let no one dare to commit this abominable act."
52. Ibid, (1851 code), chap. 3, art. 14 and 19, pp. 169, 171, 173–4. art. 14: "zahirelerine öşr vermemek içün bila-özr-i şer'i kaldıranlar hem emval-i beyt'ül-malı telef etmiş ve hem de ol zahireyi kendilerine haram eylemiş olacaklarından o makule zabıtanın haberi olmaksızın ve öşrü alınmaksızın harman yerinden zahireyi kaldırıp ketm-i aşar edenler olur ise gümrükten mal kaçıranlar haklarında iki kat gümrük alındığı misillu bunlardan dahi kaldırdığı zahireden nizaman iki kat öşr tahsiliyle haklarında mücazat oluna." "Since those who conceal their stored grain, without an Islamic law/*şer'î* excuse, in order not to pay the grain tithe, both damage the treasury and accumulate unlawful grain, let such persons who harvest their crops without the knowledge of law enforcement personnel, and who conceal their tithe dues, be punished in a way similar to those who smuggle goods past customs. Since those who smuggle goods past customs pay twice the customs duty, let those who conceal their grain stores pay twice the tithe for the concealed grain." art. 19 also mentions non-Islamic taxes to be paid.
53. Ibid, (1851 code), chap. 3, art. 12, p. 170. art. 3: "Taraf-ı Devlet-i Aliyye'den verilen evamir-i âliyye ve memurin-i saltanat-ı seniyye taraflarından ita' olunan evrak-ı resmiye ve senedat-ı şer'iye ve mürur tezkerelerine taklid ve bazı mahallerini hakk ve tağyir eden sahtekar şahsın mertebe-i töhmetine göre dört aydan dört sene ve sair nasın evrakına taklid eden üç aydan üç seneye kadar kürek ve pranga ve şahsa göre nefy ve tagrib ile te'dib kılına ..." "let those who counterfeit high orders given by the Sublime State, or who replicate official documents or Islamic law/*şer'î* certificates, or who transfer permits delivered by the functionaries of the Imperial sultanate, or who erase or spoil certain parts of these documents

receive, according to their guilt, four months to four years of hard labor and let them be put into fetters. Let those who counterfeit other people's documents receive three months to three years and be put into fetters. Let these people also be banished and exiled."

54. One exception to this rule was the spread of the local council phenomenon and the circumscribing of the role of the governor somewhat.
55. Out of a total of fifteen documents, including twenty cases involving murder, wounding, and corruption, for example, 62% contain Islamic law writs, and 39% do not. Further, 35% are legitimized according to Islamic law precepts, 12% according the code, 41% according to both, and 12% according to neither. As for the method of proof, it is difficult to establish a meaningful number in this subsection, as only four of the cases make specific reference to proof of any kind. For the sake of uniformity, however, of these four, two reference Islamic law and two the code. Finally, when looking at the sentences passed, 57% are *kısas* or *diyet,* 21% are regular, and 21% are *siyasî.* For a more detailed analysis of this data, please see: Miller, *From Fikh to Fascism,* pp. 123–5.
56. İradeler—MV 16982, 9 1274, MV 11568, 18 S 1270; MV 11154, 24 Za 1269.
57. İradeler—MV 16180, Gurre-i R 1273. "İşkodra sancağı dahilinde katl ve cerh maddesinden dolayı beynlerinde kan da'vası olanlar umumen barıştırılacaktır ve her bir katl için katil tarafından maktulün varisine ikibin guruş diyet verileceği misillu cerh için dahi mecruhun cerhine göre tensip olunacak bir meblağ mecruha ita' olunarak huzur-u şer'de ibra olunacaklardır ve ol babda bir kıt'a hüccet-i şer'iyye dahi tanzim ve tahrir kılınacaktır. Kazalar dahilinde mevcud olan bu misillu kan da'vası balada muharrer olan vechile barıştırılmak üzere tarafeyn bir an evvel İşkodra'ya celb ile icra-yı icab-ı hale ibtidar olunacaktır. İşbu musalaha-i umumiyeden sonra vuku'bulacak kaffe-i katl ve cinayat-ı saire şer'an ve kanunen rü'yet olunduktan sonra terettüp edecek ceza her neyse hükumet marifetiyle icra olunacağı cihetle hod be hod hakkını almak seydasıyla hasmını öldürmeye ve cerh etmeye cür'et edenlere katil ve carih nazarıyle bakılacaktır."
58. İradeler—MV 8340, 27 B 1268. "Rumeli kıt'asının ekser mahallerinde eshab-ı töhmetin darb ile mücazat olundukları ve Üsküp valisi devletlu Tosun Paşa hazretleri dahi şunu bunu darb etmekte olduğu ifadesiyle Silistre Valisi devletlu paşa hazretleri tarafından varid olan tahrirat Meclis-i Vâlâ'nın mazbatasıyla beraber manzur-i âli buyurulmak içün takdim kılındı. Mealinden müsteban olduğu vechile ba'dezin hadd-ı şer'i lazım gelen eshab-ı töhmetten ma'ada öyle darb ettirilmeyip ber-mucib-i kanun-i ceza pranga ve habs ile mücazat olunmaları . . ." "A dispatch sent by His Excellency the governor of Silistra stating that in many parts of Rumelia accused individuals have been punished by beatings, and that the governor of Üsküp, His Excellency Tosun Paşa, has been beating various individuals is submitted along with a Meclis-i Vâlâ memorandum [on this subject]. Given the contents of this memorandum, from now on, accused individuals—aside from those to be punished by the application of Islamic law/*şer'î* punishment—should not be beaten, but sentenced to hard labor and imprisonment according to the legal code."
59. Ibid, "Tanzimat-ı hayriyenin mugayiri," "hadd-ı şer'i lazım gelen eshab-ı töhmetten ma'adasının öyle darb ettirilmeyip ber-mucib-i kanun-i ceza pranga ve habis ile mücazat olunmaları . . ."

NOTES TO CHAPTER FIVE

1. Donovan, p. 400.
2. See, for example, D. George Boyce, "From Assaye to the Assaye: Reflections on the British Government, Force, and Moral Authority in India," *Journal of Military History* 63 (1999): 643–668. p. 653.
3. Freitag, p. 231.
4. Heidborn, p. 381.
5. Ibid, p. 246.
6. A. Bertram, "The Legal System of Turkey," *Law Quarterly Review* 25 (1909). p. 26.
7. France, "Code pénal napoléon," Napoléon Bacqua de Labarthe, ed. *Codes de la législation française.* Paris: Auguste Durand, 1849, and "Code pénal ottoman," G. Young, ed. *Corps de Droit Ottoman.* Oxford: Clarendon Press, 1905–6. vol. vii.
8. See, for example, Stanley Grupp in Enrico Ferri, *The Positivist School of Criminology: Three Lectures.* Stanley E. Grupp, ed. Pittsburgh: University of Pittsburgh Press, 1968. p. xviii.
9. In fact, it is mentioned twice in articles 8 and 74–75, but only briefly, and without a definition or extended explication. "Code ottoman."
10. See J. Schacht. "Katl," *Encyclopedia of Islam.* Vol. 4. Leiden: Brill, 1997. p. 768.
11. "Code Ottoman," Art. 169–172, "Code napoléon," Art. 297. It is worth pointing out that when Egypt adopted the same French criminal code in 1875, *kısas* and *diyet* were not mentioned anywhere. Baer, "Transition," p. 141.
12. Of the other sections not included in the Ottoman code, most are not particularly relevant to this study. Those concerning attacks on liberty, attacks on the civil status of a child, and crimes related to the exercise of public rights, for example, refer primarily to laws which existed in France at the time of the publication of the criminal code—i.e. a constitution and civil code—but did not exist in the Ottoman Empire circa 1859.
13. "Code napoléon," art. 199–200.
14. Ibid, art. 201–206.
15. Since the Ottoman code is much shorter than the French code, a simple numerical comparison will not furnish particularly useful results. In order to gauge the interest which one government or the other had in any one section of the text, therefore, it is more useful to look at the percentage of the total code which that one section occupies. In other words, in the French code, the section on corruption and crimes by functionaries contains 33 articles and takes up a total of 6.8% of the total text. In the Ottoman code, the same section contains 35 articles and takes up 13.3% of the total text. One can consequently speculate that the Ottoman drafters were more interested in corruption than the French drafters had been. Likewise, the section on kidnapping and the status of children contains twenty articles in the French code and takes up a total of 6.4% of the text, whereas the same section of the Ottoman code contains four articles and takes up 1.5% of the text. The French state would therefore seem to have been more interested in such matters than the Ottoman.
16. Respectively, 6.2%/6.9%, 6.8%/13.3%, 0%/3.4%, 0%/2.3%, 7%/7.6%.
17. Respectively, 7.3%/7.1%, 6.4%/1.5%, 6.4%/4.1%, 3.6%/0%, 3.9%/3.8%.

18. When not taking into account those articles of the Ottoman code which exist solely to ensure the primacy of Islamic law/*şer'î* jurisdiction.
19. Neither the Ottoman nor the French percentages will add to 100, as many articles in both codes relate to general dispositions, or to the other legal texts, or to areas which fall into neither of the above two categories.
20. Hurewitz, vol. 1, p. 115.
21. Hatt-ı Hümayun of Gülhane, art. 8, as presented in *Osmanlı Ansiklopedisi*, vol. 6, p. 114.
22. One should continue to bear in mind that all of the edicts and codes reinforced the supremacy of Islamic law in these matters as well, and stated that any and all reform would not infringe on its jurisdiction or authority.
23. "Hatt-ı Hümayun," in İrfan Bingöl, *Ülkemizde Anayasa Hareketleri*. Ankara: Atak Ofset, 1993. pp. 37–39.
24. "Islahat Fermanı," in *Osmanlı Ansiklopedisi*, vol. 6, p. 166. Another edict, promulgated earlier, in 1845, demonstrates similar if not quite so obvious tendencies. Since this edict, unlike the two others, is not concerned quite so explicitly with defining further the ruler/ruled relationship, its place in the gradual conflation of criminal and political law is not immediately obvious. When we examine what precisely its stated goals were, however, we do see some continuity. Sultan Abdülmecid introduced a new set of goals by arguing that with the exception of the military reform, none of the projects outlined in the 1839 edict had been undertaken effectively. (Recai G. Okandan, *Amme Hukukumuzun Ana Hatları*. Istanbul: Fakülteler Matbaası, 1957. p. 73.) He then continued by urging his ministers to consider what especially is necessary to assure the material well being of "his people." In particular, he notes that the establishment of new schools is imperative in lifting the ignorance of "the religious order as much as the temporal order." (Engelhardt, *La Turquie et le tanzimat*. Paris: Cotillon, 1882. p. 75.) Finally, he calls for the establishment of a system of representative assemblies in various provinces in order to put the state's "legal necessities" more firmly in place. (Okandan, p. 74.) Although criminal law concepts are not prominent in this edict, it is worth noting that the foundation of the reforms is still the Sultan's relatively paternalistic duty to protect the well being of his subjects. In addition, the temporal and the religious sides of the equation, if not completely synonymous as in other edicts, do occupy, once more, equal and balanced rhetorical space in the Sultan's speech. Indeed, it is only after these two more classical elements of the ruler/ruled relationship are re-affirmed, that the quasi-liberal concept of representative assemblies is mentioned—and only within the context of the earlier ideology. Although this 1845 edict is not so explicitly linked to the themes of the 1839 and 1856 texts, it is undoubtedly a product of the same legal and political environment.
25. *Osmanlı Ansiklopedisi*, vol. 7, p. 72.
26. Ibid, vol. 7, p. 72.
27. See below for a definition of "critical liberal" as opposed to "liberal" in which responsibility figures more prominently than rights. The absence of a "liberty" concept in the trio used in these edicts and the constitution makes a great deal of sense in the context of critical liberal as opposed to liberal thought.
28. "Hatt-ı Hümayun Sureti," in S.A. Kahraman, Galitekin, A.N, Dadaş, C., ed. *İlmiyye Salnamesi*. Istanbul: İşaret Yayınları, 1998. p. 19. "mukaddime-i ıslahat

ve ahkam-ı mukaddese-i şer'-i şerife muvafık olarak umumun emniyyet-i can ü mal ve ırz u namusunu mu'lin ["revealer"] olmak üzere Tanzimat Hattı'nı ilan etmişdi."

29. Ibid.
30. "Veraset-i Saltanat ve Hilafet"
31. "Zat-ı Hazret-i Padişahî, hin-i cülusunda Meclis-i Umumi'de ve Meclis müctemi' değilse, ilk ictima'ında şer'-i şerif ve Kanun-i Esasi ahkamına ria'yet ve vatan ve millete sadakat edeceğine yemin eder." "Upon his succession to the throne, His Imperial Majesty shall swear before Parliament, or, if Parliament is not in session, at its first meeting, to respect the provisions of *şeriat* and the Constitution, and to be loyal to the fatherland and nation." "Kanun-i Esasi," art. 3. Kahraman, et. al., p. 21.
32. "... Kavanin ve nizamatın tanziminde mu'amelat-ı nasa erfak ve icabat-ı zamana evfak ahkam-ı fikhiyye ve hukukiye ile adab ve mu'amelat esas ittihaz kılınacakdır." "In the drawing up of laws and regulations, care shall be taken to base them upon the provisions of the judgments of *fikh* and *kanun* and upon public morals and customs, which should be in accordance with the interest and needs of the people at the time." "Kanun-i Esasi," art. 118, ibid, p. 39.
33. Art. 87 ought also to be mentioned here. It reads "de'avi-i şer'iyye mehakim-i şer'iyyede ve de'avi-i nizamiyye, mehakim-i nizamiyyede rü'yet olunur." "*şer'î* cases will be heard in *şer'î* courts and *nizamî* cases will be heard in *nizamî* courts." "Kanun-i Esasi," ibid, p. 34. Although this article would seem to be evidence against the idea of a merging of *şer'î* and *nizamî* ideas, one ought to recall that "*şer'î* cases," and "*nizamî* cases" are never specifically defined as separate anywhere, and that often one case fits into both categories. In addition, at this point the *şer'î* courts as well as their functionaries had been incorporated so effectively into the *nizamî* system (see chapter 1) that the differentiation between the two cannot be as stark as such an interpretation of this article implies.
34. Xiaoqun, p. 2.
35. Ibid, p. 3.
36. Ibid, p. 15. A few years earlier, the KMT had thus begun to "partyize" the judiciary. p. 9.
37. Nathan Brown, "Brigands and Statebuilding: The Invention of Banditry in Egypt," *Comparative Studies in Society and History* 32 (1990): 258–281. p. 258.
38. Ibid, p. 266.
39. Ibid, p. 259.
40. Ibid, p. 267.
41. Ibid, p. 262
42. Ibid, p. 279.
43. Ibid, p. 279.
44. Freitag, p. 231.
45. Ibid, p. 233.
46. Ibid, p. 246.
47. Ibid, p. 247.
48. Ibid, p. 260.
49. See further examples of the "discovery" of banditry in Zhou, p. 445.
50. With regard to France in Algeria, for example, see Michael Brett, "Legislating for Inequality in Algeria: The Senatus-Consulte of 14 July 1865," *Bulletin of the School*

of Oriental and African Studies, 51 (1988): 440–461. p. 443. "a civilized system, the religious law and its application by the qadi was an 'influence bienfaisant et éclairée' which could, if properly used by the French, overcome the barbarism of the tribes as once it had restrained the tyranny of the Turks. While carefully excluding both the public and the penal form of the qadi's domain, Bedeau, the commandant in question at Constantine, nevertheless envisaged as system along the lines of the Décret of 1854, in which the qadi's jurisdiction would be progressively extended to 'the tribes'. The savage beast would then be soothed by that respect for the religious law evinced by all Muslim peoples. In the longer term, a different benefit could be anticipated from qadis converted to bureaucrats."

51. İradeler—MM 2028, 19 R 1290. "Prizren vilayeti ahalisinin ekseri huşunet ve cehaletleri iktizasınca min-el-kadim birbirini katl ve cerh etmek ve hetk-i ırz ve namus eylemek gibi cinayatı i'tiyat ederek ve bu fi'illerin ilca'at ve icbaratıyla yekdiğerlerinden ahz-ı intikam için kan da'vasına düşerek şu da'iye-i vahiye miyanelerinde müteselsil ve mütevaris ve enva' vuku'at-ı feci'aya bais olmakta olduğuna ve eğerçi işbu hallerden münb'ais da'valar oralarca kan barıştırmak ismiyle ittihaz olunan bir kaide-i sulhiye dairesinde tesviye edilmekte ise de bu kaide zaten gayr-ı meşru' ve süver-i icraiyesi bir takım sebükmağzan kesanın arayı hodseranesine mevdu' olmasıyla onun devamı ef'al-ı cinaiye mütecasirlerinin ahkam-ı adile-i şer'iye ve kanuniyeden istisnasını mü'eddi ve tekerrür-i vuku'at-ı muzırraya badi olarak sınuf-i teba'a arasında muhasemat ve mukatelatın hudus ve temadisi ise min-küll'il-vücuh tecviz olunamaycağına mebni buna bir nihayet verilmesi vilayet-i mezbure valisi devletlu paşa hazretlerine yazılmış idi. Ol babdaki teşebbüsattan bahisle mebhus-i anha olan ve mahallince Lekë Dukagjini namıyla usul-i mahsusa hükmünde tutulan kaide-i sulhiye ba'dezin külliyen men' ve ilga olunarak katl ve cerh da'valarının hükm-i şer' ve kanuna tatbikan rü'yeti hakkında şedid'ül-müfad bir kıt'a ferman-ı mehabet-nişan ısdar ve tesyarı vali-i müşarileyh tarafından iş'ar edilmiş." "From days of old, the majority of the inhabitants of the province of Prizren have been accustomed to committing such crimes as the violation of honor and rape, because of their roughness and ignorance. These acts compel and oblige individuals to undertake blood feuds with one another for the sake of revenge, and this silly motive has been causing all sorts of successive and ongoing tragic incidents among these people. Such cases have been settled according to a customary peace-making rule there called blood reconciliation. This rule, however, is essentially unlawful, and its execution is left in the hands of a few obstinate and silly people. In addition, the continuation of this practice will allow those who venture to commit criminal acts to escape from the application of the just judgments of the *şeriat* and law. Since the development and continuation of mutual hostilities between subjects and the killings cannot be permitted, a dispatch has been sent to the paşa, the governor of the aforementioned province, requesting that he put an end to this practice. The aforementioned paşa has communicated a message detailing his efforts toward this end and has requested the issuance of an awe-inspiring imperial edict with strong language and carrying weight as law, which might permanently abolish and annul this practice, locally known as [kanuni i] Lekë Dukagjini, and place murder and assault cases henceforth under the jurisdiction of *şeriat* and law."

52. The institutions created in the 1860s and 1870s to elaborate the new legal system illustrate this take on the religious/regular relationship clearly. In 1868, for example, the central judicial council, the *Meclis-i Vâlâ-yı Ahkam-ı Adliye,* was divided into legislative and judicial sections. Both prior to and after its division, it was composed of regular legal functionaries, civil bureaucrats, and judges of Islamic law. (İradeler, Dahiliye 40040 12 M 1285. "Divan-ı Ahkam-ı Adliye'nin mazbatalarını suret-i matlubede kaleme almak içün tarik-i ilmiyye ve kalemiyyeden on iki nefer müsevvid intihap ve ta'yin olunmak . . ." "in order to pen the reports of the *Divan-ı Ahkam-ı Adliye* in the desired manner, 12 secretaries from the ulema and clerical staff will be chosen and appointed . . ." See also Savvas Paşa, *Le tribunal Mosulman.* Paris: Mechal et Billard, 1902. p. 76, "Une cour, nommé Conseil Suprème de justice (meclis-i valai-i adliye [sic]) composés: 1° de personnages arrivés aux plus hautes grades de la hiérarchie des juges et jurisconsultes de l'ordre sacré 2° de dignitaires civils du plus haut rang . . ." "a court, called the Supreme Council of Justice consisted of: 1) people from the highest levels of the hierarchy of judges and jurisconsultants of the sacred order, 2) of civil dignitaries of the highest rank . . .") Similarly, the provincial councils that served as blueprints for the eventual regular courts proper were composed, as of 1864 (1281), of a judge of Islamic law as president, and a council of Muslim and non-Muslim functionaries and officials. (Heidborn, p. 223. ". . . composés de juge du chériat (naib) comme président et d'assesseurs par moitié Mosulmans et non-Mosulmans.")
53. "tahkikat/tedkikat-i nizamiyye ve mürafa'a-yı şer'iyye . . ." cf. for example, İradeler—DAA 577, and DAA 296.
54. The sample consists of fifteen documents, containing 25 cases of murder, theft, and corruption, for instance. 47% contain Islamic legal writs and 53% do not. As for legitimization, 16% are by the requirements of Islamic law alone, 19% are by the requirements of the code alone, 62% are legitimized upon both, and 4% are legitimized upon neither. Moreover, when one looks at the method of proof, 29% are tried by the rules of Islamic law, 29% are tried according to the precepts of the code, and 41% follow a combination of the two. Finally, as for the sentences passed, 20% are Islamic law sentences, 76% are sentences from the code, and 4% are *siyasî* sentences. For a more detailed analysis of this data, please see Miller, *From Fikh to Fascism,* pp. 123–125.
55. Although the execution of sentences was never an interest or a prerogative of the religious establishment.
56. İradeler, Meclis-i Mahsus 1943 5 S 1290, ". . . fakat riyasetlerin merkez naiblerine tefviziyle onların yerine dahi birer bab naibi ta'yini tertibat-ı mutasavvere cümlesinden . . . divan-ı temyizlerin vezaifi ise yalnız vilayetce mehakim-i sairede görülen de'avi-i hukukiye ve cinaiyenin istinafen veya tedkiken rü'yeti suretine münhasır olduğu[ndan] . . . divan riyasetine nakl edilerek yerlerine diğer naib ta'yin kılınmak üzere . . ." "with the handing over of the presidencies to the central *naibs* other bab *naibs* [will be] appointed in their place . . . the only assignment of the *divan-ı temyiz* is to hear the common law and criminal cases which were heard at other provincial courts as an appeals court or [to function] as an investigative [council] . . . those local *naibs* whose competency is proven by experience and documented will be transferred to the presidency of the *divan* and other *naibs* will be appointed to their [former] positions." See also İradeler, Dahiliye 46700 5 Ca

1290, "vilayetlerdeki divan-ı temyiz riyasetlerinin tebeddülü vuku'buldukca tarik-i ilmiyye mensubatından ehl ve erbabına tevcihi . . ." "when presidencies of the provincial cassation councils become vacant, they will be conferred to members of the ulema corps . . ."

57. "mahkeme-i kebire-i merkeziyyenin teşkili cihetle divan-ı temyiz-i vilayet bittabi ona mülhak ve munzam olacaktır" and "mahkeme-i kebire-i merkeziyye merkez-i vilayet olan sancak dahilinde vuku'a gelen cinayet da'valarını bidayeten ve gerek mülhak kazalar mecalis-i de'avisinde ve de'avi-i şer'iyeden başka olarak kabil-i istinaf olmak üzere hükm olunan da'valarıisti'da üzerine istinafen rü'yet eder." "upon the formation of the central high court, the ***divan-ı temyiz*** of a province will naturally be attached and appended to it." and "The central high court will hear murder cases that took place in the central sancak of a province as a first instance court and in addition to the justice councils and Islamic law/*şer'î* courts, it will hear, as an appeals court, upon request, [criminal cases] that took place in the capital of the province and in the districts attached to it." İradeler, Dahiliye 45362, 17 N 1289.
58. See, for example, Ahmad, p. 16. "Sultan Abdülhamid II . . . pursued a pan-Islamic policy at home and abroad . . ."

NOTES TO CHAPTER SIX

1. Xiaoqun, p. 18.
2. Ibid, p. 15.
3. Ibid, p. 22.
4. John, pp. 126–7.
5. Weber, vol. 2, pp. 784–5.
6. There is some confusion over the precise date of the opening of the Law School. Without question, students were enrolled and attending classes by 1878. The Regulation for the Law School in the *Düstur*, Istanbul: Matbaa-yı Amire, 1295/1878. vol. 4, p.445 (page numbers differ in other versions of the *Düstur*), is dated March 1293/1876. There is, however, an earlier mention of the establishment of the Law School in a text dated 1291/1874 (*Düstur*, vol. 3, p. 439). Likewise, there is a later version of the official regulation opening the Law School in the archival document, İradeler, Şura-yı Devlet 2204, 10 C 1295/1878.
7. Yahya Akyüz, "Tanzimat Döneminde Eğitim Biliminde ve Öğretim Yöntemlerinde Gelişmeler," *Tanzimat'ın* . . . p. 506.
8. Lewis, p. 182.
9. David Kushner, "Career Paths," *Tanzimat'ın 150. Yıl Dönümü Uluslararası Sempozuyumu*. Ankara: Türk Tarih Kurumu Yayınları, 1994. p. 168.
10. Lewis, p. 182.
11. Fortna notes a similar process in elementary education over the Hamidian era.
12. "Règlement de l'École de Droit," in Gregoire Aristarchi, *Législation ottomane, ou recueil des lois, reglèments, ordonnances, traites, capitulations et autres documents officiels de l'empire ottoman*. Constantinople: Frères Nicolaides, 1873–88. part 5. pp. 242–246, 1878.
13. *Düstur*, vol. 4, p. 446.

14. In 1913, Mahmut Cemal Efendi was teaching *Mecelle, Usul-u Fıkıh* (Procedure of Islamic Jurisprudence), and *Sak* (Legal Formulas) at the Law School, while simultaneously teaching *İlm-i Fıkh* (The Science of Islamic Jurisprudence) at *Dar-ül Fünun.* In exactly the same year, 1913, Mehmet Arif Efendi was teaching *Usul-u Fıkh* in exactly the same department as Mahmut Cemal at the *Dar-ül Fünun.* (Sadık Albayrak, *Son Devir Osmanlı Uleması.* Istanbul: Medrese Yayınevi, 1980. vol. 3, pp. 25, 107) Mehmet Esat Efendi had started teaching first year Hadith and *İlm-i Usul-u Hadis* there two years previously. (Ibid, vol. 3, pp. 202–3) Finally, there is Mehmet Fehmi Efendi, who between 1910 and 1911 was appointed to teach *İlm-i Fıkh* (Islamic Jurisprudence) in the Department of Religious Law, Arabic in the Literature Department, and *Mecelle* in the Legal Sciences Department (*Ulum-i Hukukiyye Şübesi*) at the *Dar-ül Fünun.* (Ibid, vol. 3, pp. 224–5)
15. ". . . duhul imtihanında tamam numaranın nısfından ziyadesini ihraz edenler medreseye kabul olunurlar." "those getting more than half marks on the entrance examination are accepted to the school." "Medresetül-Kuzat Ta'limat-ı Dahiliyesidir," art. 8, p. 685 and in Kahraman, et. al., p. 563.
16. See below and previous footnote. According to Heidborn, p. 275, the *mekteb-i nuvvab* (*naib*s' Law School) was established in 1856.
17. Article 12 of the regulation, for example, states that the "period of instruction will be four years, and the *şer'î* and *kanunî* classes to be studied will be under special instructions." "müddet-i tedrisiyyesi dört seneden ibaret olup, okunacak dürus-i şer'iyye ve kanuniyye talimat-ı mahsusasına tabi olunacakdır." "Medresetül-Kuzat . . ." Art. 12, p. 685 and in Kahraman, et. al., p. 564.
18. "Medresetül-Kuzat Nizamnamesi Zeyli," Ibid, p. 568.
19. "Règlement de L'École du Droit," in Aristarchi, pp. 243, 246.
20. İradeler, Şura-yı Devlet 2204, 10 C 1295. "üçüncü madde [Hukuk Mektebi nizamnamesi]: derslerin enva'ı zirde muharrerdir ve bunların müddet-i tahsiliyesi üç senedir: Mecelle-i Ahkam-ı Adliye, arazi kanunu, tapu ve emlâkın nizamnameleri, ceza kanunu, ticaret-i beriyye ve bahriyye kanunları, usul-u mehakim-i hukukiye ve cezaiye kanunları, usul-u tanzim-i ilam, ilm-i hukuk-u milel, mu'amelat-ı ecnebiyeye müteallik uhud ve nizamat ve mukavelat." "third article [Law School regulation]: the types of classes are listed below and the period of duration of these is three years: *Mecelle,* land law, real estate and property law, criminal law, land and naval commerce law, laws of civil and criminal court procedure, preparation of writs, international law, issues relating to the behavior of foreigners and their regulations."
21. Heidborn, pp. 280–1.
22. İradeler, Dahiliye 65344, 7 R 1297. "hukuk mektebine devam arzusunda olanların usul-u imtihaniyyelerini bi'l-icra seksen beş zat intihap olunmuş ve sami sıfatıyla dahi haylice zevat kabul edilmiş . . ."
23. In 1897, 334 Muslims and thirty-eight non-Muslims were attending the Law School. Güran, ed., p. 98.
24. MV 122/18, 11 ZA 1326. "Mekteb-i Hukuk'a girmek isteyüb dersten mücaz olan talebe-i ulumun bila-imtihan kayd ü kabulleri muktazi göründüğünden mukaddema bi'l-murakabe dahil olanlar ile me'zun bulanların nizamen musarrah hukuk ve imtiyazatına dokunulmamak üzere ba'dezin Dar'ül-fünun ulum-u diniye şubesine alınacak talebenin kemafissabık duhul imtihanına tabi tutulması . . . ve Mekteb-i Hukuk'a mekatib-i âliye ile Mekteb-i Sultani'ye ve yedi senelik

mekatib-i idadiyeden me'zun olanların ... bi'l-imtihan kaydları" "Graduates of religious schools who want to enroll in the Law School should be accepted and enrolled without an examination. From now on, those students who will be accepted by the by the divinity department of the university should be required to take an entrance examination; the privileges of those students who had previously enrolled and graduated, however, should be honored. The graduates of all of the colleges, the Mekteb-i Sultani, and the seven year high schools will be enrolled at religious schools."

25. MV 18/53, 1304.B.2 "... ders cetveline ilave edilen ulum ve fünun yolunda olduğu gibi müddet-i tahsiliyenin dahi dört seneye iblağı münasib olup ancak ifadat-ı vakı'adan müsteban olduğuna göre zikr olunan mektebe devam edenler içinde birçok talebe-i ulum efendileri bulunduğuna ve bunlardan kısm-ı azamı fukaradan olduğuna nazaran mülazimet müddetinin ale-l-ıtlak bir seneye temdidi şiddet-i zaruriyetlerini istilzam edeceği cihetle müddet-i merkumenin kemakan altı ay olmak üzere ..."
26. "müdür-i mektebin hemen azliyle yerine dindar ve muktedir ve müstakim bir zat intihap ve arz olunması ..." İradeler, Dahiliye 86579, 24 S 1306.
27. İradeler, Dahiliye 97756, 4 R 1309. Respectively "ihrac edilen," "bu defa tedrisi kararlaştırılan," and "tedris olunmakta olan."
28. Heidborn, p. 245.
29. Ibid, p. 251. Heidborn notes that a separate law also required that judges at the appeals and cassation levels have a degree from the Law School. According to the "Mehakim-i Nizamiyenin Teşkilatı Kanun-i Muvakatı," in *Düstur,* Istanbul: Matbaa-yı Amire, 1295/1878. vol. 3, p.241 (again, page numbers differ in other versions of the *Düstur*), the requirements for employment at the level of first instance were: having reached twenty-five years of age, not having been convicted of a crime, having been elected by the Justice Ministry (by examination), or having worked in a different court for four years. To be employed at the higher levels, an individual had to have reached thirty or forty years of age, depending upon the position, and had to have worked for four years at a lower level court. A temporary article does mention a degree from the Law School, but does not invalidate the other paths to employment in the regular court hierarchy.
30. Heidborn, p. 251.
31. For variations on this theme see, for example, Stanford Shaw, *History of the Ottoman Empire and Modern Turkey.* London: Cambridge University Press, 1977. vol. 2 p. 119; Bozkurt, p. 282; Dejan Aleksic, "Le Tanzimat comme intention de transformer l'Empire Ottoman en un etat de droit," in *Tanzimat'ın ... ;* and others. Also, Findley, in his article in the *Encyclopedia of Islam,* notes that there were attempts—for the most part unsuccessful—by the Ottoman government to regulate the appointment of non-*şer'î* judges to regular posts in 1879 and 1910. The 1910 attempt under the Young Turks, he argues, was more successful than the earlier one.
32. Heidborn, p. 239. And others.
33. Given a sample of approximately 265 appointments and transfers contained within 100 documents
34. See Bernard Lewis, "Efendi," *Encyclopedia of Islam,* vol. 2. Leiden: E.J. Brill, 1986. p. 687. "In the nineteenth century the Ottoman government made attempts to

regulate the use of Efendi . . . the distinction between Efendi and Bey in Turkey finally became one between religious and secular, the former for men of religion or religious education, the latter for military or civilian laymen." In the nineteenth century, Efendi was also used for non-Muslim government functionaries and male members of the royal house. Clearly the distinction between the two cannot be absolute, but an argument such as mine above I think can nonetheless stand. It might be claimed, for example, that the total absence of a Jewish or Christian name followed by "bey" in the documents indicates at least to some extent the accuracy of Lewis' argument.

35. See below, note 44.
36. Sadık Albayrak's compilation of biographies follows in the same vein. It becomes clear, in fact, when examining his work that in the Tanzimat and immediate post-Tanzimat periods, members of the religious establishment were becoming part of the regular system in quite systematic ways. An examination of the compilation further suggests that as many *ulema* found work in the regular courts as they did in the Islamic law courts. Perhaps of more interest, however, is the fact that these same *ulema* habitually took positions in large urban centers, such as Bursa, Beirut, Damascus, Diyar-i Bekir, Aleppo, and Selanik (See also İradeler, Dahiliye 63896, 12 Ca 1296, in which the İstinaf Presidents appointed to the newly formed Manastır and Selanik vilayet courts are explicitly to be the *naib*s of the same vilayets.) and that they filled posts in these courts at every available level of the hierarchy. (Albayrak. See biographies in vol. 3 of Es-Seyit El-Hac Kamil Efendi, p. 6; Kemaleddin Efendi, p. 8; Mahmut Efendi (Diyarbakırlı), p. 15; Mehmet Efendi (Şamlı), p. 70; Mehmet Âbid Efendi, p. 81 and many others.) Even posts in the Istanbul regular courts appear to have been easily acquired, given that members of the *ulema* corps became everything from scribes in the Istanbul appeals court (Ibid, vol. 3, biography of Mehmet Cemal Efendi, who in 1871 became a zabıt katibi in the İstanbul İstinaf Mahkemesi, p. 138.) to members of the Justice Ministry's Section on Legal Courts. (Ibid, vol. 3, biography of Mazhar Efendi, who in 1877 was appointed a member of the Adliye Nezareti Mahkeme-i Hukuk Dairesi. p. 49.) Finally, the line between criminal and civil jurisdiction—with the *ulema*'s authority restricted to the civil alone—seems to have been spurious as well: in addition to the de facto *ulema* jurisdiction described above over virtually all of the lower level courts, the posting of religiously trained legal scholars to positions at all levels of the regular criminal system seems to have been entirely welcome by the Ottoman government as well. Albayrak's biographies indicate, for example, that even after the opening of the state Law School, traditionally trained members of the *ulema* corps were consistently taking positions as everything from scribes in courts of inquiry to presidents of the highest provincial criminal councils. (Ibid, vol. 3, biography of Lütfi Efendi, 1884 Leskovik Bidayet Mahkemesi Ceza Dairesi Zabıt Katibi, p. 11; Mahmut Efendi, 1895 Ceza Mahkemesi Reis Vekili among others, p. 15; Mahmut Aziz Efendi, 1883 Mahkeme-i Teftiş Kalemi, p. 19; Mehmet Aziz Efendi, 1879 Bursa Vilayeti Meclisi Temyiz Reisliği, p. 119; Mehmet Emin Efendi, 1879–1896 Kerbelâ, Kerkük, and Hama Ceza Reisleri, p. 166; and others.)
37. For example in İradeler, Dahiliye 45932, 20 C 1289 or İradeler, Meclis-i Mahsus 1819, 2 S 1872.

38. For example in İradeler, Dahiliye 40840 26 Ş 1285.
39. For example in İradeler, Dahiliye 46008 9 Za 1289.
40. That is, criminal law appointments which had no background in the civil and commercial aspects of the regular system.
41. It is worthwhile to establish a control: it would be unlikely for a drastic change to occur over time in the proportion to the whole of deaths or even perhaps resignations. In fact, if these numbers were to change in any large degree, they would cast doubt on the validity of the rest of this information. As it is, the number of deaths relative to the total number of openings remains at a constant 7%, 6%, and 6%, and the number of resignations remains equally constant at 2%, 4%, and 4%. With this in mind, we can look at the other categories.
42. See the *terâcim-i ahval* included in the following documents: İradeler, Dahiliye, 66090, 66297, 66643, 67180, 67770, 68570, 68124, 69158, 67613, 67856, 69080, 70697, 70386, 71445, 71139, 69466, 69409, 71948, 72064, 73256, 72390, 72465, 75981, 74655, 79209, 74897, 74398, 76829, 78249, 79039, 81305, 80747, 80746, 80512, 79962, 79959, 79471, 91790, 92607, 91866, 96776, 97273, 93126, 96345, 93917, 93473, 93281, 97629, 97754, 98070, 99204; İradeler, Adliye ve Mezahib, 1310-C-21/5, 1310-Ra-6/11, 1313-S-5/5, 1313-M-18/10, 1313-C-23/12.
43. Ibid.
44. Ibid.
45. Ibid.
46. This tendency becomes even clearer when looking at the employment background of regular functionaries. Nearly two thirds of those appointed to positions in criminal law courts had held other positions in the regular legal system. Almost one third of the appointments had been working in Islamic Law courts or in the largely religious councils of cassation. [See İradeler, Dahiliye 46292, 26 Ca 1290, which states that the presidents of the *Mecalis-i Temyiz* are from the *Tarik-i İlmiye,* appointed by the *Meşihat,* and ought to be *naib*s. "vilayatta teşekkül eden mecalis-i temyiziye riyasetlerinden ba'dezin açılacak olanlara tarik-i ilmiyeden münasiblerinin intihab ve ta'yini bi'l-istizan müteallik ve şerefsudur buyurulan irade-i seniyye-i cenab-ı padişahi mukteza-yı âlisinden bulunmuş . . . Trabzon ve Hüdavendigar ve Edirne ve Bosna ve Cezair-i Bahr-i Sefid vilayetleri temyiz meclisleri riyasetleri açılarak bunlardan Trabzon'a Mekke payelilerinden Erzurum naibi Mehmed Celaleddin ve Hüdavendigar'a Brusa naibi Mehmet Kamil ve Edirne'ye Mustafa Faik ve Bosna'ya Ömer Fehmi ve Cezair-i Bahr-i Sefid'e dahi hâlen merkez naibi Mehmed Nurullah Efendiler intihap edilmiş . . ." "A decree ordering the selection and appointment of those connected to the *tarik-i ilmiye* to the open presidencies of the *mecalis-i temyiz* which are being formed in some vilayets was issued. For the open presidencies of the cassation councils in Trabzon, Hüdavendigar, Edirne, Bosna, and Cezair-i Bahr-i Sefid, the following are selected: For Trabzon, from the Meccan rank, the Erzurum naib Mehmed Celaladdin, for Hüdavendigar, the Bursa naib, Mehmet Kamil, for Edirne, Mustafa Faik, for Bosnia, Ömer Fehmi, and for Cezair-i Bahr-i Sefid, the current naib, Mehmed Nurullah Efendis.] Of the rest, 4% came from purely bureaucratic positions, and 5% came from the office of the *Şeyhülislam.* Again, therefore, specialization was essential. There was a definite preference for people who had worked in and therefore knew the regular system. But incorporating *ulema* who had been

in purely Islamic Law courts was also a possibility, provided they could function properly. Contrarily, entering the regular court hierarchy from the outside was, by the end of the nineteenth century, next to impossible.

47. This conclusion and those of the next two paragraphs are drawn from the following documents. Dahiliye: 1402, 1836, 32168, 39013, 41072, 43291, 40072, 40040, 40067, 40870, 40840, 45005, 45893, 45932, 45448, 45587, 46008, 46152, 46253, 46700, 47122, 46945, 47443, 4991, 47366, 48866, 50612, 50508, 60705, 63291, 64263, 64444, 64161, 63583, 63712, 64080, 64631, 64690, 64700, 66797, 66449, 66568, 65875, 65163, 65164, 67692, 67997, 67832, 68860, 69323, 68783, 68124, 68459, 68006, 69394, 69718, 71287, 71404, 69857, 69573, 69442, 72036, 81477, 85244, 84119, 82674, 83461, 84989, 86560, 98813, 99860, 100466, 100367, 95480, 95149, 99204; MV: 16306, 7948, 9397, 25790; MM: 1557, 1817, 1819, 1943; AM: 1312-C-11/310, 1313-S-5/5, 1313-M-18/10, 1313-C-23/2, 1314-Ş-12/8, 1314-Ş-12/11, 1316-N-29/7, 1316-R-20/11, 1316-Za-9/8, 1323-Ş-24/4, 1325-R-5/17, 1325-B-1321. For a more detailed analysis of this data, please see Miller, *From Fikh to Fascism*, pp. 26–31.
48. *Ulema* found bureaucratic positions in such areas as provincial assemblies, refugee committees, salary bureaus, military conscription committees, dispatch offices, and others. Albayrak, vol. 3, pp. 46, 121, 137, 165, 173, 214, etc.
49. See İlber Ortaylı, *Hukuk ve idare adamı olarak osmanlı devletinde kadı*. Ankara: Turhan Kitabevi, 1994. p. 74. "[z]amana uyum sağlayan fıkıh öğrenimi dolayısiyle, me'zunların bürokrasinin çeşitli dallarına girdikleri gözleniyordu. Bizzat Ahmed Cevdet Paşa bu duruma örnek teşkil eden asrın tipik bir ilmiye mensubdur."
50. In Albayrak, vol. 3, Kemaleddin Efendi, p. 9; Mehmet Cemal Efendi, p. 138.
51. Ibid, vol. 1: Ahmet Şükrü Efendi—Mecelle Meclisi'nin Katibi (1885), Adliye Nezareti Müsteşarı (1898), pp. 228–9. vol. 3: Mehmet Cemaleddin Efendi—Adliye Nezareti İstanbul Birinci Ceza Dairesi Muharrerat Şubesi Muavini (1872), Temyiz-i Hukuk Kalemi Mümeyyizi (1877), p. 140; Mehmet Elîf Efendi—Divan-ı Ahkam-ı Adliye Mazbata Odası Muavini (1873), p. 151; Mehmet Halit Efendi—İstanbul Mahkemesi Vekayi Odası Katib Muavini (1876), p. 245. vol. 4: Mehmet Sahib Bey Efendi—Şura-yı Devlet Muhakemat Dairesi İkinci Reisi (1885), p. 79, and Mehmet Şükrü Efendi, "Şura-yı Devlet Reisi Akif Paşa'nın riyaseti altında teşekkül eden komisyona Fetvahane tarafından aza ta'yin edilmiştir." p. 126.
52. Those *ulema* who held the above mentioned positions were: Mehmet Rıza Efendi, Mahkeme-i Temyiz Azası (Albayrak, vol. 4, p. 59); Mehmet Sahib Bey Efendi, Temyiz Mahkemesi Reisi (Albayrak, vol. 4, p. 80); Mustafa Hayri Efendi, "Adliye Nezareti ile Şura-yı Devlet Riyasetine asaleten . . . ta'yin olunmuştur," (Albayrak, vol. 4, p. 208); Ömer Hilmi Efendi, Mahkeme-i Temyiz Reis-i Evveli (Albayrak, vol. 5, p. 359); Ahmet Tevfik Efendi, Mahkeme-i Temyiz Azası (Albayrak, vol. 1, p. 240); Ali Haydar Efendi, Temyiz Mahkemesi Azası and Temyiz-i Hukuk Dairesi Reisi, (Albayrak, vol. 1, p. 262); Hasan Hülki Efendi, Temyiz Mahkemesi Azası (Albayrak, vol. 2, p. 94); and İbrahim Edhem Efendi, Mahkeme-i Temyiz İkinci Reisi (Albayrak, vol. 2, p. 210).
53. İradeler, Dahiliye (all eventually ended up working as functionaries in regular courts): 66090 11 M 1298, Ziya Efendi in the war commission, mazbata odası, and muhakemat dairesi; 66643 13 C 1298, Hamid Efendi in the ticaret ve ziraat

mektubu, umur-u hukukiye hakimiye; 67613 29 M 1294, Ali Rıza Efendi worked as inspector in mücazat office, meşihat; 69080 17 Z 1299, Abdi Efendi worked as court secretary, in Bosna tahkikat memuriyet, meclis-i kebir baş katib; 70697 2 S 1300, Mahir Efendi was katib in evrak odası; 71948 4 R 1301, Veleddin Bey in tahrirat kaleme, zabıt katibi; 72064 29 R 1301, Mehmed Hamdi Bey was Adliye nezareti katibi; 72465 9 Ca 1301, Ahmed Rüşdi Bey was Adliye nezareti mücazat dairesi katib, Yanya Vilayet Mukavelat Muharriri; 75981 5 S 1302, Sehamaddin Efendi was in meclis-i kebir kaleme, mektub-u vilayet kaleme, maarif commission member, Erzurum adliye müfettiş; 74655 29 Ca 1302, Mahmud Bey in meclis-i tahkik, divan-ı ahkam-ı adliye ceza dairesi zabıt katibi; Mehmed Mahlus Bey was Şura-yı Devlet muhakemat dairesi mulazımı; 79209 4 R 1302, Osman Edip Efendi was Adliye commission katibi, umur-u tahrirat memuru; 74897 19 Ca 1302, Tahir Efendi was tahrirat baş katibi; Mehmet Ali Efendi was in the mektubî-i vilayet kalemi, islahat commission; 74398 28 R 1302, Hafiz Ahmed Efendi was vilayet merkez tahrirat katibi; 78249 8 S 1303, was in Halep sancağı mecelle kalemi, muhasebe baş katibi; 79959 29 R 1304, Tevfik Efendi was tahrirat müdürü; 97273 4 S 1309, Mehmed Nazim Bey was in the Şura-yı Devlet muhakemat dairesi kaleme, Mehmet Rüşdi Efendi was on the justice commission; 93473 9 S 1308, Ömer Lütfi Bey was divan-ı muhakemat mazbata kalemi mulazımı; and İradeler, Adliye ve Mezahib, 1313.M.18/10, Hüseyin Fehmi Efendi was in the Istanbul bab-ı muhakemat.

54. For example, Ziya Efendi, whose father was an alim, and whose early training took place solely in Quran schools: İradeler, Dahiliye, 66090 ("ismim Yusuf Ziya Efendi, şöhretçe Müftizade, pederimin ismi Mustafa Âsım Efendi ... zaman-ı tahsilde mekatib-i resmiyenin fıkdanıyla sıbyan mektebininde Kur'an-ı Azim ve tecvid ve ilm-i hal okuduktan sonra ma'lum'ül-esami hocalardan sarf ü nahiv ve Farsi ve mantık ve adab ve akaid ve fıkh ve ma'ani ta'allüm eyledim." "My name is Yusuf Ziya Efendi, I am known as Müftizade, my father's name is Mustafa Âsım Efendi ... during my education, official schools were lacking; therefore, I learned the Holy Qur'an, reciting it with proper pronunciation, and catechism at a [private] primary school. Then I learned grammar and syntax, Persian, logic, literature, tenets of the Islamic faith, canonical law and explanatory lexicology from well known professors." And Hüseyin Fehmi Efendi, whose father was also an *ulema* corps member, but who attended more civil schools: İradeler, Adliye ve Mezahib, 1313.M.18/10 ("rüşdiye mekatibinde müretteb olan derslerile Fatih Cami'-i şerifinde şehr-i akaid okuyup mezkur rüşdiye mektebinden şehadetname ve bi'l-imtihan Mekteb-i Hukuk'tan me'zuniyet-i ruus almıştır." "along with classes which were prepared at the *rüşdiye* schools, he read religious studies at Fatih Mosque, graduated from the *rüşdiye,* and graduated with honors by examination from the Law School.")
55. For example, Ali Rıza Efendi, whose sole schooling was as an alim, İradeler, Dahiliye, 67613 29 M 1299.
56. For example, Osman Edip Efendi and Tahir Efendi, also from *ulema* families, İradeler, Dahiliye, 79209 4 R 1302, 74897 19 Ca 1302, and Hafiz Ahmet Efendi, whose father was a *şeyh,* İradeler Dahiliye, 74398 28 R 1302, or Mehmet Rüşdi Efendi, whose father worked as a *şer'i* court secretary, and whose training took place in religious private schools, İradeler, Dahiliye, 97273 4 S 1309.

57. MV 40/10, 1306.C.5. "zikr olunan encümen hey'etinin beşi hükkam-ı adliyeden ve biri Bab-ı Fetvapenahi memurininden ve diğeri dahi Mekteb-i Hukuk müdirinden mürekkeb olarak . . ." "teşkili memurin-i adliyenin hüsn-i intihab ve ta'yini maksadına müstenid olmasıyla yolunda görülüb ancak hey'et-i mezkureyi terkip edecek aza meyanında Bab-ı Fetvapenahiden yalnız bir memur bulunmasından ise umur-i adliyeye vakıf olanlardan bir iki zatın huzuru münasib olacağı . . ." "the aforementioned council will be composed of five justice ministry judges, a *Meşihat* functionary, and the Director of the Law School . . ." "since its establishment aims at selecting and appointing justice functionaries properly, this seems acceptable; however, it would be [more] reasonable to have a few individuals who are familiar with the concerns of justice among the people who will compose the aforementioned council instead of having only a single functionary from the *Meşihat* . . ."
58. İradeler, Dahiliye, 67692 9 M 1299 ("Mahkeme-i temyizin münkasım olduğu iki dairede bir müddetten beri ve işlerin tedahül etmesinden dolayı ashabı tarafından şikayat-i mütevaliye vuku'bulmakta olmasıyla bunun esbab-ı hakikiyesi tedkik olunarak çaresi aranılmakta olup ancak esbab-ı mezbureden birisi dahi mahkeme-i mezkure hey'etinin tertib-i kanuniyesinden nakıs bulunması olduğundan ve bunun ikmaline dahi hal-i hazır müsa'id olmadığından mahkeme-i mezkure azasının adedi karşılık bulundukça mikdar-ı kanunisine iblağ olunmak üzere şimdilik yeniden bir azanın ta'yinine lüzum-i acil göründüğü beyanıyla Meclis-i Tedkikat-ı Şer'iye ve Mecelle Cemiyeti azasından ve Mekteb-i Hukuk mu'allimlerinden olup ma'lumat ve ehliyeti mücerreb olan Abdülsettar Efendi'nin mahkeme-i mezkure azalığına ta'yini ile . . ." See also Adliye ve Mezahib Nezareti, 267 "Mahkeme-i temyizin münkasım olduğu iki dairede bir müddetten beri işlerin fevkalade surette tedahül etmesinden dolayı alakadarları tarafından şikayat-i mütevaliye vuku'bulmakta olmasıyla bunun esbab-ı hakikiyesi tedkik olunarak çaresi aranılmakta olup ancak esbab-ı mezbureden biri de mahkeme-i mezkure hey'etinin tertip-i kanuniyesine muvafık surette bulunmaması yani aza-yı mevcudesinin added-i kanunisinden nakıs bulunması olduğundan ve bu noksanın ikmaline ise hal-i hazır müsa'id olmadığından mahkeme-i mezkure azasının adedi karşılık bulundukça mikdar-ı kanunisine iblağ olunmak üzere şimdilik müceddeden bir azanın ta'yinine lüzum-i acil ve sahih görüldüğüne Meclis-i Tedkikat-ı Şer'iye ile Mecelle Cemiyeti azasından ve Mekteb-i Hukuk mu'allimlerinden olup ma'lumat ve ehliyeti mücerreb olan Abdülsettar Efendi'nin mahkeme-i mezkure azalığına ta'yin ile . . .")
59. İradeler, Dahiliye 85244 18 L 1305, ". . . yerine iktidar ve ehliyeti cihetiyle Mecelle Cemiyeti azasından sabıkan fetva emini ve hâlen Evkaf-ı Hümayun müfettişi faziletlu Ömer Hilmi Efendi Hazretleri'nin ta'yini . . ." See also İradeler, Dahiliye 84989 9 R 1305, which discusses the same appointment.
60. İradeler, Dahiliye, 84989 9 R 1305 ("Mahkeme-i temyize ilaveten ta'yini ba-irade-i seniyye mukarrer olan iki azalıktan birine memuriyet-i haliyesi müddetinin hitamı tarihinden mu'teber olmak üzere zaten mahkeme-i temyizin aza-yı sabıkasından bulunan Evkaf-ı Hümayun müfettişi faziletlü Ömer Hilmi Efendi hazretlerinin ve diğer azalığa mahkeme-i istinaf hukuk reisi Hilmi Efendi'nin ve bundan açılacak mahkeme-i istinaf hukuk dairesi riyasetine de mülga hey'et-i ittihamiye reisi Saadetlu Emrullah Efendi hazretlerinin intihab edilmiş olduğuna . . ." "The investigator at the Imperial Foundations [Ministry], Ömer Hilmi Efendi who is

already a cassation court member, upon his time of service being completed, is assigned to one of the two vacant membership openings added to the cassation court by decree, and to the other membership is assigned the appeals court president Hilmi Efendi, and to the open appeals court presidency is assigned the abolished *hey'et i ittihamiye* president, Saadetlu Emrullah Efendi."

61. With the exception of Ahmet Hulusi Efendi to a membership in 1867. İradeler, Meclis-i Mahsus, 1557 Selh Ca 1286.
62. And were very quickly placated. The apparently unwelcome use of a salary system for *kadı*s in the Balkans was revoked little more than a year after its original institution. Halil İnalcık, "Application of the Tanzimat and its Social Effects," Lisse: Peter de Ridder Press, 1976. p. 115.
63. Heidborn, p. 265. One assumes that this payment scale changed over time with inflation.
64. Ibid.
65. Also, the pension system for regular functionaries was based on that of other civil functionaries after 1310/1893 and not the *Meşihat*'s system. Heidborn, p. 265
66. Ibid, p. 245.
67. Ibid.
68. MV 61/52, 1308.C.3.
69. Ibid. "' . . . istihsal-i me'zuniyet eden memurinin müddet-i me'zuniyetleri maaşları dahi nısf olarak verilecek ve bunlar ile taht-ı muhakemeye alınan memurin maaşlarından tevkif olunacak nısftan yerlerine ta'yin olunacak vekiller memurin-i muvazaffadan ise zammı değil ise nısf maaş verilecektir' diye muharrer ise de ifa-yı farize-i hac için tahsil-i me'zuniyet edenlerin farize-i mezkureyi ba'd-el-ifa avdet edinceye değin maaşlarının nısf olarak ifası kendileri hakkında lazım'ül-ifa olan hürmetle mütenasip olamayacağı gibi . . ."
70. See docs. AM: 1319-M-18/8; 1319-C-4/5; 1320-Ca-18/9; 1305-Ra-25; 1310-Ş-9/3; DAA: 834, 825. And also Bayraktar, p. 320: "suivant l'article premier du dit code [de 1858] ceux qui sont condemnés par les tribunaux de Nizamiye doivent être jugés ensuite par les tribunaux de şer'iye." "following the first article of the above mentioned [1858] code, those who were condemned by the regular tribunals have to be judged afterward by the Islamic law/*şer'î* tribunals."
71. In Dick Douwes and Norman N. Lewis, "The Trials of Syrian Ismailis in the First Decade of the Twentieth Century," *International Journal of Middle East Studies* 21 (1989): 215–232.
72. Douwes and Lewis, p. 220.
73. Ibid, p. 223.
74. Ibid, p. 221.

NOTES TO CHAPTER SEVEN

1. I should emphasize here that when I refer to "positivism" I am referring to the sociological movement as a whole and not to the more narrowly defined "legal positivism." The two are related, but not the same. See below for an elaboration of the role of sociological positivism in the legal sphere.
2. Hanioğlu, p. 204.

3. Gölcüklü in Tuğrul Ansay and Don Wallace Jr., eds. *Introduction to Turkish Law.* Boston: Kluwer Law and Taxation, 1987. p. 173. See also Enrico Ferri in Stanley Grupp, ed., *The Positivist School of Criminology: Three Lectures.* Pittsburgh: University of Pittsburgh Press, 1968. p. 6. Although Enrico Ferri was not directly connected to the Young Turks, his interpretation of positivism for criminal law purposes was very much in keeping with their general philosophy.
4. For example, "Abdullah Cevdet and İshak Sükuti took another initiative before fleeing to Europe. At a private elementary school, which they had established in Mamuret el-Aziz, they attempted to instill a collective sense of responsibility by punishing every student in class whenever someone failed an exam." Hanioğlu, p. 204. See similarities in Enrico Ferri, *Sociologie criminelle,* p. 239.
5. See their adherence to the theories of Gustave le Bon in Hanioğlu, p. 206. See similarities in R. Battino, *Les doctrines juridiques contemporaines en Italie.* Paris: A. Pedone, 1939. p. 46.
6. For example, "as Ahmed Rıza expressed it, 'society is a complex organism dependent solely upon natural laws. This body is subject to cyclic illnesses.' According to him, social problems could be healed through an application of scientific methodology. One of his opponents described his extradition from the CUP in 1897 as the 'amputation of a gangrenous organ from the body of the CUP.'" In Hanioğlu, p. 208. See also Ferri, *Sociology criminelle,* p. 97.
7. It is worth noting that there was to some extent a split in the school over this last issue. Enrico Ferri, for example, believed in the value of rehabilitation. (Grupp, ed. p. 4.) But he also argued in his *Sociologie criminelle* that since much criminal behavior is the result of what he saw as physical abnormality, "many criminals are incapable of reform," and reform should not be the goal of criminal law. (Ferri, p. xviii.) The only alternative to rehabilitation for the positivists, however, was removal—a criminal individual was an impurity within the social organism and had to be destroyed. Ferri writes, for example, that "the positivists are unanimous in declaring [the death penalty] legitimate, and only a few contest its practical efficacy." At the same time, however, "for the death penalty to have that sort of positive effect [i.e. being 'in agreement with natural laws ... by the elimination of anti-social and incongruous individuals'] one would have to apply it on a huge scale," which was in his view impracticable. (Ferri, p. 239–240, 245.)
8. See for example, Ahmed Lütfi, 1840 code, p. 128: "Gülhane'de kıra'at olunan hatt-ı hümayun-i ma'delet-makrun-i hazret-i şahane mucibince kaffe-i teba'a-i Devlet-i Aliyye bila-istisna emniyet-i can ve mal ve mahfuziyet-i ırz ve namus hukuk-i mefruzasına ez-ser-i nev nail olmuş ve ber-mukteza-yı hürriyet-i şer'iye huzur-i şer' ve kanunda ve mevadd-ı hukukiyede herkesin yeksan ve siyyan olması ..." ("According to the imperial decree read at Gülhane, to which justice is joined, without exception, all subjects of the Sublime State have attained the obligatory rights of security of life and property and protection of chastity and honor by the decree of Providence and everybody has become alike and equal before the *şeriat* [Islamic law] and law according to the liberties [granted by] the *şeriat.*")
9. For example, Lütfi, 1840 code, art. 4: Taşralarda dahi vuku'buldukta memleket meclis-i meşveretinde marifet-i şer'le şeriat-i muharrereye tatbikan da'vası görülüp ba'dehu ilam-ı şer'isi ve meclis mazbatası Dersaadet'e irsal ve taraf-ı fetvapenahiye takdim ile tasdik olunup ondan sonra dahi kezalik hakipa-yı hümayuna arz ile

ferman-ı âli sadır olmadıkça icrası caiz olmaya." ("When [murders] occur in the provinces, the implementation [of verdicts of execution] may not be permitted unless such cases are heard at provincial councils by means of the *şeriat* and other written rules; a *şer'î* verdict and a memorandum by the [provincial] council are then sent to Istanbul to be submitted to the *Şeyhülislam*, and upon his approval, they are submitted to His Imperial Majesty and an imperial decree is issued in the same manner.")

10. See the 1859 "Code pénal Ottoman," G. Young, ed. *Corps de Droit Ottoman.* Oxford: Clarendon Press, 1905–6. vol. vii, and France, "Code pénal napoléon," Napoléon Bacqua de Labarthe, ed. *Codes de la législation française.* Paris: Auguste Durand, 1849.
11. *Düstur.* Dersaadet (Istanbul): Matbaa-yı Amire, 1295/1878, 1330/1912, 1333/1915. vol. 4, p. 310, no. 128. 6/6/1330.
12. Ibid, vol. 4, p. 735, no. 200. 16/9/1329.
13. It is also worth pointing out that "the people" were no less "guilty" than the individual was in Young Turk thought. As Hanioğlu notes, "le Bon's antipathy toward revolution, especially the French Revolution, became intrinsic to the Young Turk *Weltanschauung,* which viewed 'the people' as a 'foule' . . . In their private papers 'people' were labeled 'senseless.' The inability of a crowd to reach correct decisions was contrasted with the value of superior individuals, culminating in a condemnation of the people. Eventually people were judged guilty: 'to whom does the guilt belong? To the people! Because every nation is worthy of the government that administrates it.'" p. 206. It need not be pointed out that the notion of "superior individual" is far removed from the abstract civic notion of "the individual" in liberal thought.
14. *Düstur,* vol. 4, p. 114, no. 72. 24/4/1330.
15. In a regulation a few years later, which discusses procedure in Islamic law courts, there is a similar interest in getting not just the name, but the "identity" of various actors in a trial or suit—to their "true essence." *Düstur,* vol. 7, p. 230, no. 85. 1333.
16. Hanioğlu, p. 71.
17. Ibid, p. 208.
18. Ibid, p. 21.
19. Ibid, p. 201, 203.
20. Ibid, p. 203.
21. *Düstur,* vol. 5, p. 629, no. 258. 11/9/1331.
22. This is a completely different take on the crime than that which we see, for example, in mid nineteenth century Ottoman legislation, where kidnapping, marriage, and assault are all understood according to social class and the damage that might be done to the individual or the individual's family. Lütfi, 1851 code, chap. 2, art. 6: ". . . ve o misillulerden birisi kaçırdığı kızı kaza-yı aher mahkemesine götürür ise kefaet maddesi bilinemeyeceğinden hükkam efendiler tarafından akdi hususuna mesağ gösterilmeyerek mülkiye memuru tarafından bi'l-ihbar tutturulup mahalli mahkemesine götürtüle." (". . . And if one of these people takes a girl abducted by him to a court in another district, the judges should not permit a marriage since they may not know whether they are socially equal and the civil authorities ought to be asked to apprehend them and send them to their own local court.")

23. *Düstur,* vol. 7, p. 76, no. 9. 20/12/1332.
24. Ibid, vol. 7, p. 407, no. 110. 17/4/1333.
25. Ibid, vol. 7, p. 631, no. 262. 18/8/1333.
26. Ibid, vol. 4, p. 735, no. 200. 16/9/1329.
27. Ibid, vol. 7, p. 407, no. 110. 17/4/1333.
28. Ibid, vol. 3, p. 467, no. 156. 7/6/1329.
29. Ibid, vol. 4, p. 632, no. 246. 12/10/1330.
30. Ibid, vol. 4, p. 632, no. 246. 12/10/1330.
31. Although one could argue that the First World War created an extraordinary situation in the Ottoman Empire, the fact is that the Ottoman government had been "at war"—in the Balkan Wars of 1912–1913 or in various nationalist separatist wars from the 1870s onward—for a half century by this time. The militarization of law and society thus happened in a perfectly "ordinary" context, given historical circumstances.
32. See for example, İradeler—MV 294, 7 S 1257 from the Başbakanlık Archive, and Brown, pp. 258–281.
33. *Düstur,* vol. 3, pp. 19–20, no. 14. 22/12/1328.
34. Ibid, vol. 4, p. 632, no. 246. 12/10/1330.
35. Ibid, vol. 7, p. 407, no. 110. 17/4/1333.
36. Ibid, vol. 4, p. 628, no. 240. 3/10/1330.
37. Ibid, vol. 5, p. 62, no. 47. 4/3/1331.
38. See Douglas Hay, "Patronage, Paternalism, and Welfare," *International Labor and Working Class History* 53 (1997): 27–48; "Master and Servant in England and the Empire: A Comparative Study," *Labour* 31 (1993): 175–184; "War, Death, and Theft in the Eighteenth Century: The Record of the English Courts," *Past and Present* 95 (1982): 117–160.
39. *Düstur,* vol. 7, p. 631, no. 262. 18/8/1333.
40. See R. Porter, *The Greatest Benefit to Mankind: A Medical History of Humanity,* New York: Norton, 1998. pp. 397–427 and P. Weindling, "A Virulent Strain: German Bacteriology as Scientific Racism, 1890–1920," W. Ernst, B. Harris, ed. *Race, Science, and Medicine, 1700–1960,* London: Routledge, 1999. pp. 218–235.
41. If we track the careers of *ulema* who began working in regular courts before the Young Turk Revolution, and then retired after the Committee of Union and Progress (CUP) came to power, for example, we can indeed see that there is absolutely no slowing of their career advancement. Of five representative examples (out of more than 100): Mahmut Efendi began working in the Court of First Instance in 1895 in Diyar-i Bekir. After moving into the criminal section of this court in 1901, he was then promoted to membership and then the position of chief attorney in the Criminal Court of Appeals in 1908, following the accession of the Young Turks. Finally, three years later, in 1911 he took on a final position of chief public prosecutor in the same court (Albayrak, vol. 3, p. 15). Mehmet Ali Efendi likewise started out in the Selanik Central Court of First instance in 1902, and then in 1909 was appointed a member of the Selanik *Vilayet* (provincial) Court of Appeals (Albayrak, vol. 3, p. 91). Mehmet Bahaeddin Efendi, took the position of assistant to the public prosecutor in the Humus Court of First Instance in 1901. After holding the same position in a number of other courts at the same level, it was only in 1909 that he finally was appointed president of the Mersin Criminal

Court of First Instance (Albayrak, vol. 3, p. 124). Mehmet Bilâl Efendi acted as *naib* in a number of locals between 1901 and 1903, and it was only in 1908 that he became a member of the Edlip Court of First Instance (Albayrak, vol. 3, p. 133). And finally, Mehmet Münib Efendi, after acting as a *naib* with similar frequency between 1896 and 1908 finally, in 1914, was appointed a member of a provincial high court of appeals (Albayrak, vol. 3, p. 318).

42. In Albayrak, for example, vol. 1: Ahmed Hamdi Efendi—Adliye Dairesi Ceza Kalemi Memuru (1905), p. 148, Ahmet Pertev Efendi—Adliye Nezaret Sicili Memuru (1914), p. 200. vol. 2: İsmail Hakkı Efendi—Adliye Nezareti Umuri Hukukiye Memuru (1917), p. 268. vol. 3: Mahmut Aziz Efendi "Adliye ve Mezahib Nezaretine geçmiş," (1917), p. 19, Mehmet Emced Efendi, "Bağdat İstinaf Mahkemesi azası ol[duktan sonra] [1910] . . . Adliye'ye geçmiş," p. 152, Mehmet Hamdi Efendi—Adliye Nezareti Muhasebe Kalemi Katibliği Memuru (1917), p. 248.
43. Ibid, vol. 1, p. 201.
44. For example, every fifteen days, the school would conduct a mock court in which students would play the roles of defendant, plaintiff, prosecutor, secretary, and *kadı*. "ve onbeş günde bir defa, bir mes'eleyi muhakeme şeklinde, yani talebeden müdde'i ve müdde'i-i aleyh ve katib ve kadı ta'yin ederek temsil etdirip . . ." "Medresetül-Kuzat Ta'limat-ı Dahiliyesidir" art. 17.
45. "Medresetül-Kuzat Ta'limat-ı Dahiliyesidir," (1914) art. 17, 19. p. 685.
46. "Tanzim-i ilamat-ı hukukiyye ve cezaiyye muallimleri, usul ve kavaidi-i sakk-ı nizamiyyeyi beyan ve mesail-i kanuniyyeyi muhakeme şeklinde temsil ve derecat-ı mehakim itibarıyla bidayeten ve istinafen ve temyizen tanzim olunacak ilamat ve vesaik-i kanuniyyenin suret-i tanzimini ta'lim eyleyeceklerdir." Ibid, art. 20, p. 685.
47. *Düstur*, vol. 5, p. 352, no. 166. 19/5/1331.
48. Ibid, vol. 5, p. 629, no. 258. 11/9/1331.
49. Ibid, vol. 7, p. 300, no. 105. 15/4/1333.
50. See next chapter.
51. Alfredo Rocco, "Les postulats du régime fasciste dans la nouvelle législation pénale," *Centre international d'études sur le fascisme* 3 (1930). p. 10. "Le dogme de la liberté individuelle, véritable fétiche adopté jusque dans ses conséquences les plus exagérées, légitimait, sauf dans les limites citées plus haut, toute activité du citoyen, meme quand elle était contraire aux intérets les plus vitaux de l'Etat. . . . Le nouveau Code pénal pose comme principe que non seulement la sécurité de l'Etat—sa seule personnalité juridque stricto jure—doit faire l'objet d'une protection pénale, mais encore tout un vaste ensemble d'intérets politiques de nature diverse, tous d'une importance fondamentale, et dont l'Etat assume la charge comme condition de sa personnalité politique." "The dogma of individual liberty, a veritable fetish adopted in the most exaggerated way, legitimizes, except in the most extreme cases, all activities of the citizen, even when they are contrary to the most vital interests of the state. . . . The new penal Code poses as a principle not only that the security of the state—its sole juridical personality stricto jure—should be the object of penal protection but also a vast collection of political interests of a diverse nature, all off a fundamental importance, and of which the State assumes their charge as a condition of its political personality."

52. Ibid, p. 19. "Le régime fasciste ne conçoit pas la possibilité d'une incompatibilité entre le culte de la patrie el le culte divin. Il estime que le sentiment religieux, facteur essentiel de l'élévation morale de l'individu aussi bien que de la société, doit etre protégé, non seulement dans sa manifestation extérieure, c'est à dire dans l'exercice du culte, mais aussi dans sa source, dans la croyance religieuse elle-meme. . . . C'est ainsi que non seulement le droit individuel du libre exercice du culte se trouve protégé par la loi pénale, mais encore le sentiment religieux en soi, considéré comme d'intéret collectif." "The fascist regime does not concede the possibility of an incompatibility between the cult of the state and the divine cult. It asserts that religious sentiment, an essential factor in the moral elevation of the individual as well as society, should be protected, not only in its external manifestation, that is in the exercise of religion, but also in its source, in religious belief itself. . . . It is thus that not only the individual right to practice religion is protected by the penal law, but also religious sentiment itself, considered as a collective interest."
53. Raffaello Battino, *Les doctrines juridiques contemporaines en Italie.* Paris: A. Pedone, 1939. p. 141, 138.

NOTES TO CHAPTER EIGHT

1. See, for example, Woolfe, in Woolfe, ed. p. 43.
2. Among others, Stanley G. Payne, *Fascism: Comparison and Definition.* Madison: University of Wisconsin Press, 1980. p. 23.
3. Although the Italian fascists were anti-liberal and anti-socialist, they nonetheless adopted many aspects of both of these earlier philosophies into their ideology. (Alexander de Grand, *Italian Fascism.* Nebraska: University of Nebraska Press, 1982. p. x.) An argument has in fact been made that fascism in Italy occurred because liberalism had never completely taken hold, (For example, Roger Griffin, *The Nature of Fascism.* London: Routledge, 1991. p. 211.) making it more "non-liberal" than "anti-liberal" in its origins.
4. The importance of nationalism and a hierarchy of elites and masses—concepts very distant at least in theory from socialist ideology—was simultaneously at the heart of Italian fascism. (De Grand, p. x.)
5. At least one scholar has seen the emergence of "liberal" ideas in Italy at the time of unification not as a bourgeois revolution against internal conservative enemies, (Nolte, p. 194.) but rather as a "victory of critical liberalism." It was a critical liberal as opposed to liberal movement, he argues, primarily because of the suspicion directed at the individualistic ideals of the French Revolution and the foreign elements which had prevented Italian unification. It was not, to emphasize, a revolution against some sort of enemy within. (Ibid, p. 195.) A number of scholars have also pointed out that although the theory of a violently resurgent industrialized bourgeoisie—that is, liberalism gone awry—as the primary impetus to fascist movements is still alive and well, this theory does not take into account the rise of fascism in agrarian or primarily agrarian societies such as Finland, Romania, Austria or, for that matter, Italy. (Woolfe in Woolfe, ed. p. 6, Also see David Forgacs, ed., *Rethinking Italian Fascism: Capitalism, Populism and Culture.* London: Lawrence and Wishart, 1986. p. 3: Unlike Germany or Great Britain, Italy was a society in transition to modernity with one half of the working population still

employed in agriculture. In Eastern Europe, in fact, far from being seen as a revolutionary break from "normal" political functioning, fascism has been described as "an attempt to transform an already existing authoritarian regime into a fascist dictatorship from within." Woolfe in Woolfe, ed. p. 8.)

6. Although the liberal government in Italy run by Giolitti in the early twentieth century had to some extent replaced authoritarian political processes with parliamentary ones, some historians note that the corruption inherent to the self described liberal regime made actual liberalism impossible. Both the political opposition and the people of Italy had realized early on in the "liberal" era that the only true form of expression or political problem solving lay outside of the parliamentary process. (Paul Corner, "Liberalism, Pre-Fascism, Fascism," Forgacs, ed. p. 16, 19. also, Rocco in 1913 promoted "a new post-liberal order in Italy rooted in a philosophy of history which focused on the decline of state authority allegedly brought about by the diffusion of liberal and socialist principles in the wake of the French Revolution." The latter was seen as one cause of the corruption. Griffin, p. 58.) As a result, although liberal thought did to some extent influence post-unification Italian politics, the ideology had not, as one scholar notes, developed "deep functional roots." (Payne, p. 175, Griffin, p.221.) Nor had it seriously infiltrated the political environment of the day.
7. Mussolini himself saw fascism as a rejection of the liberal ideas of the French Revolution, (Ernst Nolte, *The Three Faces of Fascism.* Trans. Leila Vennewitz. New York: New American Library, 1963. p. 51.) despite the fact that he used the petite bourgeoisie—those who had supposedly benefited the most from the emergence of liberal ideology—as the foundation for his movement. (De Grand, p. x)
8. See below for further elaboration.
9. Griffin, p. 38. "Nationalism is practically the only common denominator of all previous accounts of fascism's definitional characteristics."
10. Payne, p. 14. Juan J. Linz in "Political Space and Fascism as a Late Comer: Conditions Conducive to the Success or Failure of Fascism as a Mass Movement in Inter-war Europe," Larsen, Hagtvet, and Myklebust, ed. *Who Were the Fascists: The Social Roots of European Fascism.* Bergen: Universitetsforlaget, 1980. p. 174. defines "proto-fascist" as a situation in which "the traditional legitimacy of crown, church, and the bureaucratic military state is increasingly questioned, but the new forms of democratic, liberal, legal, and rational legitimacy are far from being general accepted. Proto-fascist politics attempts a contradictory synthesis of tradition with modernity, attacking many of the values of the Establishment and at the same time rejecting its modern challenges." This situation, he argues, can also create a loyalty to the nation over the state.
11. Payne, p. 175.
12. For example, Alfredo Rocco. See also John F. Pollard, *The Vatican and Italian Fascism, 1929–1932.* Cambridge: Cambridge University Press, 1980. p. 40.
13. Nolte, p. 194. Germany also went through this process.
14. Both Mussolini and Rocco saw Catholicism as a possible aid in their national imperial aims (John Maloney, *Political Catholicism in Italy: Partito Popolare, 1919–1926.* London: Croom Helm, 1977. p. 91, Pollard, p. 39), and as at least one scholar has noted, Mussolini, unlike Hitler, was quite willing to use religion as a part of Italy's mythic past. (H.R. Trevor-Roper, "The Phenomenon of Fascism," Woolfe, ed.

p. 30). It might also be noted that religion, and Catholicism in particular, played a very important role in the myths created by East European fascist groups (In Linz p. 164 on Romania; Joseph Baglieri, "Italian Fascism and the Crisis of Liberal Hegemony: 1901–1922," Larsen, et. al., ed. p. 362; Yeshayahu Jelinek, "Clergy and Fascism: The Hlinka Party in Slovakia and the Croation Ustasha Movement," Larsen, et. al., ed. p. 374 on Slovakia.). Again, however, the complicated relationship between religion and state in the Italian fascist movement will be discussed in more detail later on.

15. Marco Revelli, "Italy," David Mühlberger, ed. *The Social Basis of European Fascist Movements*. London: Croom Helm, 1987. p. 8.
16. Woolfe, p. 43. This second phenomenon will be developed in more detail below.
17. Renzo de Felice, *Fascism: An Informal Introduction to its Theory and Practice*. New Brunswick: Transaction Books, 1976. p. 55.
18. Pollard, p. 1.
19. It ought to be emphasized once more that the Vatican and the Ottoman and Turkish religious establishments were not identical entities. Even before the dismantling of the *Meşihat*, the Vatican, as an internationally recognized, independent state capable of conducting its own foreign and financial policy, was far more powerful than any Ottoman *Şeyhülislam* had ever been. Moreover, the Ottoman *Şeyhülislam* to some extent shared his religious influence with the Sultan, who was also the Caliph. Although it might be argued that the earlier European concept of the divine right of kings also granted European monarchs a certain religious sway, it did not in any way equal that of the Sultan/Caliph in the Ottoman context. Consequently, while the head of the religious establishment in the Ottoman Empire may have been less powerful vis-à-vis the temporal leader, it can be argued that religion and politics in general were more intertwined. Bearing the above in mind, it also ought to be noted that the temporal power held by the Vatican, although still far greater than that held by any Ottoman or Turkish counterpart, was greatly circumscribed with the unification of the Italian state. Indeed, the new and uncomfortable relationship between unified Italy and the Vatican prompted Mussolini and many Italian fascists to see Catholicism and its temporal representatives as a useful tool in their political strategy.
20. An argument of course can be made that this sort of "separation" neither happened, nor was desired in any modern nation state, be it liberal, socialist, or fascist.
21. Pollard, p. 39.
22. Ibid, p. 41.
23. Ibid, p. 40.
24. Ibid, p. 191.
25. In October of that year he had said that "Catholicism could be used as one of our strongest national forces for the expression of our Italian identity in the world" (Maloney, p. 91), and in June he had noted that helping the church to build schools, hospitals, and churches would in turn help the Italian state. (Maloney, p. 106.)
26. Pollard, p. 71.
27. John Whittam, *Fascist Italy*. Manchester: Manchester University Press, 1995. p. 78.
28. This attitude on the part of pro-clerical fascists did not mean, of course, that nationalization was something the Vatican particularly wanted. And it is the tension

between Mussolini's stated goals and the independent activities of the Catholic church which can be blamed primarily for the eventual failure of Mussolini's Vatican policy. Again, it was to a large extent by means of an alliance with the Church and other conservative powers that the fascists consolidated their authority after 1922. (Pollard, p. 27. See also, Pollard, p. 28. "the ecclesiastical measures announced in November 1922 were the logical development of that change in Mussolini's religious policy which dates from 1920–1. . . . it is absurd to suggest that there was a substantial continuity between the religious policy of the Italian Governments, liberal and fascist.") This alliance, and the changes in the church/state relationship which arose from it, were eventually embodied in the *conciliazione* of 1929. In this document, Mussolini agreed to religious instruction in schools, Catholic influence over civil law and, most damaging to fascist aims, the relatively autonomous status of Catholic youth groups and associations. (Woolfe, p. 57; "Catholicism had been granted a privileged place in the life of the nation as the only organization outside of fascism permitted to exist." Stanisloa Pugliese, ed., *Italian Fascism and Anti-Fascism: A Critical Anthology.* Manchester: Manchester University Press, 2001. p. 12, Pollard, p. 11. Also note that in 1929 the Vatican persuaded Mussolini to remove 20 September—the fall of Papal Rome to Italian troops in 1870—from the Calendar of Italian national holidays. Pollard, p. 113.) Although this last "concession" brought quite a bit of discord into the Vatican's relationship with the fascist state in 1931, (Mussolini eventually did dissolve these groups. Pollard, p. 147.) it is worth noting that the accords did grow out of a far more classically fascist, if such a term can be used, attempt to define the religious establishment's relationship to the state than might be assumed.

Indeed, as early as 1925, Mussolini had brought together a commission of pro-clerical fascists to "reform Italy's ecclesiastical legislation." This committee eventually developed a proposal which implicitly emphasized the position of the fascist state as an actor capable of legally defining the church/state relationship, while it explicitly emphasized the continuation of state control over Church property. The Pope very wisely rejected this proposal "on the grounds that the Holy See could never accept a revision of Italian ecclesiastical legislation . . . if it was imposed by a unilateral act of the Italian Parliament." (Pollard, p. 38.) The Pope, that is, saw clearly the implications of a state commission drafting an ecclesiastical law. He would not allow the Vatican to be placed in such a relationship with the political power.

29. Levy, p. 169.
30. John F. Pollard, *The Vatican and Italian Fascism, 1929–1932.* Cambridge: Cambridge University Press, 1985. p. 40.
31. Ibid, p. 10.
32. Whittam, p. 59.
33. Alberto de Bernardi, ed. "Il Fascismo: Dizionario di storia, personaggi, cultura, economia, fonti e dibattito storiografico," Bruno Mondadori, 1998. p. 488. Between 1932 and 1935 Rocco held a position at the University of Rome.
34. Woolfe, p. 56.
35. Ibid, p. 56.
36. Ibid, p. 56.
37. Griffin, p. 58.

38. Pollard, p. 40.
39. Woolfe, p. 57.
40. Such as the positivist, Enrico Ferri.
41. Quoted in Silvio Trentin, *Les transformations récentes du droit public italien de la charte de Charles-Albert à la création de l'état fasciste.* Trans. J. Bonnecase. Paris: M. Girard, 1929. p. 111. "d'intégrer et de complêter les normes du Code pré-existent, non certes de les supprimer ou de les modifier radicalement."
42. Rocco, p. 10. "Le dogme de la liberté individuelle, véritable fétiche adopté jusque dans ses conséquences les plus exagérées, légitimait, sauf dans les limites citées plus haut, toute activité du citoyen, meme quand elle était contraire aux intérêts les plus vitaux de l'Etat. . . . Le nouveau Code pénal pose comme principe que non seulement la sécurité de l'Etat—sa seule personnalité juridique stricto jure—doit faire l'objet d'une protection pénale, mais encore tout un vaste ensemble d'intérêts politiques de nature diverse, tous d'une importance fondamentale, et dont l'Etat assume la charge comme condition de sa personnalité politique." "The dogma of individual liberty, a veritable fetish adopted in the most exaggerated way, legitimized, within the limits cited above, any activity of the citizen, even when it was contrary to the most vital interests of the state. . . . The new penal code poses as a principle that not only the security of the state—its sole juridical personality stricto jure—should be the object of penal protection but also a vast collection of political interests of a diverse nature, all of a fundamental importance, and of which the State assumes their charge as a condition of its political personality."
43. Rocco, p. 19. "Le régime fasciste ne conçoit pas la possibilité d'une incompatibilité entre le culte de la patrie el le culte divin. Il estime que le sentiment religieux, facteur essentiel de l'élévation morale de l'individu aussi bien que de la société, doit etre protégé , non seulement dans sa manifestation extérieure, c'est à dire dans l'exercice du culte, mais aussi dans sa source, dans la croyance religieuse elle-meme. . . . c'est ainsi que non seulement le droit individuel du libre exercice du cult se trouve protégé par la loi pénale, mais encore le sentiment religieux en soi, considéré comme d'intérêt collectif." "The fascist regime does not concede the possibility of an incompatibility between the cult of the state and the divine cult. It considers that religious sentiment is an essential factor in the moral elevation of the individual as much as society, should be protected, not only in its external manifestation, that is in the exercise of religion, but also in its source, in religious belief itself. . . . It is thus that not only the individual right to practice religion is protected by the penal law, but also religious sentiment in itself, considered as a collective interest."
44. Nolte, p. 28.
45. Pollard, p. 8. "Despite Mussolini's hopes, Kemal Ataturk's (sic) new, secular Turkish Republic did not disintegrate, thus preventing the realisation of the Italian dream of a colony in Asia Minor." There is debate about whether Italy seriously sought to occupy the Anatolian territory it had been promised during the First World War.
46. Nolte, p. 195.
47. For example, Albayrak, vol. 3, p. 115, Mehmed Atıf Efendi; vol. 5, pp. 368–9, Ömer Lütfi Efendi, vol. 2, pp. 169–172, İbrahim Efendi.
48. Eighty-five biographies, actually, but five contain no post-Republican information.

49. Approximately eight of the twenty two.
50. Out of the twenty-two, Mehmet Rıfat Efendi (Albayrak, vol. 4, pp. 53–54) became a Religious Ministry Economics Officer. Mehmet Safvet Efendi (Albayrak, vol. 4, p. 78) became a Religious Ministry Religious Institutions Inspector. Mustafa Fehmi Efendi (Albayrak, vol. 4, p. 198) became a Religious Affairs President. Mustafa Şükrü Efendi (Albayrak, vol. 4, p. 269) became an Istanbul Müftülük Affairs Officer. Mustafa Tevfik Efendi (Albayrak, vol. 4, pp. 272–3) became a Religious Affairs Committee member. Nasrullah Fahri Efendi (Albayrak, vol. 5, pp. 285–6) became a Religious Affairs President. Abdülkadir Efendi (Albayrak, vol. 1, pp. 73–4) became a Religious Foundations administrator. Ahmet Muhtar Efendi (Albayrak, vol. 1, pp. 183–4) became a Religious Affairs President. And Ahmet Rakım Efendi (Albayrak, vol. 1, p. 201) became a Religious Affairs President. A number of others entered the Ministry of Religion without clear titles.
51. Such as Malatya Lisesi (Albayrak, vol. 3, p. 9), Bolu İmam Hatip (Albayrak, vol. 4, pp. 92–3), Çeşme Barbaros Mektebi (Albayrak, vol. 4, p. 212), İstanbul Yüksek İslam Enstitüsü (Albayrak, vol. 5, p. 380), Giresun İmam Hatip (Albayrak, vol. 5, pp. 404–5), Beypazar Mektebi (Albayrak, vol. 1, p. 173), İzmir İmam Hatip Mektebi (Albayrak, vol. 1, pp. 54–5), and İstanbul Kız Lisesi (Albayrak, vol. 1, p. 160).
52. Ömer Ferid in Albayrak, vol. 5, pp. 334–5.
53. Süleyman Sırrı Efendi in Albayrak, vol. 5, p. 456.
54. Ebul'ala Ali Zeynelabidin in Albayrak, vol. 2, pp. 30–31.
55. And the closure of the department. He continued to publish until his death in 1954. Hüseyin Avni Efendi in Albayrak, vol. 2, p. 113.
56. İsmail Hakkı Efendi in Albayrak, vol. 2, p. 270.
57. Ibid, vol. 3, p. 19. A second example is Mehmet Besim Efendi who held various religious posts before becoming a member of the Mushaflar Tetkik Hey'eti (Quranic Research Committee) in 1930 and its president in 1932, where he remained until his death in 1940. vol. 3. p. 128.
58. Ibid, vol. 3, p. 137.
59. Ibid, vol. 3, p. 200.
60. Although "echo" is perhaps not the correct word. All of these speeches were made in 1927. That is, they followed the original adoption of the 1889 code, and not the transformation of the law throughout the 1930s. Indeed, the statements of these members of parliament, "echoing" the statements of Rocco introducing his own law, were made prior even to the promulgation of Rocco's 1930 code—the text which eventually prompted the transformation of the 1926 Turkish law into its 1938 version. The fact, however, that the speeches pre-date the Turkish adoption of the fascist law, and even the drafting of the Italian version of this law merely demonstrates further that the ideas and ideologies set forth in them were without a doubt those which had arisen locally, as result of historical circumstance. They were not simply a repetition of the Italian rhetoric, but the culmination of years of Ottoman and early Republican legal development
61. Kazım Paşa in Kazım Öztürk, ed., *Türk Parlamento Tarihi: 1923–1927.* (TPT) Ankara: TBMM Vakfı Yayınları, 1993. vol. 1, p. 526
62. Ibid, vol. 1, p. 524.
63. Ibid, vol. 1, p. 527.

64. Ceza kanunumuz çok serttir. Çünkü inkılap çok kıskançtır. Ama hem sert ve hem ilmî. Bundan korkacak olanlar ve korkması lazım gelenler Türk milletinin menfa'atlarına, Türk milletinin hukukuna ve inkılabına karşı tekin olmayanlardır ve bunların korkması lazımdır." Ibid, vol. 1, p. 528
65. "milletin ne emniyeti vardı ne de masuniyeti vardı" Ibid, vol. 1, p. 529.
66. Ibid, vol. 1, p. 528.
67. Ibid, vol. 1, p. 528.
68. Ibid, vol. 1, p. 312.
69. That is, Mehmet Emin had graduated from the Ottoman Law School and then become the Kastamonu appeals court public prosecutor. After that, he rose to first instance court president. He was also a functionary in the cassation court and was a justice inspector throughout the late Ottoman period. Mehmet İhsan graduated from a military school and then took up various administrative posts in Zonguldak and Trabzon. Kazım Hüsnü went to the Law School and then became involved with the press in Konya. Mehmet Semih graduated from the Law School, became a public prosecutor, the director of the Istanbul police school, a governor, and finally a lawyer in the Republican era. Mehmet Nazmi graduated from a *rüştiye* elementary school, and then took up various Ottoman administrative posts. Fahrettin Erdoğan (I have been unable to confirm beyond a doubt this committee member's identity) went to a *rüştiye* elementary school, became a merchant, was influenced by Ottomanist ideas, and eventually became active against Sultan Abdülhamid II. He then became a leader of the *İslam Cemiyeti*, and attempted to spread Turkish nationalist ideas in the Caucasus. It might also be noted that he "fought against" the Armenians. Ali Rıza graduated from the Law School and became a member of the Selanik appeals court. He then held various other posts in the Ottoman court hierarchy as both a judge and a functionary. Finally Yusuf Kemal was a member of many Justice Ministry commissions before becoming a professor at the Republican Law School in Ankara. Mecdi is unaccounted for. (TPT)
70. Frederick T. Merrill, "12 Years of the Turkish Republic," *Foreign Policy Reports* 11, no. 16 (1935). pp. 190–2.

NOTES TO CHAPTER NINE

1. A less simple reason for the opposition might be found in the behavior of the Democrat Party in Turkey throughout the 1950s. In general, the Democrats attempted to institute authoritarian practices in both Turkish politics and law, as a means of consolidating their power against the Republican People's Party. As Ahmad points out, however, "Menderes's tightening of an already draconian penal code, his measures against the press, the confiscation of the opposition's assets, and attacks on university autonomy, all suggested that he had abandoned his promises of making Turkey more free and democratic." Ahmad, pp. 111–112.
2. Dönmezer, p. 19.
3. See, for example, Zürcher, who writes, although advancing a number of qualifications:

   "... Fascist Italy was certainly important to the Turkish leadership. The way in which Mussolini seemed to forge national unity and to energize

Italian society impressed many in Turkey. ... and a number of new laws promulgated under the Republic were straight copies of Italian legislation." p. 193. He also writes that in 1927 the Turks adopted the "penal code from Mussolini's Italy." p. 181

4. See, for example, Şensoy, p. 183, Gölcüklü in Tuğrul Ansay and Don Wallace, Jr., ed. *Introduction to Turkish Law.* Boston: Kluwer Law and Taxation, 1987. p. 175, and others. Although it ought to be noted as well that Dönmezer, p. 21, mentions the adoption of one chapter of the 1930 Italian code into the new Republican one.
5. In "Code pénal," 1927. P. viii. "Le régime républicain turc est le résultat des systèmes établis par la révolution turque; il est basé sur les principes les plus démocratiques et les plus laïcs. Il est indubitable qu'il ne saurait s'accommoder des codifications pénales de l'ère de l'absolutisme et du sultanat, qui n'avaient aucun rapport avec ces principes, auxquels ils étaient même diamétralement opposés. Car les lois sont forcément l'expression des ères, des temps et des régimes qui leur ont donné naissance."
6. Gölcüklü in Ansay, p. 175.
7. Four of these nine chapters were changed completely: These four chapters were Crimes against the Nation, Counterfeiting Seals and Stamps, Abduction/Seduction, and Abortion. All of these, in the Italian code, fall under "Crimes again the Nation/State" or "Crimes against the Race."
8. In the original 1889/1927 code, the section on attempted crime contains three articles, each describing different degrees of intent, and what the penalties for each degree might be—between three and ten years in prison overall. The same section of the 1930 Italian code contains only one article, is not overly interested in degrees of intent, and prescribes much longer sentences—between twelve and thirty years—if the attempt can be proved. The 1939 version of the Turkish law removes one article concerning degree of intent, bringing it closer to the 1930 law, and then also raises the severity of the punishment almost to the same text's level—between ten and twenty years of imprisonment depending upon the circumstances. More to the point, in a section on the concurrence of offenses committed by a single individual, of thirteen articles, eleven, or 84.6% were changed between 1936 and 1938. The sentences all became more severe.
9. "Code pénal," 1927. Art. 68. (This article, incidentally, is not from the 1889 code, but from the French.) Specifically, if an individual is convicted of more than one crime for which the penalty is imprisonment for more than five years, and of which one of the penalties is for perpetual imprisonment, cellular isolation is augmented by 1 to 3 years, and can be raised to 5 if there is more than one penalty requiring a life sentence of hard labor.
10. "Code pénal," 1939. Art. 68. Recall also that the 1889 code did not contain any capital crimes. Specifically, cellular isolation is extended by one tenth of the total penalties if there is a crime requiring a penalty of hard labor, and one twelfth of the total if the crime requires simple imprisonment. The article then continues that isolation should not last for more than two years in case of hard labor, and not more than one year and six months in case of simple imprisonment. It then finishes with the stipulation that if two of the crimes require life sentences of hard labor, the penalty is death.

11. Italy, *Penal Code of the Kingdom of Italy, as Approved by Royal Decree of October 19, 1930.* London: HM Stationery Office, 1931. Art. 72.
12. See, for example, art. 69, 73, and the chapter on recidivism. Ibid.
13. Including provisions on such issues as: acting against the territorial integrity of the state (meriting a death sentence, and therefore clearly an early change from the 1889 code which did not sanction the death penalty for any crime), serving in the army of an enemy state, bearing arms against the state, delivering land, weapons, or information to the enemy in time of war, espionage, disobeying orders having to do with state security during time of war, profiteering, exchanging information with a state with the intent of fomenting war, revealing political secrets, obtaining political secrets, political functionaries who converse about their duties, journals which reveal political or military secrets, revealing military installations, treason by political functionaries, endangering the neutrality of the state, accepting honors from an enemy state, and insulting the Turkish flag.
14. "Code pénal turc," 1927, art. 125–145.
15. Including provisions on such issues as: acting against the territorial integrity of the state, bearing arms against the state, intelligence with the intent of fomenting war against the state, hostile acts against a foreign state with the intent of fomenting war, endangering the state's neutrality, corruption of a national by a foreigner, favoring the enemy in war time, providing the enemy with supplies, participation in loans in favor of the enemy, trading with the enemy, failure to execute contracts for supplies in time of war, profiteering, sabotage of military works, tampering with documents concerning the security of the state, obtaining political secrets, espionage, clandestine penetration into military places, revelation of state secrets, utilization of state secrets, unfaithfulness in state affairs, political defeatism, instigation of soldiers to disobey laws, economic defeatism, anti-national activity of a national abroad, subversive associations, unlawful constitution of associations, and accepting honors from an enemy state.
16. For a complete list of these articles, see previous footnotes.
17. The most obvious differences between the two codes is thus the severity of their sentences and in the existence of far more crimes against the psychology and honor of the state in the latter than in the former. The new crimes include such issues as unfaithfulness in state affairs, political and economic defeatism, and anti-national activity of a national abroad. (In the Italian law, crimes against the flag constitute a separate section.)
18. Although they are not quite as obvious in their borrowing as the above. When examining the specific changes made to articles in chapters such as that on crimes against state powers, however, the same pattern does hold. Of the nine articles (or 50%) of this chapter which changed, for example, three were superficially altered from their original form, one contained excerpts from both the 1927 Turkish and 1930 Italian texts, and four were lifted straight out of the 1930 Italian text. Specifically, the one article which incorporated elements of both the 1927 Turkish and 1930 Italian philosophies was that which addressed the encouragement or incitement of a population to civil war.
19. In the 1930 Italian text, the punishment is life imprisonment, so one might see "not less than twenty years" as something of a compromise between the two. At the same time, all three versions of the code advocate the death penalty for those

who direct an insurrection, and so the source of that particular element cannot be clear. ("Code pénal turc," 1927, 1939. Art. 149. "Penal Code of the Kingdom of Italy," 1930. Art. 284.)

20. The Italian fascist laws on political defeatism, instigation of soldiers to disobey, economic defeatism, (from the section on "The International Personality of the State") vilification of constitutional institutions, and vilification of the Italian nation (from the section on "The Internal Personality of the State")—including all of the general measures designed to prevent and punish them—were reproduced almost completely in the Turkish text.
21. "Code pénal turc," 1927, 1939. Art. 168.
22. "Code pénal turc," 1939, art. 168. "Penal Code of the Kingdom of Italy," 1930 art. 310, 313.
23. "Code pénal turc," 1927, art. 327–338.
24. "Code pénal turc," 1939. "Penal Code of the Kingdom of Italy," 1930. Articles of the latter which correspond to the former are: Art. 316: Art. 453—identical, Art. 317: Art. 454—Identical except that the Turkish article raises the punishment from 1–5 years to 3–5 years, Art. 318: Art. 455—Identical, Art. 319: Art. 456—Identical except that the Turkish specifies an extension of the sentence and the Italian does not, Art. 320: Art. 457—Identical, Art. 322: Art. 459—Identical except that the Turkish sentence is reduced by one half, not one third, Art. 323: Art. 460—Identical except that the Turkish sentence is 2–5 years and the Italian is 2–6 years, Art. 324: Art. 461—Identical, Art. 325: Art. 462—Identical.
25. In the 1927 law, the article reads "in case of marriage with the abducted girl or woman, the public action or execution of the pronounced condemnations will differ, upon his own withdrawal of the victim, if she is 18 years of age, with the consent of her guardian, and if she is not 18 years of age, with the authorization of the judge, if she does not have that of her guardian." "Code pénal turc," art. 434. In effect, therefore, there is no punishment here, whereas in the 1938 version, there is a diminished sentence. An argument also could be made that the 1938 code is actually closer to the 1930 code, in that the punishment in the latter for abduction with the intent to marry is, in fact, one third to one half of that for abduction with the purpose of rape. But the fact that the two are separated in the 1930 code implies that the first includes only abduction and not rape with the purpose of marriage. (Art. 522–523.) Contrarily, the 1938 code, by merging the two articles together and then including an additional article at the end which clarifies the marriage issue, suggests that both abduction and rape are mitigated by a marriage proposal following the attack. Finally, it ought to be emphasized once again that these articles are not word for word translations of their 1930 Italian counterparts, as has been the case up until now, they merely appear to be inspired by the 1930 philosophy.
26. Including the sections on crimes against respect due to the dead, simulation of an offense, and a similar, but definitely not identical section on forming associations with the intent to commit crimes.
27. The one missing bit is art. 554, on negligent or deliberate infection with syphilis or blennorhagia.
28. See below for an elaboration.
29. Alfredo Rocco, "Les postulats du régime fasciste dans la nouvelle législation pénale," *Centre international d'études sur le fascisme* 3 (1930). p. 9.

NOTES TO CONCLUSION

1. Gary Morson, "The Pun of Creativity," in Fyodor Dostoevsky, *Notes from Underground*, Michael R. Katz, trans. New York: W.W. Norton, 2001. p. 196.
2. Ibid, p. 196.
3. Fyodor Dostoyevsky (sic), *Crime and Punishment*, David McDuff, Trans. London: Penguin Books, 2003. p. 632.
4. Ibid, p. 656.

Bibliography

UNPUBLISHED WORKS

Başbakanlık Arşivi (Istanbul)
1. İrade Tasnifi
Adliye ve Mezahıb
Dahiliye
Divan-ı Ahkam-ı Adliye
Meclis-i Mahsus
Meclis-i Vâlâ
Şura-yı Devlet
2. Meclis-i Vükela Mazbataları

PUBLISHED WORKS

Abderrahman, D. "Turquie," *Revue de Droit International et de Droit Comparé* 73, no. 3 (1996): 249–268.

Ahmad, Feroz. *The Making of Modern Turkey*. London: Routledge, 1993.

Ahmed Lütfi, *Mir'at-ı Adalet, yahud Tarihçe-i Adliye-yi Devlet-i Aliyye*. Istanbul: Kitapçı Ohannes. 1304 (1888).

Akarlı, E.D. "Judiciary Organization in Ottoman Lebanon as a Mechanism of Social Consolidation," *Revue d'Histoire Maghrebine* 10 (1983): 59–72.

Akgündüz, Ahmet. *Osmanlı Kanunnâmeleri ve Hukukî Tahlilleri*. Istanbul: Hilâl Matbaası, 1990.

Aklan, Mustafa. *Yeni Türk Ceza Kanunu Şerhi*. Eskişehir: Istikamet Matbaası, 1926–1928.

Akyüz, Yahya. "Tanzimat Döneminde Eğitim Biliminde ve Öğretim Yöntemlerinde Gelişmeler," *Tanzimat'ın 150. Yıl Dönümü Uluslararası Sempozyumu*. Ankara: Türk Tarih Kurumu Yayınları, 1994.

Albayrak, Sadık. *Meşrutiyetten Cumhuriyete Meşihat, Şeriat, Tarikat Kavgası*. Istanbul: Mizan Yayınevi, 1994.

——— *Son Devir Osmanlı Uleması*. Istanbul: Medrese Yayınevi, 1980.

Aleksik, D. "Le tanzimat comme intention de transformer l'empire ottoman en un état de droit," *Tanzimat'ın 150. Yıl Dönümü Uluslarası Sempozyumu*. Ankara: Türk Tarih Kurumu Yayınları, 1994: 287–293.

Ali, Hamid. "Muslim Law and Modern Turkey," *Islamic Culture* 12 (1938): 119–121.

Anderson, J.N.D. "Movement Toward Codification in Turkey," *Indian Yearbook of International Affairs* (1958): 125–42.

Andrew, Donna T. "Debate: The Secularization of Suicide in England 1660–1800," *Past and Present* 119 (1988): 158–165.

Ansay, Tuğrul, Wallace, Don Jr. *Introduction to Turkish Law.* Boston: Kluwer Law and Taxation, 1987.

Aristarchi, Gregoire. *Législation ottomane, ou, recueil des lois, règlements, ordonnances, traites, capitulations et autres documents officiels de l'empire ottoman.* Constantinople: Frères Nicolaides, 1873–88.

Atay, Falih Rıfkı. *Çankaya.* Istanbul: Dünya Yayınları, 1969.

Ayiter, Ferit. "Interpretation of a National System of Laws Received from Abroad," *AFDI* 5 (1956): 41–3.

Baer, Gabriel. *Studies in the Social History of Modern Egypt.* Chicago: University of Chicago Press, 1969.

——— "The Transition from Traditional to Western Criminal Law in Turkey and Egypt," *Studia Islamica,* 45 (1977): 139–158.

Baglieri, Joseph. "Italian Fascism and the Crisis of Liberal Hegemony: 1901–1922," Larsen, Hagtvet, and Myklebust, ed. *Who Were the Fascists: The Social Roots of European Fascism.* Bergen: Universitetsforlaget, 1980.

Bailey, Frank. *British Policy and the Turkish Reform Movement.* Cambridge: Harvard University Press, 1942

Basman, C.F. "Les infractions pénales, leur répression, leur réparation," Levy-Ullman, ed. *La vie juridique des peuples: Turquie.* Paris: Librairie Delgrave, 1939.

Battino, Raffaello. *Les doctrines juridiques contemporaines en Italie.* Paris: A. Pedone, 1939.

Baykara, Tuncer, ed. *İzmir ve Batı Anadolu.* İzmir: Akademi Kitabevi, 1994.

Bayraktar, Koksal. "L'influence du droit français," *AFDI* 42 (1979): 317–22.

Belgesay, M. R. *Ceza Kanunu.* Istanbul: Yeni Şark Kütüphanesi, 1927.

——— "La reception des lois étrangères en Turquie," *AFDI* 7 (1958): 91–98.

Bernardi, Alberto, ed. *Il Fascismo: Dizionario di Storia, Personaggi, Cultura, Economia, Fonti, e Dibattito Storiografico.* Rome: Bruno Mondadori, 1998.

Bertram, A. "The Legal System of Turkey," *Law Quarterly Review* 25 (1909): 24–43.

Bingöl, İrfan. *Ülkemizde Anayasa Hareketleri.* Ankara: Atak Ofset, 1993

Bozkurt, Gülnihal. "Tanzimat and Law," *Tanzimat'ın 150. Yıl Dönümü Uluslararası Sempozyumu.* Ankara: Türk Tarih Kurumu Yayınları, 1994: 279–286.

——— *Batı Hukukunun Türkiye'de Benimsenmesi: Osmanlı Devleti'nden Türkiye Cumhuriyeti'ne Resepsiyon Süreci, 1839–1939.* Ankara: Türk Tarih Kurumu Basımevi, 1996.

Boyce, D. George. "From Assaye to the Assaye: Reflections on the British Government, Force, and Moral Authority in India," *Journal of Military History* 63 (1999): 643–668.

Brett, Michael. "Legislating for Inequality in Algeria: The Senatus-Consulte of 14 July 1865," *Bulletin of the School of Oriental and African Studies,* 51 (1988): 440–461.

Brown, Desmond. "Abortive Attempts to Codify English Criminal Law," *Parliamentary History* 11 (1992): 1–39. pp. 2–4.

Brown, Nathan. "Brigands and Statebuilding: The Invention of Banditry in Egypt," *Comparative Studies in Society and History* 32 (1990): 258–281.

——— "Shari'a and State in the Modern Middle East," *International Journal of Middle East Studies* 29 (1992): 359–376.

Calisse, Carlo. *A History of Italian Law.* Trans. Layton B. Register. London: J. Murray, 1928.
Cappelletti, Mauro. *The Italian Legal System: An Introduction.* Stanford: Stanford University Press, 1967.
Chasiotes, Ioannes. *Landmarks and Principal Phases in the History of Modern and Contemporary Macedonia.* Thessaloniki: Parateretes, 1992.
[Çığıraçan], İbrahim Hilmi, *Memalik-i Osmaniye Cep Atlası.* Istanbul: Mahmut Bey Matbaası, 1323 (1905).
Collin, Fernand. *Enrico Ferri et l'avant-projet du code pénal italien de 1921.* Bruxelles: Vue. F. Larcier, 1925.
Corner, Paul. "Liberalism, Pre-Fascism, Fascism," David Forgacs, ed. *Rethinking Italian Fascism: Capitalism, Populism and Culture.* London: Lawrence and Wishart, 1986.
Davison, Roderic. *Essays in Ottoman and Turkish History, 1774–1923.* Austin: University of Texas Press, 1990.
Dayınlarlı, Kemal. *Les motifs d'infirmation des sentences arbitrales en droit turc.* Ankara: Afaroğlu Matbaası, 1986.
De Grand, Alexander. *Italian Fascism.* Nebraska: University of Nebraska Press, 1982.
Deny, Jean. *Petit manuel de la turquie nouvelle.* Paris: J. Haumont et cie, 1934.
Deringil, Selim. "Legalism and Political Legitimization in the Ottoman Empire," *New Perspectives on Turkey* 3 (1989): 93–96.
Devereaux, R. "Turkey's Judicial Security Mechanism," *Die Welt des Islams* 10 (1965): 33–40.
Donovan, James. "Magistrates and Juries in France, 1791–1952," *French Historical Studies* 22 (1999): 379–420.
Dostoevsky, Fyodor. *The Brothers Karamazov,* trans. Constance Garnett. New York: W.W. Norton, 1976.
——— *Crime and Punishment,* trans. David McDuff. London: Penguin, 2003.
——— *Notes from Underground,* trans. Michael R. Katz. New York: W.W. Norton, 2001.
Dougherty, Patricia M. "The Rise and Fall of L'ami de la religion: History, Purpose and Readership of a French Catholic Newspaper," *Catholic Historical Review* 77 (1991): 21–41.
Douwes, D. and Lewis, N. "The Trials of Syrian Ismailis in the First Decade of the Twentieth Century," *International Journal of Middle East Studies* 21 (1989): 215–232
Dönmezer, Sulhi. "Le cinquantenaire du code pénal turc," *AFDI* 24 (1976–7): 15–36.
——— *Ceza Hukuku, Hususî Kısım: Şahıslara Karşı ve Mal Aleyhinde Cürümler.* Istanbul: Istanbul Üniversitesi, Hukuk Fakültesi, 1965.
Dürey, Süheyl. "La protection des droits de l'homme dans la procédure pénal turque," *AFDI* 25 (1978): 215–234.
Eisenman, R. "The Young Turk Legislation," David Kushner, ed. *Palestine in the Late Ottoman Period.* Leiden: E.J. Brill, 1986: 59–73.
Ekrem Cemal. *Ceza Usulümüzün Esasları ve İtirazlar Üzerinde Tetkikler.* Istanbul: Burhaneddin Matbaası, 1933.
Engelhardt, E. *La Turquie et le tanzimat.* Paris: A. Cotillon et cie, 1882–4.
Ergil, D. "Secularization of Islamic Law and Institutions in Turkey," *Studies in Islam* 15 (1978): 71–142
Erman, S. "La Personalità dell'omicida," *AFDI* 3 (1954): 389–404.
Fahreddin. *Memnu Fiillerin ve Cezaların İctimaı.* Istanbul: Yeni Matbaa, 1926.

——— *Yeni Ceza Tatbikatında Rehber.* Istanbul: Yeni Matbaa, 1926.
Farmer, Lindsay. "Reconstructing the English Codification Debate," *Law and History Review* 18 (2000): 397–444.
Felice, Renzo. *Fascism: An Informal Introduction to its Theory and Practice.* New Brunswick: Transaction Books, 1976.
Ferri, Enrico. *Sociologie criminelle.* Paris: A. Rousseau, 1893.
——— *The Positivist School of Criminology: Three Lectures.* Stanely E. Grupp, ed. Pittsburgh: University of Pittsburgh Press, 1968.
Fındikoğlu, Z.F. "A Turkish Sociologist's View," *International Social Science Bulletin* 9 (1957): 65–69, 13–20.
——— "Special Aspects of the Turkish Reception of law," *AFDI* 5 (1956): 155–165.
Findley, Carter. "Mahkama," *Encyclopedia of Islam.* vol. 5. Leiden: E.J. Brill, 1986. p. 7.
Fischer-Galati, Stephen. "Italy," Larsen, Hagtvet, and Myklebust, ed. *Who Were the Fascists: The Social Roots of European Fascism.* Bergen: Universitetsforlaget, 1980.
Ford, Guy Stanton. *Dictatorship in the Modern World.* Minneapolis: The University of Minnesota Press, 1939.
Forgacs, David, ed. *Rethinking Italian Fascism: Capitalism, Populism and Culture.* London: Lawrence and Wishart, 1986.
Fortna, Benjamin. *Imperial Classroom: Islam, The State and Education in the Late Ottoman Empire.* New York: Oxford University Press, 2002
Foucault, Michel. *Discipline and Punish: The Birth of the Prison.* New York: Vintage Books, 1977.
France, "Code pénal napoléon," Napoléon Bacqua de Labarthe, ed. *Codes de la législation française.* Paris: Auguste Durand, 1849.
Freitag, Sandria B. "Crime in the Social Order of Colonial North India," *Modern Asian Studies* 25 (1991): 227–261.
Gerber, Haim. *State, Society, and Law in Islam : Ottoman Law in Comparative Perspective.* Albany: State University of New York Press, 1994.
Ghauth, Muhammad. "Torts due to Negligence: Burden of Proof," *Islamic Culture* 32 (1958): 153–163.
Ginio, Eyal. "The Administration of Criminal Justice in Ottoman Selanik (Salonica) During the 18th Century," *Turcica* 30 (1998): 185–209.
Gökbilen, M.T. "Tanzimat Hareketinin Osmanlı Müesseselerine ve Teşkilatına Etkileri," *Tarihi Muhakeme,* 1 (1919).
Goldstein, J. *Criminal Law: Theory and Process.* New York: New York Free Press, 1974.
Gregor, James A. *Interpretations of Fascism.* Morristown, NJ: General Learning Press, 1974.
——— *Italian Fascism and Developmental Dictatorship.* Princeton: Princeton University Press, 1979.
Griffin, Roger. *The Nature of Fascism.* London: Routeledge, 1991.
Gross, Hyman. *Theory of Criminal Justice.* New York: Oxford University Press, 1979.
Grupp, Stanley, ed. *Theories of Punishment.* Bloomington: Indiana University Press, 1972.
Güran, Tevfik, ed. *Osmanlı Devleti'nin İlk İstatistik Yıllığı, 1897.* Ankara: Devlet İstatistik Enstitüsü Matbaası, 1997
Hallaq, Wael B. "Was the Gate of Ijtihad Closed?" *International Journal of Middle East Studies* 16 (1984): 3–41.

Hanioğlu, M. Şükrü. *The Young Turks in Opposition.* New York: Oxford University Press, 1995.

Hay, Douglas. "Patronage, Paternalism, and Welfare," *International Labor and Working Class History* 53 (1997): 27–48.

——— "Master and Servant in England and the Empire: A Comparative Study," *Labour* 31 (1993): 175–184.

——— "War, Death, and Theft in the Eighteenth Century: The Record of the English Courts," *Past and Present* 95 (1982): 117–160.

Heidborn, A. *Manuel de droit public et administratif de l'empire ottoman.* Vienna: C.W. Stern, 1908.

Heyd, U. "Kanun and Sharia in Old Ottoman Criminal Justice," *Proceedings of the Israel Academy* 3 (1969): 1–18.

——— "Islam in Modern Turkey," *Royal Central Asia Society Journal* 34 (1947): 299–308.

——— "The Ottoman Ulema and Westernization in the Time of Selim III and Mahmud II," *Scripta Hierosolymitana* 9 (1961): 63–96.

——— *Studies in Old Ottoman Criminal Law.* V. L. Menage. ed. Oxford: Clarendon Press, 1973.

Holger Maehle, Andreas. "Assault and Battery or Legitimate Treatment," *Gesnerus* 57 (200): 206–221.

Hurewitz, J.C. *The Middle East and North Africa in World Politics: A Documentary Record.* New Haven: Yale University Press, 1975.

Imber, Colin. *Studies in Ottoman History and Law.* Istanbul: The Isis Press, 1996.

İnalcık, H. "Application of the Tanzimat and its Social Effects," *Archivum Ottomanicum* 5 (1973): 97–128.

——— "Comments on 'Sultanism' in Max Weber's Typification of the Ottoman Polity," *Princeton Papers in Near Eastern Studies* 1 (1992): 49–72.

İslam Ansiklopedesi. Ankara: Türkiye Diyanet Vakfı, 1988.

Italy, *Penal Code of the Kingdom of Italy, as Approved by Royal Decree of October 19, 1930.* London: HM Stationery Office, 1931.

Kofos, Evangelos. *National Heritage and Identity in Nineteenth and Twentieth Century Macedonia.* Athens: Hellenic Foundation for Defense and Foreign Policy, 1991

Jelinek, Yeshayahu. "Clergy and Fascism: The Hlınka Party in Slovakia and the Croatian Ustasha Movement," Larsen, Hagtvet, and Myklebust, ed. *Who Were the Fascists: The Social Roots of European Fascism.* Bergen: Universitetsforlaget, 1980.

John, Michael. "The Peculiarities of the German State: Bourgeois Law and Society in the Imperial Era," *Past and Present* 119 (1988): 105–131.

Kahraman, S.A., Galitekin, A.N, Dadaş, C., ed. *İlmiyye Salnamesi.* Istanbul: İşaret Yayınları, 1998.

Kallis, Aristotle A. *Fascist Ideology: Territory and Expansionism in Italy and Germany, 1922–1945.* London: Routeledge, 2000.

Karpat, Kemal. *Ottoman Population, 1830–1914.* Madison: University of Wisconsin Press, 1985.

Kaynar, Reşat. *Mustafa Reşit Paşa ve Tanzimat.* Ankara: Türk Tarih Kurumu Basımevi, 1954.

"The Legal Situation in Turkey," *Review, International Commission of Jurists* 26 (1981): 24–40.

Lord Kinross, *Ataturk: A Biography of Mustafa Kemal, Father of Modern Turkey.* New York: William Morrow and Company, 1965.

Knox, MacGregor. *Common Destiny: Dictatorship, Foreign Policy, and War in Fascist Italy and Nazi Germany.* Cambridge: Cambridge University Press, 2000.

Kortepeter, C.M. "Another Look at the Tanzimat," *The Muslim World* 4, no. 1 (1964): 49–55.

Kunter, N. "Les facteurs sociaux de la criminalité en Turquie," *AFDI* 1 (1951): 43–71.

Kushner, David. "Career Paths," *Tanzimat'ın 150. Yıl Dönümü Uluslararası Sempozuyumu.* Ankara: Türk Tarih Kurumu Yayınları, 1994.

Lafon, Jacques, Öktem, Niyazi, ed. *Tendences actuelles du droit turc et du droit français.* Istanbul: Institute français d'études anatoliennes d'Istanbul, Isis, 1988.

Landau, Jacob. *Pan Turkism in Turkey: A Study in Irredentism.* Hamden CT: Archon Books, 1981.

Larsen, Stein U., Hagtvet, Bernt, and Myklebust, Jan P., ed. *Who Were the Fascists: The Social Roots of European Fascism.* Bergen: Universitetsforlaget, 1980.

Ledeen, Michael A. *Universal Fascism: The Theory and Practice of the Fascist International, 1928–1936.* New York: Howard Fertig, 1972.

Lee, Keekok. *The Positivist Science of Law.* Brookfield, VT: Avebury, 1989.

Levonian, Lutfy. *The Turkish Press, 1932–1936.* Athens: School of Religion, 1937.

——— *The Turkish Press: Selections from the Turkish Press Showing Events and Opinions, 1925–1932.* Athens: School of Religion, 1932.

Levy, Carl. "From Fascism to Post Fascism," Richard Bessel, ed. *Fascist Italy and Nazi Germany: Comparisons and Contrasts.* Cambridge: Cambridge University Press, 1996.

Lewis, Bernard. "Efendi," *Encyclopedia of Islam.* vol. 2. Leiden: E.J. Brill, 1986. p. 687.

——— *The Emergence of Modern Turkey.* London: Oxford University Press, 1968.

Linz, Juan J. "Political Space and Fascism as a Late Comer: Conditions Conducive to the Success or Failure of Fascism as a Mass Movement in Inter-war Europe," Larsen, Hagtvet, and Myklebust, ed. *Who Were the Fascists: The Social Roots of European Fascism.* Bergen: Universitetsforlaget, 1980.

Logoreci, Anton. *The Albanians.* Boulder: Westview Press, 1977

Lowestein, Karl. "Controle législatif de l'etrémisme politique dans les démocraties européennes," *Revue du Droit Public et de la Science Politique en France et à l'Étranger* 55 (1938): 702–757.

MacCallum, Elizabeth P. "The Near East in 1928," *Foreign Policy Reports* 8 (1928).

Magnarella, P.J. "East Meets West: The Reception of West European Law," *Journal of International Law and Practice* 2, no. 2 (1993): 281–306.

Maloney, John. *Political Catholicism in Italy: Partito Popolare, 1919–1926.* London: Croom Helm, 1977.

Mansurnour, L.A. "Shawkani and the Closed Door of Ijtihad: Did Shawkani Possess the Key to the Reopening of the Closed Door of Ijtihad?" *Hamdard Islamicus* 11 (1988): 57–65.

Manzini, Vincenzo. *Trattato di Diritto Penale Italiano: Secondo il Codice del 1930.* Torino: Unione Tipografico-Editrice Torinese, 1933–1939.

Marufoğlu, Sinan. *Osmanlı Döneminde Kuzey Irak.* Istanbul: Evren, 1998.

Mellaerts, Wim. "Criminal Justice in Provincial England, France, and the Netherlands, c. 1880–1905: Some Comparative Perspectives," *Crime, Histoire, et Sociétés* 4 (2000): 19–52.

Merrill, Frederick T. "Twelve Years of the Turkish Republic," *Foreign Policy Reports* 11 (1935).

Miller, Ruth A. "The Ottoman and Islamic Substratum of Turkey's Swiss Civil Code," *Journal of Islamic Studies* 11 (2000): pp. 335–361.

Mihas, Talat. "Le conseil d'état et la jurisdiction administrative en Turquie," *Revue du Droit Public et de la Science Politique en France et à l'Étranger* 55 (1938): 693–701.

——— "Le tanzimat et son système legislatif," *AFDI* 17 (1967): 1–40.

Mitchell, Timothy. *Colonising Egypt*. New York: Cambridge University Press, 1991.

Mühlberger, David, ed. *The Social Basis of European Fascist Movements*. London: Croom Helm, 1987.

Mutaf, Abdülmecit. *Salnamelerde Karesi Sancağı: 1847–1922*. Istanbul: A. Mutaf, 1997.

Nolte, Ernst. *The Three Faces of Fascism*. Trans. Leila Vennewitz. New York: New American Library, 1963.

Okandan, Recai G. *Amme Hukukumuzun Ana Hatları*. Istanbul: Fakülteler Matbaası, 1957.

Orman, J. "Loi relative aux délits," *AFDI* 5 (1956): 327–330.

Ortaylı, İlber. *Hukuk ve İdare Adam olarak Osmanlı Devletinde Kadı*. Ankara: Turhan Kitabevi, 1994.

——— "Le tanzimat et le modèle français," *L'Empire Ottoman, la Republique de Turquie* (1986): 197–208.

"Ottoman Law and Sharia," *Journal of Comparative Legislation and International Law* 22 (1940): 95–98.

Özkaya, R. Y. "Tanzimat'ın Siyasi Yönden Meşrutiyet'e ..." *Tanzimat'ın 150. Yıl Dönümü Uluslararası Sempozyumu*. Ankara: Türk Tarih Kurumu Yayınları, 1994.

Özturk, Kazım. *Türk Parlamento Tarihi: 1923–1927*. Ankara: TBMM Vakfı Yayınları, 1993.

Paxton, Richard O. "France: The Church, the Republic, and the Fascist Temptation, 1922–1945," Wolff and Hoensch, ed. *Catholics, the State, and the European Radical Right, 1919–1945*. Boulder: Social Science Monographs, 1987.

Payne, Stanley G. "The Concept of Fascism," Larsen, Hagtvet, and Myklebust, ed. *Who Were the Fascists: The Social Roots of European Fascism*. Bergen: Universitetsforlaget, 1980.

——— *Fascism: Comparison and Definition*. Madison: University of Wisconsin Press, 1980.

Peters, Rudolph. "The Islamization of Criminal Law: A Comparative Analysis," *Die Welt Des Islams* 34 (1994): 246–260.

Pollard, John F. *The Vatican and Italian Fascism, 1929–1932*. Cambridge: Cambridge University Press, 1985.

Pollo, Stefanaq and Puto, Arben. *The History of Albania*. London: Routledge, 1981.

Porter, R. *The Greatest Benefit to Mankind: A Medical History of Humanity*, New York: Norton, 1998.

Postacioğlu, I.E. "Aperçu sur l'organisation judiciaire en Turquie," *AFDI* 4 (1954): 155–161.

——— "De la restriction de la preuve testimoniale dans les droit turcs, français, et italien comparés," *AFDI* 1 (1951): 102–118.

——— "Quelques observations sur la technique des codes étrangers à la lumière de l'expérience turque," *AFDI* 5 (1956): 63–74.

Pugliese, Stanislao, ed. *Italian Fascism and Anti-Fascism: A Critical Anthology*. Manchester: Manchester University Press, 2001.

Revelli, Marco. "Italy," David Mühlberger, ed. *The Social Basis of European Fascist Movements.* London: Croom Helm, 1987.

Rheinstein, M. "Types of Reception," *AFDI* 5 (1956): 31–40.

Rikkam, Stein, Hagtvet, Bernt. "The Conditions for a Fascist Victory: Toward a Geo-economic Geo-political Model for the Explanation of Violent Breakdown of Competitive Mass Politics," Larsen, Hagtvet, and Myklebust, ed. *Who Were the Fascists: The Social Roots of European Fascism.* Bergen: Universitetsforlaget, 1980.

Robertson, B.A. "The Emergence of the Modern Judiciary in the Middle East," in Chibli Mallat, ed. *Islam and Public Law: Classical and Contemporary Studies,* London: Graham and Trotman, 1993. 107–139.

Rocco, A. "Les postulats du régime fasciste dans la nouvelle législation pénale," *Centre international d'études sur le fascisme* 3 (1930).

Rossi, E. "Il Decennale della Repubblica di Turchia (29 ottobre 1923–29 ottobre 1933)," *Oriente Moderno,* 12 (1933): 541–57.

Ruggiero, Kristin. "The Devil and Modernity in Late Nineteenth-Century Buenos Aires," *Americas* 59 (2000): 221–233.

Sade. "Philosophy in the Bedroom," in *The Marquis de Sade: Justine, Philosophy in the Bedroom, and Other Writings.* trans: Richard Seaver and Austryn Wainhouse. New York: Grover Press, 1965.

Savvas Paşa. *Le tribunal Mosulman.* Paris: Mechal et Billard, 1902.

Schacht, J. *An Introduction to Islamic Law.* Oxford: Clarendon Press, 1964

——— "Katl," *Encyclopedia of Islam.* Vol. 4. Leiden: Brill, 1997.

Şensoy, N. "Le délit d'adultère," *AFDI* 3 (1954): 349–362.

——— "Reception of Foreign Codes of Criminal Law and Criminal Procedure in Turkey," *AFDI* 5, no. 6 (1956): 182–185.

Seviğ, V.R. *Ceza Muhakemeleri Usul-ü Kanunu Tatbikat ve Sakkı.* Ankara: Ankara Hukuk Fakültesi, 1930.

——— "Chronique de jurisprudence turque," *Journal du Droit International* 105 (1978): 927–935.

Soucy, Robert J. "France," David Mühlberger, ed. *The Social Basis of European Fascist Movements.* London: Croom Helm, 1987.

Stadler, K.R. "Austria," S.J. Woolfe, ed. *Fascism in Europe.* London: Methuen, 1968, 1981.

Starr, J. "Islam and the Struggle over State Law in Turkey," *Law and Islam in the Middle East.* D.H. Dwyer, ed. New York: Bergin and Garvey, 1990: 77–98.

Stephens, Luc. "Fascists and Nationalists in Belgium—1919–1940," Larsen, Hagtvet, and Myklebust, ed. *Who Were the Fascists: The Social Roots of European Fascism.* Bergen: Universitetsforlaget, 1980.

Streckfuss, David. "Kings in the Age of Nations: The Paradox of Lèse Majesté as Political Crime in Thailand," *Comparative Studies in Society and History* 37 (1995): 445–475.

Süngü, İhsan. "Mekteb-i Maarif-i Adliyenin Tesisi," *Tarih Vesikaları* 1 (1941): 212–25.

Surridge, Keith. "Rebellion, Martial Law and British Civil-Military Relations: The War in Cape Colony 1889–1902," *Small Wars and Insurgencies* 8 (1997): 35–60.

Szuchman, Mark. "Disorder and Social Control in Buenos Aires," *Journal of Interdisciplinary History* 15 (9184): 83–110

Taghizade, S.H. "Les courants politiques dans la Turquie," *Revue du Monde Mosulman* 21 (1912): 158–221.
Tanca, A. "The Public Statement on Turkey," *European Journal of International Law* 4 (1993): 115–127.
Taner, T. "Le traitement des délinquants en Turquie," *AFDI* 2 (1953): 5–33.
Tanör, Bülent. "L'État de droit en Turquie," *L'État de Droit dans le Monde Arabe* 34(1995, 1997): 389–394.
Thompson, Elizabeth. "Ottoman Political Reform in the Provinces: The Damascus Advisory Council in 1844–45," *International Journal of Middle East Studies* 25 (1993): 457–475.
Timur, H. "Views on the Transition in Turkey from Islamic Law," *AFDI* 6 (1957): 81–88.
——— "The Place of Islamic Law in Turkish Law Reform," *AFDI* 5, no. 6 (1956): 75–80.
Toledano, E.R. "Legislative Process in the Ottoman Empire in the Early Tanzimat," *International Journal of Turkish Studies* 1 (1980): 99–106.
Trentin, Silvio. *Les transformations récentes du droit public italien de la charte de Charles-Albert à la création de l'état fasciste.* Trans. J. Bonnecase. Paris: M. Girard, 1929.
Trevor-Roper, H.R. "The Phenomenon of Fascism," S.J. Woolfe, ed. *Fascism in Europe.* London: Methuen, 1968, 1981.
Tuncay, S. "Les recours contre la puissance publique," Levy-Ullmann, ed. *La vie juridique des peuples: Turquie.* Paris: Librairie Delgrave, 1939.
Turan, Ömer. "Legal Adjustments of the Tanzimat and 'Mecelle,'" *Études Balkaniques* 35(1999): 213–221.
Turkey. *Ceza Kanunname-i Humayunudur: Suret-i Hatt-ı Humayun.* Istanbul: Takvimhane-yi Amire, 1274 [1858].
——— *Ceza Kanunun Tatbiki Hakkında Kanun.* Istanbul: Maarif Kutuphanesi, 1926.
——— *Code ottoman d'instruction criminelle.* Trans. Yanco Vithynos. Constantinople: J. Pallamary, 1884.
——— *Code pénal.* Constantinople: J.A. Rizzo, 1927.
——— *Code pénal: Précédé du dépot du projet du code.* Istanbul: John Rizzo, 1939.
——— *Düstur.* Dersaadet (Istanbul): Matbaa-yı Amire, 1295/1878.
——— *La législation turque: lois promulguées par la grande assemblée nationale de Turquie.* Constantinople: Imprimerie de l'Annuaire Oriental, 1930.
——— *Türk Ceza Kanununun Bazı Maddelerini Değiştiren Kanun.* Istanbul: Cihan Kitaphanesi, 1933.
Tyan, Emile. *Histoire de l'organisation judiciaire en pays d'Islam.* Paris: Librairie du recoil Sirey, 1938.
Ural, E. *Handbook of Turkish Law for Foreigners.* Ankara: E. Ural, 1980.
Vickers, Miranda. *The Albanians: A Modern History.* London: I.B. Tauris, 1999.
Vogel, F.E. "Siyasa Shar'iyya," *Encyclopedia of Islam.* Vol. 6. Leiden: Brill, 1997. pp. 695–696
Warner, G. "France," S.J. Woolfe, ed. *Fascism in Europe.* London: Methuen, 1968, 1981.
Watson, Alan. *The Evolution of Law.* Baltimore: Johns Hopkins University Press, 1985.
Weber, Max. *Economy and Society.* New York: Bedminster Press, 1968.
Weindling, P. "A Virulent Strain: German Bacteriology as Scientific Racism, 1890–1920," W. Ernst, B. Harris, ed. *Race, Science, and Medicine, 1700–1960,* London: Routledge, 1999. pp. 218–235.

Weinzierl, Erika. "Austria: Church, State, Politics and Ideology, 1919–1938," Wolff and Hoensch, ed. *Catholics, the State, and the European Radical Right, 1919–1945*. Boulder: Social Science Monographs, 1987.

Whittam, John. *Fascist Italy*. Manchester: Manchester University Press, 1995.

Wilson, R.K. "Modern Ottoman Law," *Journal of Comparative Legislation and International Law* 8 (1907): 41–50.

Wolff, Richard J. and Hoensch, Jörg K., ed. *Catholics, the State, and the European Radical Right, 1919–1945*. Boulder: Social Science Monographs, 1987.

Woolfe, S.J. "Italy," S.J. Woolfe, ed. *Fascism in Europe*. London: Methuen, 1968, 1981.

——— ed. *Fascism in Europe*. London: Methuen, 1968, 1981.

Xiaoqun, Xu. "The Fate of Judicial Independence in Republican China, 1912–1937," *China Quarterly* 149 (1997): 1–28.

Yıldız, Hakkı. *Kütayha'nın Tarihçesi*. Istanbul: Formül Matbaası, 1981.

Young, G. *Corps de droit ottoman*. Oxford: The Clarendon Press, 1905–6.

Yurtcan, E. "Children in Turkish Criminal Law," *AFDI* 27 (1980): 237–242.

Zhou, Guangyuan. "Illusion and Reality in the Law of the Late Qing: A Sichuan Case Study," *Modern China* 19 (1993): 427–456

Ziadeh, Farhat, J. "Compelling the Defendant's Appearance at Court in Islamic Law," *Islamic Law and Soceity* 3 (1996): 305–315.

Zürcher, J. *Turkey: A Modern History*. New York: I.B. Tauris, St. Martin's Press, 1997.

Index

Q

R

S

T

U

V

W

For Product Safety Concerns and Information please contact our EU
representative GPSR@taylorandfrancis.com
Taylor & Francis Verlag GmbH, Kaufingerstraße 24, 80331 München, Germany

www.ingramcontent.com/pod-product-compliance
Ingram Content Group UK Ltd.
Pitfield, Milton Keynes, MK11 3LW, UK
UKHW022120190926
475702UK00013B/1544
* 9 7 8 0 4 1 5 6 5 5 4 2 2 *